Instructional Skills
Handbook

INSTRUCTIONAL SKILLS HANDBOOK

DAVID G. ARMSTRONG
JON J. DENTON
TOM V. SAVAGE, JR.

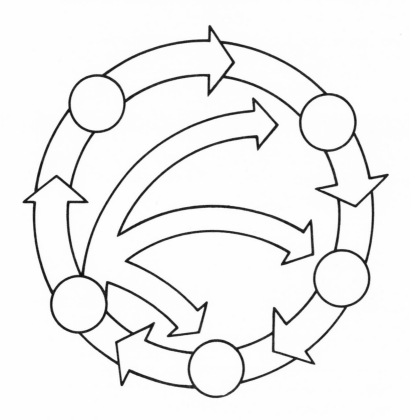

EDUCATIONAL TECHNOLOGY PUBLICATIONS
ENGLEWOOD CLIFFS, NEW JERSEY 07632

Library of Congress Cataloging in Publication Data
Armstrong, David G
    Instructional skills handbook.

    Includes index.
    1. Teaching. 2. Lesson planning. I. Denton,
John J., joint author. II. Savage, Tom V.,
joint author. III. Title.
LB1025.2A775   371.1'02   77-25986
ISBN 0-87778-102-8

Printed in the United States of America.

Library of Congress Catalog Card Number:
77-25986.

International Standard Book Number:
ISBN 0-87778-102-8.

First Printing: February, 1978.

Acknowledgments

The authors gratefully acknowledge the kindness of authors and publishers for permission to reproduce the following:

Journal of Reading and Edward Fry for permission to use Fry's "Graph for Estimating Readability," excerpted from Edward Fry, "A Readability Formula That Saves Time," *Journal of Reading* (April 1968), p. 516.

Random House, Incorporated for permission to print the following excerpts: From Charles E. Silberman, *Crisis in the Classroom*. New York: Random House, Inc., Copyright © 1970, p. 413. From Alvin Toffler, *Future Shock*. New York: Random House, Inc., Copyright © 1970, p. 398.

The University of North Carolina Press for permission to reprint the following excerpt: From David G. Armstrong, "Equipping Student Teachers to Deal with Classroom Control Problems," *The High School Journal* (October 1976), Copyright © 1976, pp. 2-9.

The Viking Press, Inc. for permission to print the following excerpts: From *The Way of the Storyteller* by Ruth Sawyer, Copyright © 1942, renewed 1970 by Ruth Sawyer. Ruth Sawyer, *The Way of the Storyteller*. New York: The Viking Press, second printing, 1966, pp. 239, 242-244, 246. Also to the Bodley Head, London for British rights to this material.

Preface

In recent years, inflation of real property values and increases in assessment rates have escalated school taxes dramatically in many parts of the country. During this same period, declines in youngsters' scores on national tests of academic achievement have been reported widely by the media. Though meanings of these score declines are still being debated in some quarters, it is clear that a sizeable segment of the tax-paying public has concluded that schools today are providing *less* real education for *more* real dollars. School officials at all levels are being called upon as never before to justify expenditures in terms of the anticipated academic progress of the children being served.

In the area of instruction, this movement has signaled the end of easy approvals of new programs and has triggered a demand for the identification of substantive benefits expected from each allocated dollar. The concern for optimizing the impact of instructional expenditures has attracted support for a systems-based approach to instructional design. Several excellent books have been written focusing on theoretical considerations implied by a systematic approach to instruction. Others have looked in great detail at individual sub-systems of integrated instructional designs. But little attention has been directed toward combining general considerations for planning an entire systematic instructional design along with descriptions of operational specifics of each sub-system. This volume attempts to fill that gap.

We have attempted to provide a systematic model of instruction composed of the interrelated sub-systems of (1) performance objectives, (2) diagnosis, (3) instructional strategies, (4) interaction patterns, and (5) evaluation. Detailed descriptions of each sub-system serve as "how-to-do-its" for beginners and as handy references for seasoned professional teachers.

Throughout the book there is an emphasis on using evaluation data to assess specific elements within the instructional program as well as to monitor learners' progress. We have found this emphasis on program component evaluation helpful in isolating problem areas within the total systematic instructional plan. Frequently, a little "tinkering" with a minor problem will result in a vastly improved program (and, not inconsequentially, at a cost well below the expensive alternative of scrapping the *entire* instructional plan).

This book does not deal with *every* possible instructional skill and sub-skill which should be in the repertoire of a teacher. No single book could possibly accomplish such a task. We have treated, however, a number of important skills, suggesting the range of competencies to be sought by the reader. We believe that this book will serve well as the base for a continuing program of professional improvement.

We are indebted to many of our professional colleagues for their helpful and considerate criticism during the preparation of this manuscript. Particularly we should like to thank Dr. Robert H. Pinney and Dr. Richard J.L. Covington of Western Washington University for their careful reading of and insightful comments regarding several chapters of this book. Finally, our very special appreciation goes out to the undergraduate education students at Texas A&M University, Western Washington University, and Whitworth College for their candid reactions to versions of this material in various stages of development.

David G. Armstrong
Jon J. Denton
    College Station, Texas

Tom V. Savage, Jr.
    Spokane, Washington
    June, 1977

Table of Contents

Instructional Skills
Handbook

Chapter 1

Toward Responsible Instruction

OBJECTIVES

This chapter provides information to help the reader to:

1. identify reasons for changes in public tolerance for deficiencies in educational programs.

2. describe how clear descriptions of teachers' roles can promote professionalism in instructional planning.

3. point out implications of clearly-defined teacher responsibility for all levels of education.

A young person born twenty-five years ago has lived through an epoch of enormous change. Sophisticated scientists and engineers, using a systems management approach, have enabled man to stride upon the surface of the moon. Poliomyelitis, the dread scourge of summer, has been conquered. The development of the transistor and integrated circuits have spawned hundreds of compact and easy to use electronic marvels. Taken as a whole the record of the past two and one-half decades reveals an accelerating rate of change that has altered the hue and intensity of much of American life.

But what of education? Contrasted to twenty-five years ago are there fundamental differences in the ways young people are taught today? Has education shared the fruits of change? The lamentable reality is that education has not maintained the pace. Fundamentally, little divides educational practices today from those in vogue a quarter of a century ago. Indeed, some evidence suggests that education has changed only minimally since the turn of the century.

The gap between rates of change in education and other sectors of American society is disquieting. Of particular concern has been a belief held by large numbers of Americans that education has the capability to do better but that educational leaders have been reluctant to use this capability to serve the needs of youngsters in the schools. An alleged lack of congruence between capability and performance has led to an increasing erosion of public confidence in and financial support for public education.

Alvin Toffler, writing in his book, *Future Shock*, captures the frustrations many Americans feel with education today:

> Today, one billion human beings, the total population of the technology rich nations, are speeding toward a rendezvous with super-industrialization. Must we experience mass future shock? Or can we, too, achieve a "soft landing?" We are rapidly accelerating our approach. The craggy outlines of the new society are emerging from the mists of tomorrow. Yet even as we speed closer, evidence mounts that one of our most crucial sub-systems—education—is dangerously malfunctioning (Toffler, 1970; p. 398).

Toffler's suggestion that education has stagnated relative to other areas of national life has been seconded by a number of other critics. Their concern has stimulated a re-examination of the proper relationship between education and the larger society of which it is a part. The decline in birth rate has changed the image of education as an institution whose possible lack of efficiency could be excused because of the burden of fitting ever-increasing numbers of youngsters into understaffed, inadequate physical plants. That day has passed. Class loads are down. Numbers of educational specialists are up. These changes have been viewed by the public as indications that the "crisis to crisis" existence that characterized education ten and fifteen years ago is no longer at hand.

For all the transformations in the nature of the problems facing education, one factor has remained constant. Costs have continued to rise. The combination of increasing expenses and decreasing enrollments has led to a demand that educators be held more clearly accountable for services rendered in exchange for tax monies. In response to these pressures, a methodology has had to evolve according to which judgments can be made regarding the extent to which education is or is not meeting its basic responsibilities.

In attempting to develop such a methodology, the problem of which sorts of data ought to be collected has been a thorny one. Should teachers' lesson plans be used? How about the "citizenship" activities of youngsters ten years after they leave school? Of all the suggestions that have been made regarding kinds of evidence to be used in assessing effectiveness of teaching performance, the most broad-based support has been generated for the idea that data ought to to be collected that focus on observable learner performances. These performances allow for relatively simple data-gathering procedures. They are designed to provide information regarding whether an individual youngster can or cannot accomplish a given task. All gathering of evidence is directed toward providing answers to the "can" or "cannot" question.

An emphasis on observable performances requires that objectives be stated in terms of what learners should be able to *do* as a result of instruction. Stating intended instructional outcomes in terms of youngsters' observable performances reasserts the primacy of purposefulness in education. Use of these performance objectives promotes responsibility by requiring teachers to identify what learners should be able to do as a consequence of instruction. This process helps develop a professional sense of direction that runs counter to the vague "mindlessness" that Charles E. Silberman, in his *Crisis in the Classroom,* described as characterizing instruction in many American schools (Silberman, 1970).

When instruction is organized around performance objectives that state in specific terms what learners are to be able to do after a given instructional sequence, teachers have a standard they can use to find out how well they are "getting through" to their youngsters. Further, the use of performance objectives permits a clearer conception of the role of the teacher. Specifically, that role takes the shape of an instructional facilitator charged with organizing learning experiences in such a way that performance objectives are mastered. This role definition puts teachers "in the driver's seat" in terms of their discretion in selecting procedures they believe to be most effective in bringing students to achieve identified performance objectives.

Teaching that focuses on clearly delineated performance objectives makes it possible for teachers to make reasoned decisions regarding which inservice and summer school programs best meet their needs. Rather than selecting at random from a potpourri of courses, teachers can insist that programs be directed toward their own instructional needs.

Unquestionably, moves toward precisely specifying intended learner outcomes through the use of performance objectives is going to result in fundamental changes in operating procedures of all agencies that traditionally have had a hand in the professional preparation of teachers. Colleges of education will be particularly influenced.

If colleges of education are to produce new teachers and enhance the effectiveness of presently employed teachers who will be held responsible for their performance, then the colleges, too, must be held responsible. Certainly, today, some teacher training institutions are not influenced notably by the publics they serve. Charles E. Silberman has articulated the feelings of many critics of present practices as follows:

> ... There is probably no aspect of contemporary education on which there is a greater unanimity of opinion than that teacher education needs a vast overhaul. Virtually everyone is dissatisfied with the current state of teacher education. ... (Silberman, 1970; p. 413).

Traditional teacher preparation programs have gone forward on the assumption that "good" or "right" techniques of teaching most appropriately are taught in methods courses on college campuses. According to this view, students who spend time on the campus learning these "secrets of teaching" are able to apply them later in real school settings. Unhappily, these expectations frequently have not worked out well in practice. As a consequence, campus methods courses have been criticized on the grounds that they are dull and unrelated to the dynamics of the public school classroom. Some critics, too, have suggested that many methods courses have focused only infrequently on coherent, systematic concepts of instruction. More typically, these critics allege, students have been introduced to unrelated sets of generalities about different aspects of teaching. When they have attempted to put these generalities into practice, many new teachers have sensed themselves to have been catapulted into a classroom world bearing little resemblance to the world of education described by their professors.

Moves toward more precise specification of educational out- comes have not enjoyed universal admiration. Some critics have suggested that increasing specificity of instructional intentions goes hand-in-hand with an undesirable mechanization of teaching, a robot-like approach that is the antithesis of humanism.

Those who support attempts to specify instructional outcomes more precisely share the concern for humane and sensitive instruction. They (and the authors) argue that identifying clear and specific performance objectives for learners operates to assure humanity in a way traditional approaches never have. Precise performance objectives reduce ambiguity of instructional intent and, hence, learners' anxieties. Youngsters know where they are headed. When teachers are well aware where their instruction is going, they are in a position to assess progress of each learner and adjust for individual differences.

By defining teachers' roles in terms of youngsters' progress toward clearly defined performance objectives, teachers' psycho- logical states and overall enjoyment of their work are enhanced. For too long, teachers passively have accepted criticisms that they should be responsible for social phenomena over which they have had little, if any, direct control.

Many of these accusations have been made because educators have failed to protect themselves by articulating reasonable and clearly-stated sets of teacher responsibilities. Having had no consensus regarding the limits of their role, teachers have had "no place to stand" when charges of the most absurd sort have been hurled in their direction. By virtue of their silence, teachers at times have seemed to apologize for a variety of social ills having little, if any, causal connection to public education.

To counteract unfounded criticisms, teachers must take care to formulate performance objectives that clearly spell out the intent of their instructional programs. Once this has been accomplished, teachers can generate role descriptions delimiting responsibilities in the instructional domain to help their learners master those performance objectives. While teachers should not shrink from making a public commitment to helping their learners achieve these performance objectives, they should, at the same time, have no hesitancy whatever in declining to be held responsible for other instructional purposes. Clearly, teachers' responsibilities must be anchored firmly to a discrete number of well-defined tasks that derive logically from performance objectives set out for their learners.

In addition to relieving pressures from certain public interest groups, clear role definitions for teachers can help clarify relationships between teachers and administrators. Much of the friction between administrators and classroom teachers results from an absence of a clear understanding of the role responsibilities of each group. Consequently, with no common understanding of "the rules of the game," a basis for dialogue is lacking. When roles are defined clearly, discussions between teachers and principals that spring from mistaken perceptions of function and responsibility can be reduced in number.

Clear role definitions for teachers have implications for all levels of education. Armed with a precise understanding of what they are expected to do, teachers increasingly can professionalize instructional planning as they focus on preparation of performance objectives, development of strategies appropriate for individual learners, and techniques for gathering evidence to validate the quality of their programs. Professional instruction implies that teachers will have in their repertoires a sophisticated array of instructional skills. The precise nature of these skills, and the tasks they imply for teachers, comprise the substance of this book. Hopefully, guidelines introduced here will provide a useful framework for teachers everywhere who see the potential for clearly-focused instructional practices.

Summary

Changes in public expectations of education have put pressures on professional educators to show evidence that instruction is having a measurable impact on learners. Continuing escalation in costs of public education at a time when enrollments are stabilizing has contributed significantly to increased public scrutiny of educators' performance.

One implication for teachers is that they need to think seriously about defining their roles more precisely. The authors suggest role definitions in terms of tasks associated with helping youngsters achieve established performance objectives. Such a move would serve the twin purposes of focusing teachers' efforts in the area of instructional planning and of preventing teachers from being falsely accused of negligent behavior in an area outside of their proper realm of responsibility.

References

SILBERMAN, Charles E. *Crisis in the Classroom: The Remaking of American Education.* New York: Random House, 1970.

TOFFLER, Alvin. *Future Shock.* New York: Random House, 1970.

Additional Professional Study

Books

EISNER, Elliot W., and Elizabeth VALLANCE. *Conflicting Conceptions of Curriculum.* Berkeley, Calif.: McCutchan Publishing Corporation, 1974.

FRYMIER, Jack R. *The Nature of Educational Method.* Columbus, Ohio: Charles E. Merrill Publishing Co., 1965.

GOODLAD, John I. and M. Frances KLEIN, ET AL. *Behind the Classroom Door.* Worthington, Ohio: Charles A. Jones Publishing Company, Inc., 1970.

GRONLUND, Norman E. *Determining Accountability for Classroom Instruction.* New York: Macmillan Publishing Co., Inc., 1974.

HAGEN, Owen A. *Changing World/Changing Teachers.* Pacific Palisades, Calif.: Goodyear Publishing Company, Inc., 1973.

HYMAN, Ronald T. *Teaching: Vantage Points for Study* (2nd Edition). New York: J.B. Lippincott Company, 1974.

MC NEIL, John D. *Toward Accountable Teachers: Their Appraisal and Improvement.* New York: Holt, Rinehart, and Winston, Inc., 1971.

SILBERMAN, Charles E. *Crisis In The Classroom: The Remaking of American Education.* New York: Random House, 1970.

TOFFLER, Alvin. *Future Shock.* New York: Random House, 1970.

WEIGAND, James E. *Developing Teacher Competencies.* Englewood Cliffs, N.J.: Prentice-Hall, Inc., 1971.

WILSON, Elizabeth C. *Needed: A New Kind of Teacher.* Bloomington, Ind.: The Phi Delta Kappa Educational Foundation, 1973.

Periodicals

CRONIN, Joseph M. "Decline of the School as an American Priority." *The National Elementary Principal* (May 1974), 39-42.

EBEL, Robert. "What Are Schools For?" *Phi Delta Kappan* (September 1972), 3.

KAPUNAN, Salvador C. "Teaching Implies Learning." *Educational Theory* (Fall 1975), 362-378.

KIRKMAN, Ralph E. "The Future of American Education." *Peabody Journal of Education* (July 1973), 261-262.

NICKEL, K.N. "Accountability: For What? For Whom?" *Clearing House* (January 1974), 303-307.

TYLER, Ralph W. "Tomorrow's Education." *American Education* (August 1975), 16-19.

Chapter 2

A Model of Instruction

OBJECTIVES

This chapter provides information to help the reader to:

1. point out specific instructional skills.

2. organize instructional skills systematically into a model of instruction.

3. describe how each component of a model of instruction relates to each other component.

4. list a logical sequence of instructional skills for use in a complete unit of instruction.

--- --- --- --- --- --- --- --- --- --- --- --- --- ---

What is this process of teaching? What are the instructional skills needed by those who work with youngsters in the classroom? The problem of specifying which instructional skills ought to be emphasized has long troubled developers of teacher preparation programs. A number of solutions have been proposed from time to time.

One response has been teacher education programs characterized by the development of long lists of specific instructional experiences through which all neophyte teachers have been expected to pass. A basic problem has been the tendency for these programs to center on "ideal teacher role behaviors" that have described well-enough the sorts of things teachers *do* in the classroom, but that have ignored the impact of these teacher behaviors on *learners.* In such programs, evaluation of new teachers' performance has been in terms of their adherence to these "ideal teacher role behaviors" independent of any assessment of how these teacher behaviors might have affected learners.

A difficulty with programs of this type is that they have produced teachers who have been sent to the field without having been judged on the degree to which their teaching helped (or even hindered) learners. This situation suggests the following question: Is it more desirable to turn out new teachers who have mastered sets of teaching behaviors their supervisors have labeled "good," or to turn out new teachers whose teaching has had a demonstrated (and positive) impact on learners? The authors support the view implied by the second half of the question.

There is no single set of teacher behaviors that represents an appropriate instructional response regardless of setting. Learners are unique. Nuances emerge from particular groupings of youngsters and from different physical settings. These differences must be addressed by "tailor-made" teaching styles that respond to the peculiar nature of each situation.

Any set of so-called "ideal teacher role behaviors" assumes a constancy of circumstances among sites and situations that simply does not exist in the real world of teaching. Given this reality, little is to be gained by training teachers to operate as though mastery of a rigid set of teaching behaviors would assure success in all situations.

If not specific sets of teacher role behaviors, then what *should* be emphasized in teacher preparation programs? Rather than "ideal teacher role behaviors," the focus should be on some groups of widely-applicable instructional processes or skills. Prospective teachers need to learn these instructional skills and be exposed to alternative procedures for implementing them. But in no sense should a list of "right" or "highly preferred" methods for putting these instructional skills into practice be presented to novice teachers.

Teachers, like the learners they serve, are unique personalities. It makes sense for them to take advantage of their own special interests, skills, and competencies as they plan for instruction. Individual strengths of teachers can be utilized most efficiently when a logical framework is employed to organize the instructional skills selected for a specific program. Such a framework can suggest how instructional skills might best be organized to promote a logical, systematic instructional program for learners.

As a framework to guide teachers' instructional practices, a model of instruction is proposed here that relates actions of teachers to achievement of learners. According to this model, major emphases are placed not specifically on what teachers do, but on what learners derive from instruction. There is no interest in evaluating teachers' modes of instruction in terms other than learners' achievement.

This model of instruction rests on a clear formulation of the teaching process. Teaching can be thought of as a series of events requiring decisions made by the teacher. Logically, these decisions can be organized into separate categories. The authors have grouped these decision categories under five general headings. Collectively, these five headings comprise all of the basic instructional skills. These skills are:

Skill one: specifying performance objectives
Skill two: diagnosing learners
Skill three: selecting instructional strategies
Skill four: interacting with learners
Skill five: evaluating the effectiveness of instruction

Each of these five instructional skills can be thought of as an element in a comprehensive model of instruction. This model provides a useful framework for teachers as they plan for classroom instruction. The model is presented in Figure 2.1.

This model provides a framework that encourages the development of individual teaching styles. Individualized styles are encouraged because evaluation of instruction is based on learners' achievement of the performance objectives. Given this criterion, teachers are free to choose procedures from their own repertoires that they believe will result in high levels of learner achievement.

Teacher responsibility is well served by this model. This responsibility comes not in terms of teachers' rigid adherence to a set of "ideal role behaviors," but rather in adapting instructional practices, as necessary, to help learners achieve performance objectives that have been selected.

A consideration of the five instructional skills included in this instructional model leads logically to the question: "How *well*

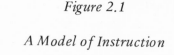

Figure 2.1

A Model of Instruction

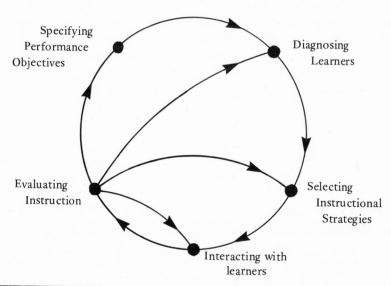

must teachers be expected to perform these skills?" The authors wish to emphasize that, with respect to criteria, this is not a prescriptive model. Different levels of acceptable performance ought to be established according to the unique characteristics of individual teaching situations. Properly, teachers, administrators, parents, and other community figures ought to be involved in any determination of what constitutes minimal levels of competency.

While the authors wish to avoid any implication that a prescribed set of "correct" teaching behaviors is suggested by this instructional model, they do recognize the need to provide general guidelines for those individuals who may be charged with determining minimal levels of acceptable teacher performance. To meet needs of these individuals, subsequent chapters will include discussions of each instructional skill in detail. Information will be provided regarding kinds of considerations that ought to go into decisions regarding establishment of criteria for teacher performance.

Some readers may have an immediate need for some "pieces" of information that are scattered throughout the remaining chapters of the book. To help focus their search, a brief summation of the general character of each instructional skill will be provided in sections to follow. Information derived from these summations may direct attention to the appropriate chapters in which matters introduced in summary fashion here are considered in much greater detail. This overview should provide a general context for remaining chapters in the book.

Specifying Performance Objectives

The decisions involved in this element of the instructional model are a key to the entire instructional process. Performance objectives determine the direction and the focus of instruction.

In some sense, whether formally stated or not, all teachers set objectives. Too frequently, these are determined by reference to a sequence developed by a textbook author with little serious thought about what is being taught and why it is being taught. There is a need to move away from such practices to specify performance objectives that are derived according to a plan founded on a defensible scheme of logic. Logic, too, needs to guide sequencing of performance objectives. When performance objectives are selected and sequenced according to a logical plan, teachers not only know where they are heading, but also are in a position to justify those ends to responsible critics.

Diagnosing Learners

Teachers need information regarding learners' readiness to begin a proposed new instructional sequence, learners' past records of achievement, and learners' individual needs and interests. A failure to diagnose often results in classrooms filled with frustrated, bored, and unmotivated youngsters. When adequate diagnostic information is in hand, teachers are well positioned to formulate learning plans that meet specific informational and emotional needs of each pupil or student. Planning that proceeds from a sound base of diagnostic information can result in programs that do much to reduce the incidence of learners' disaffection with school.

Selecting Instructional Strategies

In selecting instructional strategies, teachers properly adopt procedures that are consistent with (1) the identified performance objectives, (2) the peculiar demands of the subject or topic being taught, and (3) the learning styles of youngsters in their classrooms. No single strategy is "best" for all learners and all conditions. There are times when groups of youngsters should work together, and there are times when students in those same groups should work independently. Sometimes inductive teaching strategies prove effective in helping learners to master a given performance objective. Under other circumstances, deductive teaching strategies are more appropriate.

Because of the necessity to tie selection of a specific strategy to the unique characteristics of a given teaching situation, an understanding of the enormous range of available strategies must precede responsible choice. While neophyte teachers may not, initially, use a tremendous variety of strategies, familiarity with a wide range of options is important. There is evidence that, as teachers grow professionally, their active use of a wider range of strategies increases. With experience they become more proficient at matching individual strategies to the variables characterizing a particular instructional setting. Ideally, teachers seek a level of expertise in this area enabling them to organize the instructional environment so that learners and resources come together in the way that best facilitates each youngster's attainment of the performance objectives.

Selection of instructional strategies must be considered in relation to other elements of the instructional model. There is a need to guard against a temptation to choose a given strategy because of a personal whim or preference. If strategies are selected after a consideration of (1) the performance objectives being sought, (2) the needs of individual learners, and (3) a careful consideration of past learner performance, then teachers can feel confident that instructional strategies are being selected professionally.

Fundamentally, when teachers select instructional strategies, they act as "hypothesis makers." A range of potential approaches is surveyed, and a selection is made that is believed most likely to bring about the desired changes in learners' abilities. The appropriateness of these choices is tested during the implementation and evaluation phases of instruction.

Interacting with Learners

The most professional selection of performance objectives, diagnostic techniques, and instructional strategies must be validated not in terms of the elegance of the planning, but according to how the program "works" when it is implemented in the classroom. The "interacting with learners" component represents the "doing" phase of the instructional model. Questioning skills, reinforcement skills, classroom management skills, large and small group communications skills, and a host of interpersonal relations techniques are involved.

Learning how to interact with learners is, perhaps, the most difficult instructional skills for new teachers to master. Notable performance in this area seems to require actual experience working with pupils or students and a regular program of feedback from qualified observers. Certainly, the authors do not mean to suggest that skills associated with interacting with learners have not been identified and cannot be taught. Indeed, they can be taught, and they have been described with considerable precision. But teachers do seem to need a great deal of practice in actual classroom settings to become genuinely and comfortably proficient in this area.

Evaluating the Effectiveness of Instruction

To test hypotheses concerning the potential effectiveness of certain instructional strategies and patterns of interacting with learners, evidence needs to be gathered during and after the teaching of a given unit of work. Such information enables teachers to evaluate their performances with a view toward improving instructional practices. As implied by the instructional model (see Figure 2.1), evaluation should prompt a review of each element of the instructional planning process. If desired results were not achieved by learners, a number of questions are appropriate in the quest for identification of "weak" spots: Were the performance objectives appropriate? Was the diagnostic information adequate? Were the strategies suitable? Were there patterns of classroom interaction that may have inhibited learning? Was the information gained through the evaluation process itself valid?

Too frequently, evaluation of instruction has been narrowly conceived in terms of formalized testing procedures. Due to this misguided perception of evaluation and because such formalized testing requires a great deal of teacher preparation time, many teachers have come to view evaluation as a time-consuming appendage of instruction rather than as an integral part of the instructional process. Certainly some formal testing is necessary and important, but a number of easy-to-use informal assessment techniques also can contribute valuable information that may be used to judge the effectiveness of instruction.

Whether they recognize it or not, even those teachers who argue that they "just don't have time" for evaluation in fact *do* evaluate their instruction. A visit to any faculty room reveals teachers making informal assessments of their teaching. A visitor is likely to hear such comments as, "It seemed to be a good approach. My students were paying attention"; or "I enjoyed the lesson. It was lots of fun." The point is not whether teachers evaluate—they do—but whether their judgments are made on the basis of information that is valid and reliable.

Sometimes teachers believe a particular segment of instruction to have been effective because *they* enjoyed the lesson or had a personal interest in the subject matter. Later, when interacting with their learners, they are surprised to find that the students viewed the lesson much less positively. The point is that teachers' feelings about the worth or the "impact" of particular lessons frequently are invalid criteria for determining instructional effectiveness.

Because of personal disappointments when youngsters fail to develop an enthusiasm for a given topic paralleling their own, some teachers succumb to the temptation to take out their frustrations by suggesting that "these youngsters can't learn." Disappointing as these situations are, professionalism demands that the issue be rephrased to read: "They did not learn. Why not?" A rigorous pursuit to a reasonable answer to that question can do much to pinpoint specific problems experienced by individual learners. By focusing attention on a limited number of identified difficulty areas, teachers can work systematically toward genuine improvement of their instructional practices.

Subsequent chapters will provide specific suggestions regarding how alternative teaching skills might be deployed to shore up identified weak spots throughout the entire instructional program.

Summary

Many traditional teacher preparation programs have been premised on the assumption that a set of "ideal teacher role behaviors" have been identified. In such programs, neophyte teachers have been encouraged to master the essentials of these role behaviors on the assumption that such mastery would assure success in the classroom. Regrettably, teachers trained according to these procedures do not have their performances validated by evidence of how well youngsters in their classrooms learn when these "ideal teacher role behaviors" are demonstrated. This lack of validation has produced great frustration among many newer teachers, who have found that youngsters in their classrooms did not respond well to instruction formulated according to procedures recommended and learned well during their teacher education program.

The authors argue that variables from one instructional site to another are so great that the concept of "ideal teacher role behaviors" has little practical utility. Because of these differences, teachers ought to select instructional strategies from their own repertoires that best respond to the unique needs of their own teaching situations. This does not mean, however, that teaching ought to be random and unorganized. On the contrary, instruction ought to be systematic and focused on identified performance objectives. But, once these "ends" have been identified, individual teachers ought to draw upon their own strengths in preparing programs that meet the particular needs of youngsters in their classes.

To facilitate instructional planning of teachers, a formatting procedure has been introduced built around a five-component model of instruction. This model suggests that professional instruction must attend to planning regarding performance objectives, diagnostic procedures, instructional strategies, patterns of interaction, and evaluation. Because these components are mutually related and because each represents a separate element of the instructional planning process, use of the instructional model as a framework for unit planning makes technically feasible a post-teaching assessment of strengths and weaknesses of each component. Use of this model maximizes potentials for teachers to exercise individual choice and, at the same time, provides a mechanism for organization of choices into a professional instructional system.

Additional Professional Study

Books

DE CECCO, John Paul. *The Psychology of Learning and Instruction,* 2nd Ed. Englewood Cliffs, N.J.: Prentice-Hall, Inc., 1974,

EMMER, Edward T. and Gregg MILLETT. *Improving Teaching Through Experimentation.* Englewood Cliffs, N.J.: Prentice-Hall, Inc., 1970.

FILBECK, Robert. *Systems in Teaching and Learning.* Lincoln, Nebr.: Professional Educators Publications, Inc., 1974.

GERLACH, Vernon S. and Donald P. ELY. *Teaching and Media: A Systematic Approach.* Englewood Cliffs, N.J.: Prentice-Hall, Inc., 1971.

POPHAM, W. James and Eva L. BAKER. *Systematic Instruction.* Englewood Cliffs, N.J.: Prentice-Hall, Inc., 1970.

Periodicals

BAUMAN, Robert P. "Preliminary Model for Effective Teaching." *Physics Teacher* (May 1974), 287-291.

HAMACHEK, D. "Characteristics of Good Teachers and Implications for Teacher Education." *Phi Delta Kappan* (February 1969), 341-345.

HAYMAN, John L. "Systems Approach and Education." *The Educational Forum* (May 1974), 493-501.

HERRON, J. Dudley and Grayson WHEATLEY. "Working Theory of Instruction." *Science Education* (October 1974), 509-517.

LAVI, Aryeh. "Design for a Dynamic Learning System." *Educational Technology* (February 1975), 14-21.

ZAHORIK, John A. "What Good Teaching Is." *The Journal of Educational Research* (July-August 1973), 435-440.

Chapter 3

Specifying Performance Objectives

OBJECTIVES

This chapter provides information to help the reader to:

1. identify research-based evidence supporting the use of performance objectives.

2. distinguish among *goals, aims,* and *performance objectives.*

3. write performance objectives according to the *a,b,c,d* format.

4. point out purposes and characteristics of cognitive-dimension performance objectives.

5. point out purposes and characteristics of attitudinal-dimension performance objectives.

6. point out purposes and characteristics of psychomotor-dimension performance objectives.

_____

Clear, precise statements of performance objectives promote effective instruction. Learning occurs most efficiently when planned instructional experiences are constructed in such a way that outcomes of learning can be observed. Given this careful attention to organization, the expectation that youngsters will master new material is much better grounded than when achievement is left to depend on the presumed utility of random teacher acts.

Even teachers who reject the position that precisely-defined

performance objectives are useful *do* have objectives, and they do look for subtle indicators of learners' progress in making judgments regarding the degree to which these objectives have been accomplished. Frequently, these objectives, though clear in the minds of teachers, are not communicated to learners. This places students in the difficult situation of having to guess what the course objectives are and how a given teacher proposes to evaluate them. A second problem with this approach is that, since teachers may never bother to commit evaluation criteria to writing, these criteria may be developed in haste. The possibility that selected evaluation criteria may not be valid is a very real threat under these circumstances.

To avoid ambiguity in the minds of learners and to promote the use of valid evaluation criteria, the use of performance objectives is recommended. Performance objectives, committed to writing and typically distributed to students before a given unit of instruction begins, describe the nature of the behavior sought, the way that behavior will be measured, and the level of proficiency deemed adequate. Use of performance objectives assuages learners' anxieties regarding teachers' intentions. Further, the process of developing performance objectives in advance of instruction gives teachers an opportunity to consider strengths and weaknesses of alternative ways of measuring learners' progress. This reasoned assessment of evaluation options promotes selection of valid criteria and test instruments.

There is a need for care to be exercised in the selection of words used in a performance objective. This need is exemplified in the following deficiently-stated social studies objective:

This program seeks to promote the development of good citizenship.

The objective posits a commendable *goal*, but, as stated, the phrase provides an imprecise referent against which to measure progress. For example, what *is* "citizenship?" And beyond that, what is *good* "citizenship?" At what point does "good citizenship" begin to slip over into "mediocre" or even "bad" citizenship? Until such questions are answered, learners' progress toward the end of "good citizenship" remains difficult to measure.

This very poorly stated social studies objective is typical of many seen in old curriculum guides. In large measure, the lack of specificity reflected in this objective and others of this type results from confusion regarding the distinct characteristics of *goals, aims,* and *performance objectives.*

Educational goals function to indicate the general direction of school programs. School boards use them as rough guidelines to follow in shaping school district policies. Ordinarily, educational goals are derived from combining information from four general areas: (1) information regarding what society sees as desirable at a given time; (2) information from professional scholars in the various subject areas; (3) information from educational psychologists concerning the learning processes; and, (4) information about the characteristics of learners in the area being served. This combination frequently results in a compilation of a series of goal statements. The following are typical examples:

- *Students will develop an appreciation of the scientific method.*
- *Pupils will develop respect for our democratic institutions.*
- *Students will understand the elements of capitalism.*
- *Every youngster will learn how to accept differences in others.*

Goals have value in establishing a general universe of concern for educators. But, by themselves, they provide inadequate referents for teachers to use as they plan instructional programs. Before goals can have any utility for program planning, they need to be broken down into aims and, subsequently, into performance objectives. This sequence of steps is illustrated in Figure 3.1.

Aims of subject area curricula, the second tier of this system, express subject area generalizations relevant to educational goals in a form intended to identify specific intellectual skills to be acquired by learners. For example, consider the following aim from physics:

> *Learners will apply Newton's Laws of Motion using simple laboratory apparatus.*

This aim is derived from more general physics content generalizations known as Newton's Laws of Motion. Selection of these generalizations, along with the aims flowing from them, implies that the generalizations are serving some broader ends expressed in the adopted educational goals.

In developing aims for use in instructional planning, the key

Figure 3.1
The Relationship of Goals, Aims, and Performance Objectives

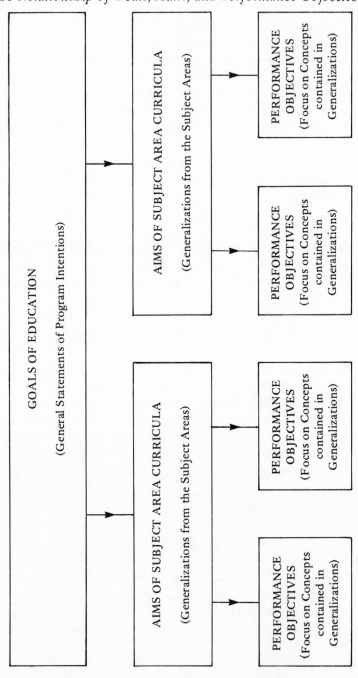

issue is the identification and selection of appropriate content generalizations. Content generalizations include laws from the sciences, theorems from mathematics, and verified theories from the social sciences. In general, content generalizations have the following characteristics:

1. They are statements implying a relationship between two or more concepts. (*Example*: The *force* applied to an object is directly proportional to the product of the *mass* and *acceleration* of the object.)
2. They are considered to be "true," given the best information available at present.

Performance objectives further refine subject matter that has been broken into aims derived from content generalizations. Performance objectives, by providing specific indications of expected learner behaviors, methods of assessment, and acceptable criterion levels, guide teachers in the preparation of new units of learning. Because there is an interest in evaluating achievement of students, it makes sense for performance objectives to describe assessment procedures that can provide valid and reliable learner progress data. There is a consensus that validity and reliability are best served when teachers assess *observable* learner behaviors. These observable behaviors can be quickly measured to provide information both about progress of individual learners and about the general impact of the program itself. Research evidence supports these claims.

Do Performance Objectives Make a Difference?

Professional journals in education contain numerous articles both supporting and opposing the use of performance objectives in planning instruction. While many of these articles provide interesting logical structures supporting one or the other position, few provide *evidence* relating to the key issue of whether use of performance objectives affects learners' achievement in any significant way. This evidence is best sought by referring to reports of controlled experimental studies. Brief discussions of several of these important investigations follow.

Olsen (1973) conducted an investigation with 14 ninth-grade physical science classes to determine the effects of providing learners with performance objectives prior to instruction. Eight classes received the lists of relevant performance objectives and then instruction on the topics of "heat and light energy," "energy transfer," and "phases of matter." Six control classes received instruction on the same topics but no performance objectives. Both groups received instruction over a period of three months. Learners in classes receiving performance objectives scored higher than learners in control classes both on achievement tests administered at the conclusion of the unit and on a retention test administered three weeks later.

A second study, involving 52 secondary school students enrolled in two separate sections of an introductory algebra course, utilized programmed instructional materials. Students in one of the classes were provided with relevant performance objectives. Students in the other class received no performance objectives. The investigator compared (1) retention and (2) rate of learning of students in the two classes. No differences were found in performances of students in the two classes either on the retention or on the rate of learning measure (Loh, 1972).

In another investigation with mathematics students, Ferre (1972) set out to compare the effectiveness of providing performance objectives at different times during an instructional unit. One hundred three mathematics students were divided into three groups. Group one received no performance objectives. Group two received performance objectives at the beginning of the unit. Group three received performance objectives on a daily basis. At the conclusion of the unit, a battery of tests was administered to the three groups. Ferre reported that optimum scores were achieved by those students who were given objectives on a daily basis. The next highest group scores were those of students provided with objectives at the beginning of the unit. The lowest scores were achieved by students who received no objectives at any time.

The findings of Olsen (1973) and Ferre (1972) have been replicated in studies using college students as subjects. Performance on a brief test was found to improve when there was a prior knowledge of relevant performance objectives. In this study, at the University of Tennessee, two randomly-selected groups were formed from 19 seniors and graduate students enrolled in an educational psychology research course. One group was presented with performance objectives for a lesson. The other group discussed an unrelated topic. Following these procedures, the two groups came together to hear the lecture. After the lecture, a short test was given over its contents. The investigators found that the group provided with the objectives prior to the lecture scored higher on the test (Huck and Long, 1973).

The following two studies, in addition to assessing the impact of performance objectives on learning, attempted to determine what effect provision of performance objectives had on learners' ability to acquire information not specifically mentioned in the objectives. A University of Georgia study involved an introductory educational psychology class with 52 students. These students were assigned at random to six treatment groups. Three of these groups received lists containing half of the performance objectives that had been developed to guide instruction in the course. The remaining three groups received no performance objectives at all. Additionally, students in these three groups were not advised that students in the other three groups had received a partial list of the performance objectives guiding instruction in the course. At the conclusion of instruction, a test was administered based on all of the performance objectives that had been used to guide instruction. The investigators found that those students who had received the partial list of performance objectives outperformed students with no performance objectives on test items related to performance objectives on their partial lists. Further, those students who received the partial lists performed as well as students who received no performance objectives on test items not related to performance objectives on the partial lists (Morse and Tillman, 1973).

Taylor (1972) conducted a similar study. One treatment group received no performance objectives, a second treatment group received a partial list of performance objectives, and a third group received a complete list of performance objectives. Consistent with other research, the groups with the partial and the complete lists of performance objectives outperformed on an achievement test the group with no performance objectives. Further, similar to the Morse and Tillman (1973) finding, students with a partial list of performance objectives scored at least as well on items unrelated to performance objectives on their partial lists as did students with no performance objectives. Taylor concluded that partial lists of performance objectives do not limit students' attention only to the content for which they have received relevant performance objectives. The work of Morse and Tillman (1973) and Taylor (1972) suggests that, contrary to the views of many writers of "opinion" articles, there is little *evidence* that pointing out important sections of content to learners through the use of performance objectives will reduce the learning of information not specifically mentioned in the performance objectives.

Investigations discussed here involved subjects ranging in age from pre-adolescents to graduate students. Further, treatments ranged in length from one class period to one semester. Regardless of the age of the subjects or length of the treatment, results consistently have favored learners who were provided with performance objectives prior to instruction. These data make a strong case for including carefully prepared performance objectives in instructional plans.

Characteristics of Performance Objectives
All performance objectives should include four elements:
1. *Audience* (the "who")—a statement concerning which learners must demonstrate a behavior.
2. *Behavior* (the "what")—a description of the skill or content the learners must demonstrate.
3. *Conditions* (the "how and when")—a statement of the circumstances and limitations that will be present during the test performance of the behavior; or, more simply, the testing conditions.
4. *Degree* (the "how well")—a phrase or statement indicating what level of performance is necessary for the objective to be achieved.

Audience
The *audience* (who is to be doing the learning) is an essential feature of a performance objective because personalization of instruction implies that all learners will not go through common experiences. Consequently, the performance objective must indicate which individuals will be asked to demonstrate the behaviors called for in the objective.

Note the differences in the audience component of each of the following phrases:

- The children will . . . (unacceptable).
- The emotionally disturbed children in the core unit of the clinic will . . . (acceptable).

Note the greater specificity with which the audience has been described in the second sample. This specificity may help other teachers evaluate an objective in terms of its potential appropriateness for inclusion in their instructional programs.

Behavior

The *behavior* component of a performance objective concerns the specific nature of the competency desired of learners as a consequence of instruction. The behavior component focuses on the question: "*What* should the learner be able to do as a result of this instruction." To provide a basis for answering that question, specific observable behaviors need to be identified that will be taken as indicators that learners are moving toward mastery of the performance objective. Consider the following examples:

1. —The student will know the basic components of research design (unacceptable).

   —Each student in freshman botany will be able to conduct an investigation and submit a report containing the five principal parts of an investigation . . . (acceptable).

2. —The student will understand the words in the story *Ten Billion Aardvarks* (unacceptable).

   —Each student in eighth grade English will construct metaphors such as the "cat was soft as . . ." with words used in the story *Ten Billion Aardvarks* (acceptable).

3. —The student will report on the material in the text on foreign policy (unacceptable).

   —Students in marketing and general economics will analyze the impact on the United States of the wheat exportation deal with the Soviet Union . . . (acceptable).

There is need to exercise great care in selecting verbs to describe observable behaviors. Verbs that are subject to a wide range of interpretation are notably unsuitable. For example, verbs such as "to understand," "to know," or "to appreciate" are subject to much broader interpretation than verbs such as "to list," "to point out," or "to compute."

Occasionally, it is difficult to decide on a verb more specific than "to appreciate" or "to understand" when developing a given performance objective. These situations require that a clear specification be made of what will be taken as evidence of "appreciating" or of "understanding." For example, will the "understanding" be demonstrated by an art project, by production of an illuminated manuscript, by a paper-and-pencil test? Acceptable indicators need to be specified by the developer of the performance objective.

No master list of tasks exists that includes all indicators of "appreciating" and "understanding." Teachers must make judgments about what might be appropriate given the unique characteristics of their own instructional situation. While the specific indicators that are chosen may vary among individuals and circumstances, there is a common necessity to *specify* the indicators selected as appropriate, whatever they may be. Clearly identified indicators make possible the continuous assessment of learners that is essential to professional program management and review.

Several verbs that may be used to pinpoint desired learner behaviors are included in Figure 3.2.

Figure 3.2

Verbs for Operationalizing Several Levels of "Knowing"

Knowledge and Understanding	Application	Analysis, Synthesis, and Evaluation
defines	computes	composes
identifies	demonstrates	creates
selects	operates	writes
converts	diagrams	compares
distinguishes	illustrates	contrasts
extends	categorizes	interprets

Conditions

Stating the *condition* under which behavior will be measured provides learners with an idea of "how and when" they are expected to demonstrate what they have learned. This component of a performance objective should provide learners with answers to questions such as the following: "What resources will be used?" "What is the general nature of the test?" The term "conditions," as it is used here, refers to *the assessment conditions, not to the nature of the provided learning experiences.* Some of the examples that follow illustrate this distinction.

1. —Given the student handbook and the guided tours provided by the student council . . . (unacceptable).

   —. . . paper and pencil test consisting of 15 true-false items given by the homeroom teacher (acceptable).

2. —After hearing the class lecture and reading the assignment on the qualifications of House and Senate members, then . . . (unacceptable).

   —. . . on a unit posttest consisting of eight multiple-choice items (acceptable).

3. —After completing the reading assignments on American writers . . . (unacceptable).

   —. . . describe how American prose differs from English prose in spelling, punctuation, and sentence structure on an essay question administered as a unit posttest (acceptable).

4. —. . . provided with the proof that "2" is an irrational number, the leader will . . . (unacceptable).

   —. . . on a unit posttest consisting of a proof of an irrational number, without text or class notes, each learner will . . . (acceptable).

5. —. . . will complete the reading assignment on acid/bases and the investigation of neutralization of acid/base solutions (unacceptable).

   —. . . submit a laboratory report following the regular format on the acid/base investigation. This report will be evaluated on the pH of each indicator . . . (acceptable).

These examples have been drawn from a number of content areas. In each of the five pairs, the first example describes the nature of the learning activity or activities that must be completed before assessment occurs. The second example in each pair specifies the testing conditions. These testing conditions include information related to type of assessment procedures to be used. A complete performance objective always includes information about these *conditions.*

Degree

The *degree* component of a performance objective indicates the extent to which a learner ought to be able to demonstrate an identified behavior as a consequence of instruction. In terms of which degree of proficiency is appropriate, there are no universal standards applicable to all teachers, classes, subject areas, or units within given courses. The research literature, too, has little to say regarding the issue. One study by Block (1972) revealed that an 80 percent criterion level (this means that objectives are presumed to be mastered when learners answer 80 percent or more of the test items correctly) results in a more favorable attitude toward learning than when the criterion level is set at 90 percent. On the other hand, greater retention of content was observed when the criterion was set at the 90 percent level.

An issue closely related to criterion levels concerns the number of questions that must be asked in a test covering any one performance objective. To assure reliability in measurement, Novick and Lewis (1974) suggest that when multiple-choice, true-false, matching, and other "non-essay" items are used, a minimum of ten items be provided for each performance objective. This would mean that if a program were organized around ten performance objectives, and the teacher wished to test with multiple-choice items, 100 items would need to be prepared (ten questions focusing on each one of the ten performance objectives).

The degree component may be stated in a variety of ways within a performance objective. The following examples illustrate some possibilities:

1. . . . answer correctly 10 of 12 questions posed orally.
2. . . . recite without error the Gettysburg Address.

3. . . . solve 80 percent of the problems on the unit posttest.
4. . . . with no more than 13 spelling or punctuation errors.

The A,B,C,D Format

As has been indicated, a complete performance objective must include references to the *audience*, the *behavior*, the *conditions*, and the *degree*. It sometimes is convenient to remember these components by coding them in memory by the first letter of each. That is, "A" for audience; "B" for behavior; "C" for conditions; and "D" for degree. A simple recall of this A,B,C,D format can prompt a quick check of a newly formulated performance objective to see that all four components are included.

In preceding sections, fragments of performance objectives have been presented to illustrate proper ways of writing each of the four essential components. In the examples provided below, all of these elements have been brought together in four sample performance objectives that properly include all essential components:

1. Each student in eighth-grade English will create metaphors such as "the cat was soft as snow" with words used in the story *Ten Billion Aardvarks.* This objective will be achieved by writing ten statements on the unit posttest, at least eight of which meet the requirements of metaphors.
2. Fred Stone, a student in the marketing and general economics class, will analyze the impact on the United States of the wheat export deal with the Soviet Union. This objective will be achieved when a two-page reaction paper has been submitted that includes specific, documented references to each of the following: (1) impact on petroleum exports of the Soviet Union; (2) impact on food prices in the United States; (3) impact on meat prices in the United States; and (4) impact on planting plans of American farmers.
3. Algebra 2 students will develop a proof demonstrating that the square root of some numbers produces an irrational number. This objective will be achieved by developing a proof of an irrational number on the unit posttest without the aid of the textbook or class notes.
4. Chemistry 1 students will demonstrate their ability to

neutralize acidic and basic solutions with a variety of indicators and a pH meter. This objective will be achieved by each student when he submits a laboratory report following the regular format. This report will be evaluated on the pH range of each indicator determined, the calibration of the pH meter, and a comparison of results using universal indicator paper.

Given these examples as models, review the following performance objectives and attempt to decide whether each is or is not written in an acceptable manner.

1. John Smith will identify, without error, a poem that has 17 syllables to the line from a group of six poems. This behavior will be demonstrated on a written posttest.
2. Each ninth-grade history student will describe five causes of the Civil War (e.g., trade agreements, economy of the North, etc.) in a short paper, maximum length four pages. Papers will be graded on spelling, sentence structure, accuracy of content, organization of content, and the inclusion of five causes of the Civil War.
3. Group four of the fifth-period class will name the capitals of the states.
4. Each student in eighth-grade music appreciation will understand music themes. This objective will be achieved by answering correctly eight of ten multiple-choice items on the posttest.

In the cases provided above, numbers 1 and 2 represent acceptable performance objectives. Each includes the key elements of *audience, behavior, conditions,* and *degree.*

Case 3 includes the audience and the behavior components of a performance objective, but the conditions and the degree are missing. Precise intent of the instructor is unclear. Is the student to name the capitals with no error at all? With five errors? Where will the capitals be named? In class tomorrow? On a self-test? On a unit posttest? To repair this objective, there is a need (1) to indicate what will be accepted as a minimum level of performance, and (2) to state how this behavior will be demonstrated for the purposes of assessment. Each of the following revisions would strengthen case three:

- ... name all of the state capitals of the United States with 100% accuracy on a matching test.
- ... name the New England states and their capitals on an oral test consisting of five questions. Each student will be expected to name each state and its capital correctly.

Case 4 also fails to meet the requirements of a complete performance objective. The audience, conditions, and degree components are satisfactory as written, but the behavior component is not specified in measurable terms. A new verb needs to be selected to replace "understand." In selecting a new verb, it is necessary to decide what behavior will be acceptable as evidence that learners do have an "understanding" of folk music themes. Either of the following revisions would be appropriate statements of the behavior component of this performance objective.

- ... will interpret popular 19th century American folk songs. This objective will be achieved by answering correctly . . . .
- ... will develop a chart on which five characteristics of folk music themes are described. This objective will be achieved by submitting this chart . . . .

Kinds of Performance Objectives

Learning can be thought of as an amalgam of cognitive, attitudinal, and psychomotor components. The *cognitive dimension* includes the intellectual, academic aspects of school experiences. The *attitudinal dimension* concerns learners' feelings about their school activities. The *psychomotor dimension* focuses on development as it relates to issues such as body muscle control and similar demands of the school curriculum.

Instructional plans that include experiences for learners in all three of these dimensions—cognitive, attitudinal, and psychomotor—facilitate learning.

Whether or not a conscious division is made, all instruction has cognitive, attitudinal, and psychomotor components. Emphases on one or another of the dimensions vary among subject areas, programs, and teachers. There is, of course, a heavier emphasis on psychomotor tasks in secondary school physical education than in English classes. But in both kinds of classes, all three components of learning are present to some degree. Consequently, regardless of the subject being taught, some consideration must be given to each of the three dimensions of learning. In the sections that follow, instructions will be provided for preparing performance objectives in the cognitive dimension, the attitudinal dimension, and the psychomotor dimension.

Cognitive Dimension

The cognitive dimension has been the subject of intense investigation. In a seminal educational document, *Taxonomy of Educational Objectives: Handbook I, Cognitive Domain*, Bloom (1956) suggests the existence of a taxonomy of cognitive learning. According to this postulated hierarchy, information is classified from the simple to the complex in a series of steps beginning with (1) memory and recall sorts of processes, and continuing with increasing sophistication through (2) comprehension, (3) application, (4) analysis, (5) synthesis, and (6) evaluation. One implication that has been drawn from this work is that teachers ought to strive for instructional procedures that enable learners increasingly to become adept at using higher level intellectual processes. As instruction unfolds, there should be an increase in learners' abilities to operate at the levels of analysis, synthesis, and evaluation. This progression is doubtful without careful planning of instructional experiences for learners.

Good planning in this area results in a systematic varying of the levels of intellectual challenges learners confront to help them move beyond reliance on mental processes demanding little more than simple recall. Without conscious attention to the need to challenge learners intellectually, there is a danger that performance objectives may demand too little of them. Memorization tasks and simple factual recitation requirements are examples of learning outcomes that, in the absence of sound planning, may be sought at the expense of those requiring application, analysis, synthesis, and evaluation.

To provide for an expanding sophistication of intellectual functioning of learners, a framework that categorizes performance objectives in terms of their conceptual difficulty is a good instructional planning tool. The following framework, an adaptation of Bloom's (1956) scheme, serves well in this regard:

Level 1:   Knowing and Understanding

Level 2: Applying
Level 3: Analyzing
Level 4: Synthesizing
Level 5: Evaluating

Under Level 1, *Knowing and Understanding*, performance objectives can be developed that:

1. require the recall of facts.
2. require an explanation for a given process or phenomenon when facts have been given previously.

Examples:

- Each pupil will write the names of at least five of the past six Presidents. This objective will be achieved . . . .
- Group six will explain orally in class, with no mistakes, which states have the highest per capita incomes according to the *Statistical Abstract of the United States.*
- Each student will write a short paper on how a bill becomes a law, mentioning at least five of the steps described in class. This paper will be evaluated . . . .

Under Level 2, *Applying*, performance objectives can be developed that:

1. require the learner to apply previously-learned information to new situations.

Examples:

- With 100% accuracy, each child will prepare maps with bodies of water depicted with the color blue.
- Each pupil will name at least five new words that start with the "p" sound. . . .
- Each student will solve for the length of the hypotenuse ten problem triangles, with 100% accuracy, using the Pythagorean theorem on the unit posttest.

Under Level 3, *Analyzing*, performance objectives can be developed that:

1. require the learner to break down known information into less complex parts.

Examples:

- Members of the seventh-period class will write a paper in which three possible causes of the 1974 petroleum shortage are discussed. Achievement of . . . .
- The student will determine the purity of the acid solutions used in experiment 15. Achievement of . . . .

- Each student in Algebra 2 will solve correctly four out of five word problems containing situations unlike those worked in class. Achievement of . . . .

Under Level 4, *Synthesizing*, performance objectives can be developed that:

1. require the learner to develop responses that go beyond a simple recitation of facts or discussion of elements of an existing situation to form an essentially new body of information.

Examples:

- The student will prepare five known solutions for colorimetric analysis. Achievement will be . . . .
- Each student will suggest six possible consequences of a change in weather that would give Phoenix, Arizona 100 inches of annual rainfall.
- Each student will write a paper in which he names the individual most likely to be the 1984 Republican candidate for President and supports his case with cited evidence. Achievement will . . . .

Under Level 5, *Evaluating*, performance objectives can be developed that:

1. require the learner to state criteria for making a judgment.
2. require the learner to make a judgment.

Examples:

- Each student will state his preference for the underhand method or the overhead method of making the basketball free throw. At least three reasons for the choice must be provided. Achievement will . . . .
- Group six will write a group paper on the effectiveness of monetary policy in slowing inflation since World War II. Positions taken will be supported by the inclusion of at least ten citations from business and economics journals. Achievement will . . . .
- Each pupil will tell why he liked or did not like the story, giving five specific reasons for his decision. Achievement will . . . .

All teachers need to write some performance objectives that fall under each of these five levels of the cognitive dimension of learning. No broad prescriptions are possible concerning the relative numbers of performance objectives that ought to be written for each level. Those decisions must be made in light of individual teaching circumstances. The important consideration is that some effort be made to plan consciously for learning at all five levels of the cognitive dimension. This assures that programs will evolve leading youngsters through a broad spectrum of learning experiences designed to increase the sophistication of their cognitive functioning. In the absence of such planning, any increases in learners' abilities to conceptualize at more abstract levels will be difficult to attribute to the instructional program.

The Attitudinal Dimension

Educators have long recognized the importance of the attitudinal dimension of learning. Statements of goals and objectives relating to attitudes and values have been a traditional feature of district curriculum guides. Despite the professed concern for values in statements of school policy, many teachers have been reluctant to develop performance objectives that focus specifically on the attitudinal dimension of learning. Teachers' hesitancy to get involved in this area stems from several traditional problems.

The first of these relates to the difficulty of evaluating attitudinal objectives. What sorts of behaviors are to be observed? What criteria can be used to establish levels of satisfactory performance? Is it even possible to measure a change in an attitude or a value? Frequently, teachers have given up the quest for answers to these thorny questions and have avoided the attitudinal dimension entirely.

A general lack of enthusiasm for developing performance objectives in this area has been reinforced by critics who contend that attitudes ought to be considered personal and private. The non-public nature of attitudes and values, they assert, means that these areas are not proper foci for instruction in schools. A difficulty with this position is that attitudes and values are bound up inextricably with the cognitive and psychomotor dimensions of learning. Since attitudes and values affect youngsters' performance on cognitive and psychomotor tasks, it is difficult to make a good case for failing to plan for learning in the attitudinal dimension. Failure to plan in the attitudinal dimension may well result in substandard learner performance on tasks relating to cognitive and psychomotor abilities as well as on specific tasks relating to attitudes or values.

There is a need to set some limits to the kinds of behaviors that ought to be sought through the use of performance objectives in the attitudinal dimension. Surely there are, for example, processes leading to the development of highly personal values that are outside the realm of the school's responsibility. On the other hand, teachers do have a proper professional role in helping youngsters develop positive attitudes toward learning. Certainly, most teachers would consider themselves ineffective should they find themselves doing a "good" job introducing content only to find that their learners had developed a distaste for the subject matter.

Abundant evidence underscores the point that educators are not doing an adequate job in the area of helping youngsters to develop a positive attitude toward learning. For instance, over one-half of our high school graduates never read a book after leaving school. Further, many elections fail to attract enough thought and discussion to bring out even half of the registered voters on election day. Teachers have a responsibility to work for development of attitudes that can change these unpleasant realities.

Attitudes are mental constructs that are inferred from observable behavior. For example, from the preceding information about voting behavior, an observer might infer an attitude of political indifference. In dealing with attitudes, teachers need to make decisions concerning which attitudes are of interest and which behaviors can be observed to infer how individual youngsters stand with respect to those attitudes. Critics sometimes are bothered by the idea that educators might want to compare youngsters in terms of how they stand with respect to certain attitudes, in much the same way that arithmetic scores might be compared. Any such use of information concerning the nature of youngsters' attitudes clearly is improper.

Youngsters' attainment of performance objectives in the attitudinal dimension must never be used for conventional grading purposes. The chief function of performance objectives in this area is to provide teachers with information concerning how their instructional programs and teaching styles are influencing attitudes of learners toward subjects they teach. This information is of great interest to individual teachers, but it is not suitable at all as a basis for determining a letter grade distribution.

The process of valuing needs to be considered as performance objectives in the attitudinal dimension are being formulated. An understanding of this process can shed light on how values come to be internalized. This information can provide a basis for preparing performance objectives that may guide instructional practices that change youngsters' feelings toward the school and the school program in a positive way.

Raths, Harmin, and Simon (1966) propose a seven-step process of valuing. The development of a value, according to their framework, involves the following seven processes:

1. Choosing freely
2. Choosing from among alternatives
3. Choosing after thoughtful consideration of the consequences of each alternative
4. Prizing and cherishing
5. Affirming
6. Acting upon choices
7. Repeating

The intent of this framework is to help individuals consider what their values are, where their values came from, and what actions they have taken reflecting their values. This information helps people to bring to consciousness values that are the bases for their decisions. When values are brought to the level of purposeful consideration, it becomes feasible for individuals to accept or reject the set of values they see themselves holding along with actions flowing logically from that set of values.

The Raths, Harmin, and Simon framework can be used to guide the development of performance objectives directed toward helping youngsters examine their values and making decisions based on those values. In most classroom situations it is not reasonable to expect students to go much beyond step five, "affirming." But objectives in the attitudinal dimension can be developed using each of the first five steps as guidelines. Some examples of such a procedure follow:

1. Choosing freely. (This level indicates that a youngster is able to make choices in the absence of pressure.)
   Example:
   When confronted with several alternative positions in a

class discussion, the group will allow each individual to
choose his position without exerting pressure on him.

2. Choosing from among alternatives. (This level indicates
that a youngster knows what other choices are available.)
Example:

When making a choice of a position, the learner is able
to name at least two other possible choices.

3. Choosing after thoughtful consideration of the consequence of each alternative. (This level indicates that a
youngster understands consequences of a choice made
from among several alternative possibilities.)
Example:

After making a choice, the learner is able to state
possible consequences of that choice.

4. Prizing and cherishing. (This level indicates that a youngster is characterized by a sincere personal satisfaction with
the choice he has made.)
Example:

After making a choice, the learner is able to state his
satisfaction with that choice through either written or
oral statements.

5. Affirming.
(This level indicates that a youngster is willing to commit
himself to his choice in a public setting.)
Example:

By the conclusion of the unit, the learner will have
made at least one public statement of his commitment
to a choice he has made.

The utility of attitudinal-dimension objectives derived through
the use of this scheme relates most directly to the interest teachers
have in identifying values learners hold and to which they are
willing to make a public commitment. This framework is less
useful as a mechanism for organizing performance objectives
directed toward promoting positive attitudes toward learning. In
this connection, teachers' interest resides not so much in determining what a student values at a given point in time as in promoting
an appreciation for learning outcomes that are valued by the
school as an institution.

As a preliminary step in developing performance objectives to promote improved attitudes toward learning, it is desirable to ask questions such as: "What do people who have an appreciation of subject 'X' do?" Take the example of music. Music buffs frequently are observed listening to recordings or to classical music stations. They read articles and books about music. They attend concerts. They go to lectures given by prominent conductors and other musical figures. Finally, they talk about music whenever the opportunity presents itself.

A comparable list of behaviors could be prepared for football fans, fisherman, skiers, or stamp collectors. All of these people spend much of their free time engaged in rather predictable sorts of activities.

This same technique can be applied to determine the degree to which educational programs are developing committed "fans." There is a need to determine the behavioral indicators that will be expected in youngsters who are "turned on" by lessons focusing on the American heritage, or chemistry, or stitchery. Performance objectives in this area should center around behaviors commonly seen in individuals who have "taken" to given subjects. For example, the following behaviors might be tried as likely indicators of a positive attitude toward reading:

By the conclusion of the unit, English 1 students will demonstrate an appreciation of reading by:
1. getting a library card at the public library.
2. choosing to read during at least 25% of "free time" periods.
3. voluntarily telling others about a "good book."
4. buying books from the book club.

True, there may not be a one-to-one relationship between each of these criteria and the general area of "appreciation of reading," but the accumulated evidence of the several behaviors taken collectively can provide valuable evidence regarding the degree of "appreciation." Information derived from these behaviors provides a useful referent for teachers considering possible changes in instructional practices.

A final area relating to the attitudinal component of learning concerns the development of performance objectives that enable learners to recognize values that undergird decisions made by others. When youngsters are taught to search for values lying behind statements of others, they become less susceptible to propaganda. An example of a performance objective of this type follows:

> Given three statements on the posttest, each seventh grade history student will list the values implied by each statement and will identify the statement most consistent with the values expressed in the Bill of Rights.

Few teachers have been grounded formally in the preparation of performance objectives in the attitudinal dimension. This situation is to be regretted because careful instructional planning, centering around well-stated performance objectives, can produce rich dividends. Hopefully, this dimension of learning will attract increasing professional attention as the intimate connection between students' attitudes and their success in the total school program becomes appreciated more widely.

The Psychomotor Dimension

The psychomotor dimension centers on the physiological aspects of learning. While motor responses obviously are an essential feature of some curriculum areas more than others (notably physical education), they play a role throughout the entire school program. The psychomotor dimension includes such important skills as hand-eye coordination and large and small muscle control. This dimension of learning plays a particularly important role in handwriting, reading readiness, music, physical education, and art.

The psychomotor dimension of learning typically focuses on a motor response of some kind. Performance objectives in this area tend to be sequenced in such a fashion that the learner, ultimately, will be able to perform specific psychomotor tasks unaided and in different situations. Three levels of behavior in the psychomotor dimension constitute a framework for systematic development of performance objectives in this area:

> Level 1: *Performs as guided.* (At this level, the learner performs an activity properly when directions and help are provided.)
> *Examples*:
> • Each pupil will write one row of the small letter "o" in which no part of any letter extends above the "beltline."

- John will perform successfully at least two somersaults, aided by the teacher.
- Each pupil will tie his own shoelace, at least once, aided by the teacher.

Level 2: *Performs unaided one time.* (At this level, the learner has internalized the new behavior to the extent that he can perform at least once without teacher help.)

Examples:

- Each student will raise at least one six-inch pot on the potters wheel.
- Pupils will print two rows of small "n's" with no parts cutting through the "beltline."
- Each pupil will do at least one backward roll unaided by the teacher.

Level 3: *Performs unaided repeatedly and in different settings.* (At this level, the behavior should be internalized so well that the learner can perform at will in a variety of situations.)

Examples:

- Each pupil will catch a ball from a distance of ten feet at least eight out of ten times on at least three different days selected at random.
- Each student will make at least six out of ten free throws in basketball on at least three different days selected at random.
- Students will walk at least 12 feet on the balance beam on at least three different days selected at random.

The emphasis in performance objectives in the psychomotor domain is on helping youngsters to develop internal motor control over various physical acts. Teaching activities in this area need to be sequenced to assist learners in moving from aided to unaided performance. The timing and exact nature of activities provided will vary from situation to situation. A determination of the appropriateness of instructional plans in this area must be made in the light of a careful consideration of available diagnostic information. Some mechanisms for gathering such information will be provided in the next chapter.

Summary

Experimental studies reveal that instructional programs guided by performance objectives result in higher achievement levels for learners. These performance objectives, in a complete instructional program, need to focus on learning in (1) the cognitive dimension, (2) the attitudinal dimension, and (3) the psychomotor dimension. In this chapter, procedures for developing performance objectives in each of these areas were described, and examples of acceptable performance objectives in each area were provided. Consonant with the model of instruction introduced in Chapter 2, performance objectives were described as essential components in a systematic plan of instruction in which expected outcomes of instruction become an integral part of the planning process.

References

BLOCK, James H. "Student Learning and the Setting of Mastery Performance Standards." *Educational Horizons* (Summer 1972).

BLOOM, Benjamin S. (ed). *Taxonomy of Educational Objectives; Handbook I: Cognitive Domain.* New York: David McKay Company, Inc., 1956.

FERRE, Alvin V. *Effects of Repeated Performance Objectives Upon Student Achievement and Attitude.* Ed.D. Dissertation, New Mexico State University, 1972.

HUCK, Schuyler W. and James D. LONG. "The Effects of Behavioral Objectives on Student Achievement." *The Journal of Experimental Education* (Fall 1973), 40-41.

LOH, Elwert L. *The Effect of Behavioral Objectives on Measures of Learning and Forgetting in High School Algebra.* Ph.D. Dissertation, University of Maryland, 1972.

MORSE, Jean A. and Murray H. TILLMAN. "Achievement as Affected by Possession of Behavioral Objectives." *Engineering Education* (June 1973), 124-126.

NOVICK, Melvin R. and Charles LEWIS. "Prescribing Test Length for Criterion-Referenced Measures." In *Problems in Criterion-Referenced Measurement.* C.W. Harris, M.C. Alkin, W.J. Popham (eds.). Los Angeles: Center for the Study of Evaluation (UCLA), 1974.

OLSEN, Robert C. "A Comparative Study of the Effects of Behavioral Objectives on Class Performance and Retention in Physical Science." *Journal of Research in Science Teaching* (No. 3, 1973), 3.

RATHS, Louis F., Merrill HARMIN and Sidney B. SIMON. *Values and*

Teaching. Columbus, Ohio: Charles E. Merrill Publishing Co., 1966.

TAYLOR, Curtis L. *et al*. "Use of Inferred Objectives with Non-Objectives-Based Instructional Materials." Tempe, Arizona: Arizona State Univeristy, Research Sponsored by Air Force Human Resources Laboratory, Williams Air Force Base, Arizona Flying Training Division, October 1972.

Additional Professional Study

Books

BLOOM, Benjamin S. (ed.). *Taxonomy of Educational Objectives; Handbook I: Cognitive Domain*. New York: David McKay Company, Inc., 1956.

CLARK, D. Cecil. *Using Instructional Objectives in Teaching*. Glenview, Ill.: Scott, Foresman and Company, 1972.

FERRE, Alvin V. *Effects of Repeated Performance Objectives Upon Student Achievement and Attitude*. Ed.D. Dissertation, New Mexico State University, 1972.

GRONLUND, Norman E. *Stating Behavioral Objectives for Classroom Instruction*. New York: Macmillan Publishing Co., Inc., 1970.

HARROW, Anita J. *A Taxonomy of the Psychomotor Domain*. New York: David McKay Co., Inc., 1972.

HOOK, Julius N. *et al*. *Representative Performance Objectives for High School English*. New York: Ronald Press, 1971.

KAPFER, Miriam B. *et al*. *Behavioral Objectives in Curriculum Development*. Englewood Cliffs, N.J.: Educational Technology Publications, Inc., 1971.

KIBLER, Robert J., Larry L. BARKER and David T. MILES. *Behavioral Objectives and Instruction*. Boston: Allyn and Bacon, Inc., 1970.

KRATHWOHL, David R. *et al*. *Taxonomy of Educational Objectives; Handbook II: Affective Domain*. New York: David McKay Company, Inc., 1964.

LOH, Elwert L. *The Effect of Behavioral Objectives on Measures of Learning and Forgetting High School Algebra*. Ph.D. Dissertation, University of Maryland, 1972.

MAGER, Robert F. *Preparing Instructional Objectives*. Palo Alto, Calif.: Fearon Publishers, 1962.

MC ASHAN, Hildreth H. *Writing Behavioral Objectives: A New Approach*. New York: Harper & Row, Publishers, 1970.

NOVICK, Melvin R., and Charles LEWIS. "Prescribing Test Length for Criterion-Referenced Measures." In *Problems in Criterion-Referenced Measurement*. C.W. Harris, M.C. Alkin, W.J. Popham (eds.). Los Angeles: Center for the Study of Evaluation (UCLA), 1974.

PLOWMAN, Paul D. *Behavioral Objectives: Teacher Success Through Student Performance*. Chicago, Ill.: Science Research Associates, Inc., 1971.

POPHAM, W. James and Eva L. BAKER. *Establishing Instructional Objectives*. Englewood Cliffs, N.J.: Prentice-Hall, Inc., 1970.

RATHS, Louis F., Merrill HARMIN and Sidney B. SIMON. *Values and Teaching.* Columbus, Ohio: Charles E. Merrill Publishing Co., 1966.

Periodicals

BLOCK, James H. "Student Learning and the Setting of Mastery Performance Standards." *Educational Horizons* (Summer 1972).

CAFFYN, L. "Behavioral Objectives: English-Style." *Elementary English* (December 1968), 1073-74.

CONSALVO, R.W. "Evaluation and Behavioral Objectives." *American Biology Teacher* (April 1969), 230-260.

EISNER, Elliot W. "Educational Objectives: Help or Hindrance?" *The School Review* (Autumn 1967), 250-260.

ENGMAN, Bill D. "Behavioral Objectives: Key to Planning." *The Science Teacher* (October 1968), 86-87.

ESBENSEN, Thorwald. "Writing Instructional Objectives." *Phi Delta Kappan* (January 1967), 246-247.

FREY, Sherman. "Behavioral Objectives: Attitudes of Teachers." *The Clearing House* (April 1974), 487-490.

HABERMAN, M. "Behavioral Objectives: Bandwagon or Breakthrough?" *The Journal of Teacher Education* (Spring 1968), 91-94.

HUCK, Schuyler W. and James D. LONG. "The Effects of Behavioral Objectives on Student Achievement." *The Journal of Experimental Education* (Fall 1973), 40-41.

MORSE, Jean A. and Murray H. TILLMAN. "Achievement As Affected by Possession of Behavioral Objectives." *Engineering Education* (June 1973), 124-126.

OLSEN, Robert C. "A Comparative Study of the Effects of Behavioral Objectives on Class Performance and Retention in Physical Science." *Journal of Research in Science Teaching* (No. 3, 1973), 271-277.

Chapter 4

Diagnosing Learners

OBJECTIVES

This chapter provides information to help the reader to:

1. describe general strengths and weaknesses of selected diagnostic data-gathering procedures.

2. derive specific "information needs" from performance objectives.

3. identify diagnostic data sources most suitable for meeting specified "information needs."

4. prepare and utilize "test out" procedures.

5. develop master lists of remediation possibilities for use when learners are discovered to have entry-level deficiencies.

6. develop prescriptions for individual learners.

_____

"Begin where learners are" is a time-honored phrase in education. Serious attempts to respond programmatically to individual differences must be preceded by a systematic gathering and ordering of diagnostic information. This information serves as a data base for teachers to draw upon as they begin to make decisions regarding how learners' needs might best be met.

In instructional programs constructed in such a way that each new unit of work builds logically upon the unit just completed, final evaluation data from the "just completed" unit serves well as a source of diagnostic information. In such cases, an examination of learners' performances on this completed work helps teachers to identify students who failed to acquire skills and knowledges they must have before they can be expected to deal adequately with new material. Once such individuals are identified, prescriptions can be prepared, designed to help them overcome deficiencies.

In other instances, proposed new learning experiences bear little direct relationship to work just finished. Under these conditions, records of learners' performances on prior learning tasks are not helpful in pinpointing potential areas of difficulty individual students may experience with the new material. Given these circumstances, teachers must look to other sources of diagnostic information as they attempt to identify individuals lacking the prerequisite knowledges and skills necessary for success. In the next section, a number of potentially useful diagnostic data sources will be introduced along with suggestions for judging the usefulness of each.

Though an integral and important part of the instructional process, diagnosing learners must be accomplished relatively quickly. Priorities must be established so that time allotted for the purpose of gathering and interpreting diagnostic information is much shorter than that for interacting with learners during the actual implementation of strategies selected to support performance objectives.

In this connection, the authors would point out that *it is not necessary to consider the use of every source of diagnostic information for every student in the classroom.* Because of past experiences with a class, teachers frequently have reliable information about how most will fare with planned new material. Further, as professionals, few teachers set out deliberately to plan something so sophisticated that most students will lack necessary entry-level knowledges and skill. Teachers should begin the process of diagnosing learners by focusing attention on those few students who, they suspect, may have some problems.

Diagnostic information should be gathered first about those students that teachers have identified as "possibly deficient" in terms of needed entry-level competencies for the new work. Then, if time permits, additional diagnostic information can be obtained on others as a means of checking teachers' initial impressions that they have the necessary prerequisite knowledges and skills.

Professional diagnosis begins with identification of the performance objectives that will guide development of a new unit of instruction. By referencing diagnostic procedures to performance objectives, teachers can pinpoint specific prerequisite knowledges and skills students will need to deal successfully with material to be introduced in the new unit. Additionally, performance objectives suggest hoped-for attitudes that the teacher would like learners to have at the conclusion of the instructional sequence.

For the purpose of illustrating how performance objectives may be used to guide selection of appropriate diagnostic procedures, two sample performance objectives are provided below. Diagnostic techniques discussed throughout the remainder of the chapter will be evaluated in terms of how teachers might view them, assuming an instructional program that included these two performance objectives.

- *Objective 1: cognitive dimension (application level)*
  Each student in eight-grade English will create metaphors with words used in the story "The Peddler of Ballaghadereen." This objective will be achieved by writing ten statements on the unit posttest, at least eight of which meet the requirements of metaphors.

- *Objective 2: attitudinal dimension (prizing and affirming)*
  Each student in eighth-grade English will rate folk tales higher after reading "The Peddler of Ballaghadereen" than before as measured by changes in ratings on an attitude inventory given before and after the story is read. Further, each student will write a few sentences after each rating on both pre- and post-administrations of the inventory, explaining his rating of each choice.

An examination of a set of performance objectives can suggest specific prerequisite knowledges and skills students will need for success in a new unit of work guided by those objectives. Further, the nature of the performance objectives may imply certain hoped-for attitudes. For example, a careful consideration of these two sample performance objectives might result in the identification of the following prerequisite knowledges, prerequisite skills, and hoped-for attitudes:

Prerequisite knowledges suggested by performance objectives 1 and 2.
1. The term "figure of speech" (used in defining "metaphor").

2. The term "analogy" (used in defining "metaphor").
3. The term "literal" (used in defining "metaphor").
4. The term "denotation" (used in defining "metaphor").

Total prerequisite knowledges = 4

Prerequisite skills suggested by performance objectives 1 and 2.
1. Ability to read material written at a grade seven or eight level of readability (level of "The Peddler of Ballaghadereen").
2. Ability to write sentences free of mechanical errors.
3. Ability to verbalize personal concerns (lack of understanding, etc.).
4. Ability to absorb information through listening (teacher instructions and explanations, teacher-learner discussions, etc.)

Total prerequisite skills = 4

Hoped-for attitudes suggested by performance objectives 1 and 2.
1. Increased interest in reading.
2. Willingness to make known personal decisions in a public setting.
3. Increased interest in folk tales.
4. Increased interest in the use of metaphors.

Total hoped-for attitudes = 4

By using these dozen areas of prerequisite knowledges and skills and hoped-for attitudes, a narrowing of focus results, enabling an efficient and purposeful selection of diagnostic data sources. Specification of these informational needs adds a great deal of precision to the task of extracting "necessary" information from the various data sources that might be potentially useful. Clearly, some of these sources will yield much more pertinent information than others. An assessment of the relative merits of alternative sources related to the two sample performance objectives will be provided as each of the diagnostic data collection procedures is discussed in the pages that follow.

The Work Sample

Old examinations, notebooks, papers, projects, laboratory reports, and other examples of learners' previous work can provide insights relating to students' development. In selecting work samples as a source of diagnostic data, teachers need to choose those that reflect learners' competencies and attitudes in pertinent areas. For example, if a teacher were to gather diagnostic information relevant to the two sample performance objectives that have been introduced here, work samples taken from the areas of language arts and reading would be the most appropriate.

Once relevance has been determined, the issue of quantity must be faced. Regrettably, there is no simple standard for determining when "enough" work samples have been examined for instructional decisions to be made with some confidence. In general, there is a need to look at several pieces of past work so that common patterns emerge that appear to be of a persistent nature. For example, if sentence structure tends to be shaky on four or five papers a given student has written, the likelihood that the student has a real problem in this area is much greater than if only a single piece of former work reflected this difficulty. (All learners have their "good" and "bad" days.)

In addition to the general principle of examining several work samples before rendering a judgment, it also makes good sense to select as many work samples as possible that reflect learners' more recent work. Hopefully, the instructional program is changing learners' behavior over time. If this is the case, a distorted view of levels of attainment may result if judgments are made on the basis of dated work samples.

Regarding the information needs derived from the two sample performance objectives, work samples would be most useful as sources indicating relative abilities in the area of writing sentences free of mechanical errors. In some instances, work samples may also provide insights regarding learners' capacity for verbalizing personal concerns, absorbing information through listening, enjoying reading, and making known personal decisions. Other information needs suggested by the two sample performance objectives would not be well served had teachers to rely only on work samples.

When teachers *do* decide that a given diagnostic data source can provide information of interest, there is a need to process that information and establish procedures for making decisions about individual youngsters. As an example, consider the information need relating to learners' "ability to write sentences free of mechanical errors." Were a given student found to be weak in this area, how much "evidence" would be required to establish the need for a special learning prescription?

The authors suggest a system according to which learners who show evidence of experiencing problems with writing mechanics *on more than one-half* of the work samples examined be identified as in need of special help. This is an arbitrary standard. Another decision-rule might serve equally as well so long as it were applied consistently. For learners identified as deficient, using whatever standard is adopted, teachers will wish to develop special learning prescriptions. Procedures for accomplishing this task will be introduced later in the chapter.

The Anecdotal Record

Anecdotal records are brief written summaries that focus on specific classroom incidents. Typically, behaviors of a single learner or group are described. For the purpose of serving as a valuable data source, anecdotal records are of use only when teachers conscientiously set out to record information that is pertinent to the demands to be placed on students in a new unit of work.

Examining the information needs suggested by the two sample performance objectives, how might anecdotal records best serve as a data source? The procedure would be of doubtful utility as a vehicle for gaining useful information regarding learners' understanding of such prerequisite knowledges as the terms "figure of speech," "analogy," "literal," and "denotation."

In the area of prerequisite skills, an anecdotal record might be of some value as a source of information regarding learners' abilities to deal with printed material written at a grade seven or grade eight level of readability. However, use of an anecdotal record procedure to get this information requires that judgments be made only on the basis of learners' oral reading skills. (There is no way to observe *visually* whether reading level difficulties are interfering with learners' progress during silent reading sessions.)

A serious difficulty in making decisions about learners' problems with reading textual material based only on observation of oral reading is that there are many explanations for oral reading problems that have little to do with the issue of grade level readability. A given learner may simply be nervous when reading in public. Another may understand terms visually that he has never heard pronounced and which he will stumble over in an oral reading session. Because of such possibilities, teachers should consider use of an anecdotal record to determine learners' levels of reading competence only when more suitable data sources are not available.

In the prerequisite skills area, the most appropriate use of the anecdotal record would be as a data source for information about ability to verbalize personal concerns. After class discussions, when individual youngsters have spoken their thoughts about issues of personal concern, teachers might take time to recall and record recollections of what was said. There is no need to be verbose. A few lines will do. Until there is time to evaluate these notations and make selective comments in the folders of one or two students, a running anecdotal record book can be maintained in which all notations are kept.

Teachers might use the anecdotal record to gain information regarding increasing interest in reading. But probably a better data source would be an interest inventory or some other procedure providing a more direct measure than is possible through the use of an anecdotal record.

Perhaps the best use of the anecdotal record in the hoped-for attitudes area would be as a source of information about a student's willingness to make known personal decisions. Many opportunities occur during class meetings when learners find themselves caught between attractive options. Frequently, the selection of any one of these will have both negative and positive consequences. In such situations, many learners seek to escape the dilemma by avoiding a decision entirely. Social psychologists suggest that the ability to make a decision in full knowledge of the consequences is a hallmark of the maturely integrated personality. Data gathered about learners' abilities to make decisions, therefore, are of high interest.

In attending to this matter in the anecdotal record, a brief notation should be made about the nature of the decision-making opportunity and whether the learner chose to make a public decision or chose not to do so. As time permits, it is desirable that several entries be made for each person. It is useful to organize entries in the anecdotal record book under headings directly related to the information needs derived from program objectives. Ordinarily, one or two pages will suffice for information about a given student. In the example provided below, there has been an attempt to organize information related to (1) ability to verbalize personal concerns, and (2) willingness to make known personal decisions.

Given an anecdotal record notebook filled with entries such as those in Figure 4.1, there is a need for a decision-rule regarding

---

Figure 4.1

Sample Page from an Anecdotal Record Notebook

Abrams, Adolph

Time span covered = 5 days, 10/21 - 10/25

Verbalize Concerns	**Make Decisions**
10/21 Asked for help on homework.	10/21 Adolph was asked to run for president of either the varsity club or the student council. He declined, saying he couldn't decide.
10/23 Adolph, Steve, and Joe engaged me in a long discussion after class about vocabulary problems.	10/22 Decided the "tramps" were the heroes and the "merchants" the villains in the story.
10/24 Adolph volunteered three times today to make personal comments on the story.	10/23 Said he couldn't decide whether the class should read a novel or write a play next.
10/25 Adolph "took on" Barbara and Sam to defend his feeling that we should slow down and do more vocabulary work.	10/24 Refused to referee a basketball game. Said he didn't want to call the "close ones."

when special prescriptions are necessary for individual learners. If problems occur on more than one-half of the days during the time span covered, a special learning prescription would be in order.

In the case of learner Abrams (see Figure 4.1), an observer might note that he was able to "verbalize personal concerns" on four out of the five days under consideration. Since this represents well over one-half of the days under review, logically there would be no need for a special prescription for this individual in this area. But regarding "willingness to make known personal decisions" quite a different conclusion emerges concerning the desirability of special help. On three out of the four days for which data was recorded in the anecdotal record notebook, this student showed evidence of having great difficulty in making decisions. This pattern suggests a need for a prescription designed to help him feel more comfortable about making his personal conclusions known. Given this situation, the teacher would probably wish to make a notation in this student's folder and to begin thinking about prescriptive possibilities.

The Conference

In form, the conference represents nothing more sophisticated than a planned conversation between the teacher and a student. The utility of the conference as a source of diagnostic data depends directly on the degree to which the teacher can structure the dialogue. By referring to performance objectives that will be guiding the design of new learning tasks, a teacher can assure a conference of substance (that is, a conference from which *useful* information can be derived) by preparing a series of focal questions in advance.

Certainly, conferences should not be reduced to mechanical performances in which teachers ask planned questions, learners respond, and both teachers and learners move forward woodenly like programmed puppets. Spontaneity ought to be encouraged. Issues not addressed by focal questions that may be of great importance to learners need to be aired.

The function of focal questions is not to restrict the range of the dialogue, but rather to prompt teachers to probe for answers to issues that performance objectives suggest are important at some point during the discussion. Teachers may never have to ask directly any of their planned focal questions. Frequently, answers to these questions will emerge as a natural part of the ebb and flow of the conversation. Teachers do have, however, a responsibility to get this "essential" information, and sometimes thay may have to resort to the more direct focal questions to accomplish that objective.

The conference is a one-on-one procedure. As such, it extracts a heavy "cost" in terms of time. For this reason, use of the conference ought to be restricted to information that the conference can gather better than other available diagnostic techniques.

With regard to the two sample performance objectives, the conference has the capability to yield information concerning learners' mastery of the identified prerequisite knowledges (learner understanding of the terms "figure of speech," "analogy," "literal," and "denotation"). But using the conference to provide this information represents a time-consuming, inefficient use of the technique.

In the prerequisite skills area, the conference would not be a useful tool to help teachers assess learners' reading levels or their ability to write sentences free of mechanical errors. On the other hand, the conference would be well suited as a vehicle for providing information relating to abilities to verbalize personal concerns. The conference is a better choice than the anecdotal record in providing information about this general area. In the conference, the teacher, by careful selection of questions, can assure a supply of information relevant to this issue.

In the area of hoped-for attitudes, the conference can be moderately useful as a source of information regarding learners' levels of interest in reading in general, and in reading folk tales in particular. Probably, though, this information could be obtained more conveniently through the use of a preference inventory administered to the entire class at the same time.

As a technique for providing information about learners' willingness to make known personal decisions in public, the conference is a poor choice. The conference involves only a teacher and a single learner, not exactly a private setting but certainly an arrangement that strains the intent of the phrase "public setting."

Additionally, the conference requires too much teacher time to be considered an appropriate tool for determining levels of learners' interest in metaphors. Other techniques could provide this information much more efficiently.

Of all the information needs suggested by the two sample performance objectives, the conference seems best suited to provide data relating to learners' "ability to verbalize personal concerns." If Betty Benz, for example, had been selected for a personal conference to elicit information regarding this ability, the teacher would begin by preparing some focus questions. These questions would be designed with a view to prompting the learner to talk about potential difficulties and concerns. A set of questions prepared for use with Betty Benz might look something like the following:

1. Do you have any problems or concerns about what we are studying in class now?
   ... (If *Yes*) Can you describe the specific nature of these problems?

2. Do you have any worries about speaking up in class?
   ... (If *Yes*) Can you describe the specific nature of these problems?

When replies indicate problems on more than half of the questions asked about a given topic area, there is a need for special learning prescriptions to be prepared. Special notations ought to be made in the folders of learners for whom remedial action is indicated.

The Observation Checklist

The observation checklist has versatility as a source of diagnostic data because teachers can develop categories that "capture" information about very specific behaviors of interest. But for all of its adaptability to wide-ranging informational needs, the checklist presents problems in the area of implementation. The basic difficulty centers on the problem of keeping a running tally on learners' behaviors in several categories at the same time the class is being taught. Teachers frequently attempt to resolve this dilemma by inviting in a second party to serve as observer. This procedure, however, introduces the perceptions of someone other than the teacher between the behavior itself and the recorded evidence of the behavior.

These difficulties suggest that the checklist is a tool teachers ought to use when students in their own classes are involved in seat-work of some kind. At such times teachers are free to observe and record the behaviors of their own youngsters without, at the same time, having to engage in a formal verbal presentation.

Regarding the information needs suggested by the two sample performance objectives, the checklist would not be suitable as a source for data providing information about learners' grasp of the identified prerequisite knowledges. Likewise, the checklist would not serve well as a vehicle for providing information about prerequisite skills. These knowledges and skills are not likely to show themselves as behaviors that can be classified and logged in terms of frequency of occurrence on a checklist.

In the area of hoped-for attitudes, the checklist would be a poor choice as a source of diagnostic data relating to (1) "willingness to make known personal decisions in a public setting" (this could be reduced to a behavior on a checklist, but the situation suggests a great deal of interaction, demanding time-consuming teacher involvement), and (2) "increasing interest in metaphors" (how does one "act out" this behavior so its frequency of occurrence can be tallied?).

The observation checklist would serve well as a data source in the remaining two areas of the hoped-for attitudes category, namely (1) "increasing interest in reading," and (2) "increasing interest in folk tales." Since teachers wish to see an "increase" in both of these areas, it is desirable to obtain baseline data about interest in reading and in folk tales before the new instructional program begins. Use of a checklist can provide this baseline information.

Preparatory to using a checklist for this purpose, it would be necessary to arrange for a classroom situation in which learners are permitted to select activities from among several options. This might involve establishment of a "free study time" in which students might work on mathematics problems, go to listening carrels, read books, or engage in other learning options. A large number of books should be provided. Among these books, a good sprinkling of folk tales would be included.

Since learners require a few minutes to settle into a new activity, no attempt should be made to tally behaviors for the entire 20-minute period. Tallies should start only after students have settled into a relatively stable activity pattern. A checklist something like the following would serve well as a vehicle for organizing the tally marks.

Figure 4.2

A Sample Observation Checklist

	Reading: Folk Tales	Reading: Not Folk Tales	Doing Math Problems	Doing Art Work	Not Working
Abrams	111	111			1111
Benz			THL THL		
Cole	THL	11		111	
Denny		THL THL			
Ender		1111		THL 1	
Fogg					THL THL
Howar	1111		THL 1		
Islip	1111	THL 1			
Judd			THL THL		
Kent	11	THL 1			11
Lee	THL		11	111	

In gathering data for inclusion in a checklist such as the one depicted in Figure 4.2, tallies need to be made at regular clock intervals. A rate of one tally per learner per minute generates a great deal of information. Although this sounds very fast, it can be accomplished with little difficulty. Once the procedure is underway, little time is required to glance at an individual, see what he is doing, and place a tally mark under the appropriate heading.

Decisions about individuals ought not to be made on the basis of a single day's observation. When feasible, checklists should be kept for three or four days (a week is even better). When several days' data have been collected, it is necessary to collapse information from the several checklists to make up a "master checklist." The "master checklist" includes a total for each learner of the number of tallies in each category taken over the entire observation period. For example, looking only at the row with data on a hypothetical learner, Adolph Abrams, part of a completed "master checklist" would appear as indicated in Figure 4.3.

To determine this student's relative interest in reading, the first step is to compare the total number of tallies for non-reading activities (doing math problems, doing art work, not working) to the total number of tallies across all categories. Since the non-preferred behavior (something other than reading) occurred more than half the time, it would be logical to conclude that this student might profit from a special prescription designed to enhance his interest in reading. Even more pointedly, his ex-

---

Figure 4.3

Illustration of One Learner's Tallies
on a Master Observation Checklist

	Reading: Folk Tales	Reading: *Not* Folk Tales	Doing Math Problems	Doing Art Work	Not Working
Abrams	4	20	10	11	5

tremely low frequency of free-choice selection of folk tales (four of 50 tallies reflect this behavior) suggests the desirability of systematic work to build his interest in this area. It would be well to put notations in this student's folder regarding patterns revealed by the "master observation checklist."

The Interest Inventory

As a source of diagnostic data, the interest inventory is particularly useful when teachers wish to gather information regarding learners' relative ranking of a subject or topic before a new unit of instruction begins. Interest inventories can be prepared according to a variety of formats. One simple procedure involves a listing of statements to which learners are required to respond with a "yes" or a "no" answer. Other forms include listings of statements that students are asked to arrange in order of preference.

In terms of the information needs suggested by the two sample performance objectives, the interest inventory would be a poor source of diagnostic data relating to learners' prerequisite knowledge. By its nature, the interest inventory does not work well as a collector of data relating to understanding of cognitive concepts (such as, for example, "figure of speech," "analogy," "literal," and "denotation"). Similarly, the interest inventory would be of little use in obtaining information regarding prerequisite skills.

However, since by design the interest inventory probes concerns that are a function of attitudes, it is an outstanding procedure to use to gather data relating to hoped-for attitudes. Indeed, the interest inventory can be used to gather information about all hoped-for attitudes that can be written in such a way that they "make sense" as part of a preference rating scale. Of the hoped-for attitudes suggested by the two sample performance objectives, only "willingness to make known personal decisions in public" does not lend itself well to inclusion on that kind of a scale. Interest inventories would be apt choices for gathering diagnostic information about each of the remaining hoped-for attitudes ("increased interest in reading," "increased interest in folk tales," "increased interest in the use of metaphors").

Examples of how interest inventories might be used to provide baseline information with regard to each of these hoped-for attitudes are included in Figure 4.4.

Figure 4.4

Examples of Interest Inventories

1. Interest in Reading   Name: Daniel Denny

Directions: On the paper below are several activities you might be able to do during a free study time. Write the number "1" in the blank before an activity you would *most* like to do, a "2" before the activity with the next highest interest to you. Continue in this way until you finish with an "8" in front of your *least preferred* activity. (Note to the teacher: With younger children, directions would have to be simplified and given orally.)

1	tool leather	6	build models
4	read stories	7	draw pictures
3	do math problems	2	make clay projects
5	write stories	8	do science experiments

2. Interest in Folk Tales   Name: Daniel Denny

Directions: You will have a chance to choose different kinds of stories during free reading time. Look at the following list. Place a "1" before your *first choice*, a "2" before your *second choice*. Continue on until you conclude with an "8" in the blank before your *last choice*.

1	reading mystery stories	7	reading plays
8	reading fairy stories	2	reading travel stories
5	reading folk tales	6	reading poetry
3	reading biographies	4	reading adventure stories

3. Interest in Metaphors   Name: Daniel Denny

Directions: During the next few weeks, we will study some terms used in analyzing prose and poetry. Some of these terms may be of more interest

(Continued on next page)

Figure 4.4
(Continued)

to you than others. Look at the following list of terms. Place a "1" in the blank before the term of *highest personal interest*, a "2" in the blank before the term with the *next highest personal interest*. Continue in the same way until you conclude with an "8" in the blank before the term of *lowest personal interest* to you. (Note to the teacher: Use of this inventory presupposes that learners have an understanding of the meanings of these terms.)

6	caesura	7	iambic pentameter
1	simile	4	personification
2	metaphor	5	alliteration
8	alexandrain	3	onomatopoeia

Procedures for assessing needs of individual learners from an analysis of data gathered by interest inventories parallels those suggested previously for use with other diagnostic data gathering techniques. First a determination needs to be made of the relative standing of the topic of interest (for example of "metaphor" in sample test 3 in Figure 4.4 above). If more than one-half of the remaining topics were rated higher than the topic of interest, this may suggest the need for developing a special prescription designed to stimulate greater enthusiasm for that topic. Notations need to be made in the folders of students showing little initial enthusiasm for issues identified as important by hoped-for attitudes derived from performance objectives. These notations ought to include references to the specific nature of any teacher-developed learning prescriptions.

Prerequisite Knowledge Tests

As vehicles for gathering data about learner's understandings of prerequisite knowledges, tests which teachers develop themselves are apt choices. Such tests enjoy the particular advantage of focusing specifically on knowledge identified as essential for learners' success on a contemplated new unit of instruction.

Rarely can teachers find commercially-developed tests that are designed to provide information relating to the unique information needs derived from the performance objectives that have been selected to guide the instructional program.

The multiple-choice test is a particularly reliable instrument for teachers to use to assess learners' mastery of entry-level knowledges. Multiple-choice tests would serve well as devices to gather information about prerequisite knowledges developed from the two sample performance objectives ("figure of speech," "analogy," "literal," "denotation"). Several multiple-choice tests and identification tests are provided in Figure 4.5 as illustrations of the use of teacher made tests for determining learners' relative standings on prerequisite knowledges. (Text continues on page 74).

Figure 4.5

*Samples of Teacher-Made Tests
for Assessing Prerequisite Knowledges*

1. Identification: "figure of speech."   Name: Daniel Denny
                                                       ....

Directions: Webster's New Collegiate Dictionary (G & C Merriam, Springfield, Massachusetts, 1974) defines "figure of speech" as "a form of expression . . . used to convey meaning or heighten effect often by comparing or identifying one thing with another that has a meaning or connotation familiar to the reader or listener."

Look at the following passages. Two phrases have been italicized in each. Circle the letter identifying the phrase that is an example of a "figure of speech" as the term is defined in *Webster's.*

1. The tiny vessel separated the waters *like a plow* as it moved *eastward toward Liverpool.*

    b.

2. The *newly appointed* commander, *happy as a lark,* announced, "48 hours liberty for all hands!"

    a.

Figure 4.5
(Continued)

3. Jennings, the *long time* mayor of the little city, ruled with *an iron hand.*

    a.

4. The old man with a *heart of gold* spent Saturdays *reading to children* in the hospital.

    b.

5. The reserve halfback stomped *like a spring stallion* in his *eagerness to get into the game.*

    b.

6. Robin's arrow flew *fast as the wind* and neatly split the cherry *into two equal halves.*

    b.

7. Anderson, a *gruff old bear* most of the time, could turn on the charm *when a customer appeared interested* in placing a large order.

    b.

8. *Like a group of eager monkeys,* the five-year-olds scampered up the rope nets *strung across the end* of the gymnasium.

    a.

    b.

Figure 4.5
(Continued)

2. Multiple-Choice: "analogy."   Name: Daniel Denny

Directions: For each item, there are four sentences. One of these sentences represents an example of an *analogy* that is superior to the other three possibilities. Circle the letter before the sentence that represents the *best example of an analogy.*

1. a. In terms of food value, pole beans and bush beans are identical in every respect.

    b. There are no parallels at all between the operation of the legislatures of France and Ghana.

    c. Neurosurgeons' training bears little in common with greenhouse attendants' training.

    (d.) The Maine State Education Department resembles, to a degree, the Texas Education Agency.

2. (a.) Cacti have many features in common with succulents.

    b. Reactions of litmus paper to acidic and alkaline solutions differ.

    c. In Montana, one does not need a permit to carry a handgun so long as it is visible.

    d. Geese are used for pest control in mint fields.

3. a. Birds of a feather flock together.

    (b.) Ducks and geese share many, but not all characteristics.

    c. Out of sight, out of mind.

    d. American bison and South African water buffalo have few, if any, shared genetic characteristics.

4. a. Sugar is sweet, and lemon is sour.

    b. An apple a day keeps the doctor away, but three a day can create problems.

    c. Black is the absence of color.

Figure 4.5
(Continued)

d. This court case is similar to the case of U.S. vs. Smith (1956).

5. a. Many of the actions of DeGaulle were reminiscent of those of Clemenceau.

   b. Opposites attract; likes repel.

   c. What goes up must come down.

   d. Not all fish have large scales.

6. a. Opium and heroin, derived from poppy seeds, share certain characteristics in common.

   b. Aspirin is often taken for headaches.

   c. Some bridges are high, but others are low.

   d. Paper and plastics are not derived from the same raw materials.

7. a. Pine trees are evergreens, and maple trees are deciduous.

   b. Plans for invasion of Southeastern Europe from the Mediterranean in World War II were based to a large degree on a similar plan from World War I.

   c. Okra tends to be preferred more in the American South than in the American North.

   d. Courage and cowardice are opposites.

8. a. Some modern plastics fulfill many of the functions of natural leather.

   b. Birds in the Southern Hemisphere migrate North in the winter; birds in the Northern Hemisphere migrate South in the winter.

   c. Many books are imported from England.

   d. One side of Mercury is very hot, and one side is very cold.

Figure 4.5
(Continued)

3. Multiple-Choice: "literal."   Name: Daniel Denny
....

Directions: For each item, there is a brief passage describing a *literal* event.
Circle the letter of the response that *best explains* what literally happened.

1. Pierre pushed open the door, shuddered, and forced himself to face the
   howling Montana January wind. He was gone not ten minutes. When he
   returned, stomping his feet, clapping his hands, and hooting in
   discomfort, we could see that the cold had literally frozen the tips of
   his ears.

   What happened to his ears?

   a. They only seemed to be frozen.

   (b.) They were really frozen.

   c. He pretended they were frozen.

   d. They weren't frozen, but just felt as though they were.

2. Alphonse took a tentative step out on the swinging guy wire. The
   crowd hushed as three lions paced in the open pit below. Clenching his
   teeth, Alphonse edged his shaky foot forward. Then, struck from the
   side by an unexpected gust of wind, he slipped to the left and literally
   plunged to his death.

   What happened to Alphonse?

   a. He only imagined he had fallen.

   (b.) He was killed.

   c. He finished his act and went on to perform another day.

   d. He thought he was killed, but he was mistaken.

3. If elected, I shall go to Korea. You may take that promise as literal.

   If elected, this candidate says he will

   a. stay in Washington.

Figure 4.5
(Continued)

b. do no traveling at all.

c. keep his promise and go to Korea.

d. abandon his campaign promise.

4. Slim dismounted. Keeping his eyes peeled for signs of smoke rising from Indian campfires on a distant butte, he started to sit down. Suddenly, cursing, he literally leaped into the air, having made an unfortunate choice of a prickly pear cactus as a cushion.

Slim

a. just felt like leaping into the air, but really didn't.

b. just cursed and continued to sit in the same place.

c. felt nothing at all when he sat down.

d. really did leap into the air.

5. Snorting wildly, the peccary tore at the ground with front feet pounding a frantic staccato beat. Breathing nervously, I felt my muscles tense—almost creaking—as I strung the arrow and began my draw. Then, with no warning, the beast snorted, dropped its head low, and literally charged my exposed position.

The beast

a. started shaking as though it might charge later.

b. really did charge.

c. did not really charge.

d. might or might not have charged.

6. The plane droned on. Lights were out. The critical final approach for the bombing run drew near. Suddenly, solid walls of anti-aircraft shells began to form a lethal curtain around the plane. And then . . . an orgiastic play of white-hot light for just a second before the darkened hulk literally was pulled back, dead, to the breast of its earth mother.

Figure 4.5
(Continued)

The plane

a. continued on to target.

b. was damaged slightly by anti-aircraft fire.

(c.) was destroyed and fell out of the sky.

d. returned to base having made no contact with the enemy.

7. Soft mellow rhythms pushed softly between the open balcony doors. Outside, a couple or two savored the biting late October air. Inside the overheated ballroom, couples continued to glide swan-like across the polished surface. In one corner, two young men ministered to a matronly chaperone who had literally fainted in the hot still air.

The matronly chaperone

a. started to faint, but didn't.

(b.) really did faint.

c. at no time lost consciousness.

d. wanted to faint, but couldn't.

8. Flames licked tentatively at the edges of the newspapers stacked in the corner. Then, in a flash, the entire room was afire. The building literally burned to the ground.

The fire

(a.) really did burn the building to the ground.

b. perhaps did and perhaps did not burn the building to the ground.

c. did not burn the building to the ground.

d. was quickly extinguished by the fire department before doing any damage.

Figure 4.5
(Continued)

4. Identification: "denotation."   Name: Daniel Denny
                                                 ....

Directions: Each item features a short phrase followed by a brief explanation of the meaning of the phrase. If the explanation is a proper example of the *denotation* of the phrase, place a + in the space provided. If the explanation is not a proper example of the *denotation* of the phrase, place a - in the space provided.

1. Stabbed in the back

   ...⁺.... a knife really has been thrust into the back.

2. Kicked the bucket

   ...⁻.... died

3. Stick in the mud

   ...⁺.... a piece of wood in the mud

4. Stars in her eyes

   .... in love

5. A piece of cake

   ...⁺.... a small part of a sweet, light pastry

6. Looking through rose colored glasses

   ...⁻.... looking at the world in such a way as to see just the "nice" things

7. Ear-splitting scream

   ...⁺.... a scream of such intensity that the ear physically is split

8. An eye opener

   ...⁻.... some surprising news

Learners' scores on teacher-prepared tests can be evaluated according to the same general system suggested for use with diagnostic data gathering techniques introduced earlier in the chapter. That is, prescriptions are in order for learners missing more than one-half of the items designed to test their proficiency on any one prerequisite knowledge item.

Prerequisite Skills Tests

Tests of this type focus on specific skills suggested as important by the performance objectives selected to guide a given unit of instruction. With respect to prerequisite skills identified from the two sample performance objectives, several teacher-prepared tests would be appropriate. One of these tests might be directed at providing information regarding learners' "ability to write sentences free of mechanical errors." Assessment of this ability might be accomplished through providing students with a visual stimulus of some kind (a painting or a photograph would do) and asking them to write a description of what they see. Each youngster should be encouraged to write at least 20 sentences. Following the usual decision rule, learning prescriptions would be in order for youngsters making mechanical errors on more than one-half of the sentences. Notations would be added to the folders of learners with identified problems in this important skill area.

Another teacher-developed procedure would be appropriate for determining learners' "ability to absorb information through listening." To test for this ability, a short audio tape or lecture is prepared and presented to learners. About ten minutes of new information ought to be provided on a topic with which learners are not familiar. No more than three new concepts should be introduced in any one such presentation. At the conclusion of the tape recording or lecture, a short test of concept understanding, preferably multiple-choice, can be administered. This test ought to have at least eight questions for each concept introduced. Learning prescriptions would be in order for students missing more than one-half of the items associated with any concept.

Two Special Procedures Focusing on Readability

One of the most nettlesome problems teachers face concerns difficulties their learners experience with reading. Several useful teacher-administered procedures are available that can pinpoint youngsters with serious difficulties in the area of reading comprehension. A device that is particularly useful in determining the grade reading level of a given prose selection is the Readability Graph developed by Fry (1968). Fry's Readability Graph and directions for use are provided in Figure 4.6.

Figure 4.6.

Fry's Readability Graph and Directions for Use

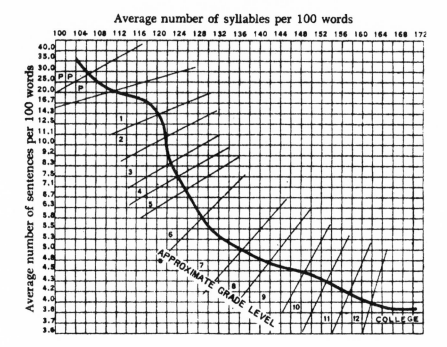

FRY'S READABILITY GRAPH
EXTENDED THRU PREPRIMER LEVEL

Directions:
1. Select three 100-word passages from near the beginning, middle, and end of the book. Skip all proper nouns.

2. Count the number of sentences in each 100-word passage. (Estimate to the nearest tenth of a sentence.) Average these three numbers.

3. Count the total number of syllables in each 100-word sample. There is a syllable for each vowel sound. (For example, cat = one syllable, blackbird = two syllables, continental = four syllables. Don't be fooled by word length. (For example, *polio* has three syllables, whereas *through* has only one syllable.) Average the total number of syllables for the three samples.

4. Plot on the graph the average number of sentences per hundred words and the average number of syllables per hundred words. Most plot points fall near the heavy curved line. Perpendicular lines mark off approximate grade level areas. (Fry, 1968.)

As an illustration of the use of Fry's procedure, look at the following passages selected at random from "The Peddler of Ballaghadereen" (a selection in Ruth Sawyer's *The Way of the Storyteller*, 1966 edition). Each of the three passages is 100 words in length (remember that proper nouns are *not* counted).

Sample 1
More years ago than you can tell me and twice as many as I can tell you, there lived a peddler in Ballaghadereen. He lived at the Crossroads, by himself in a bit of a cabin with one room to it, and that was so small that a man could stand in the middle of the floor and, without taking a step he could lift the latch on the front door, he could lift the latch on the back door, and he could hang the kettle over the turf. That is how small and snug it was.

Outside the cabin the peddler . . . . (Sawyer, 1966; p. 239.)

total sentences = 3.5
total syllables = 113

Sample 2
Spring followed winter in Ireland, and summer followed close upon the heels of both. And winter came again and the peddler grew old. His pack grew lighter and lighter, until the neighbors could hear the trinkets jangling inside as he passed, so few things were left. They would nod their heads and say to one another: "Like as not his pockets are empty as his pack. Time will come, with winter at hand, when he will be at our back doors begging crumbs, along with the blackbirds."
The time did come, as the neighbors had prophesied it would, smug and . . . . (Sawyer, 1966; pp. 242-243.)

total sentences = 5.3
total syllables = 125

Sample 3

Back to Ballaghadereen went the peddler, one foot ahead of the other. How he got there I cannot be telling you. He unslung his pack, took up a mattock lying near by, and dug under the cherry tree. He dug deep and felt at last the scraping of the mattock against something hard and smooth. It took him time to uncover it and he found it to be an old sea chest, of foreign pattern and workmanship, bound around the bands of brass. These he broke, and lifting the lid he found the chest full of gold, tarnished and clotted with . . . . (Sawyer, 1966; p. 246)

total sentences = 5.5
total syllables - 124

To find the average for all these passages, add totals together and divide by three, as follows:

	total sentences	*total syllables*
passage 1	3.5	113
passage 2	5.3	125
passage 3	5.5	124
	14.3	362

$$\frac{14.3}{3} = 4.8 \qquad \frac{362}{3} = 120.7$$

Averages = 4.8 sentences and 120.7 syllables

These averages are used to enter Fry's Readability Graph to determine approximate grade-level difficulty of the material. This process would begin by finding 4.8 on the vertical axis at the left-hand side of the chart. Beginning at point 4.8, it is necessary to move to the right across the chart until the line extending to the right from 4.8 intersects the line running down from the 120 syllables point at the top of the chart. Since the average number of syllables was not 120 but 120.7, it is necessary to move slightly to the right of the point of intersection of the line dropping down from the 120 point. Once this has been done, a dot is placed on the line extending to the right from the 4.8 mark on the left-hand side of the chart.

The location of this dot pinpoints the approximate grade-level readability. The grade-level is read directly from the graph. To get this information, it is necessary to observe which sets of lines perpendicular to the heavy, wavy diagonal line running from the upper left-hand corner to the lower right-hand corner of the graph enclose the dot. In this instance, the dot is almost on the line separating grade six and seven. One could conclude that this material roughly is of a grade six or seven level of reading difficulty. (For those who may have difficulty following the discussion of these procedures, a dot has been placed at the appropriate point on Fry's Readability Graph in Figure 4.6 for material characterized by 4.8 sentences per 100 words and 120.7 syllables per 100 words.)

This analysis would indicate that, from the standpoint of reading difficulty, "The Peddler of Ballaghadereen" should be an appropriate choice for use with the eighth-graders who are the target population for the two sample performance objectives. Readability levels reveal little about abilities to deal with concepts introduced in the material and with classroom activities built around the reading. But they do provide a rough indication of the degree to which decoding problems may be a source of learning difficulty.

A limitation of the Fry procedure is that it yields a grade-level readability figure that is referenced to averages. That is, material rated to be at fifth-grade level of difficulty is assumed to be material that average fifth-graders can decode without great difficulty. The problem is that teachers have no way of knowing the degree to which a given class matches those average capabilities. Even if such information were available and teachers were lucky enough to have students closely matching these averages, they still would be faced with an enormous range of abilities on both sides of a measured class mean reading ability. A technique which, unlike the Fry Readability Graph, provides information regarding the potential problems each youngster in a class may be expected to have with a given prose selection is the Cloze Procedure developed by Taylor (1953).

In very general terms, the Cloze Procedure provides information about the capabilities of an individual in terms of his ability to deal with the level of reading difficulty of a given prose selection.

In using the technique, a sample is selected from the prose selection. It is a good idea to select a sample that is fairly long, 500 words or more if possible. (Shorter samples will work, but reliability of scores is better when longer samples are used.) From this sample, a test is prepared consisting of the sample being typed with every fifth word omitted. Blanks are provided where the fifth word would normally be found. Students are asked to complete the blanks with words that "give the passage sense." Correction consists of comparing words written in by learners with the words deleted from the original package. Depending on the number of words written in that are different from the original, an assessment is made regarding the reading difficulty an individual learner is likely to have with the material from which the passage is drawn. Specific Instructions for using the Cloze Procedure are described in Figure 4.7.

Teacher Tests and Hoped-for Attitudes

As a source of information regarding hoped-for attitudes that have been derived from performance objectives selected to guide a given unit of instruction, teacher-made tests do not represent a good choice. This attitudinal information does not lend itself well to the formats of multiple-choice, true-false, matching, and essay examinations. The observation checklist, the anecdotal record, and the interest inventory are much more appropriate for gathering information related to this important area.

Comparative Strengths and Weaknesses of
Alternative Data Sources

To this point, basic operational features of a number of diagnostic data-gathering techniques have been described. Additionally, merits of each of these techniques in terms of information needs derived from two sample performance objectives have been discussed. In a real instructional setting, once these information needs have been determined from a consideration of the selected performance objectives, it may be desirable to prepare a summary chart displaying the relative strengths and weaknesses of alternative diagnostic data-gathering techniques. An example of such a summary chart, based on information needs from the two sample performance objectives, is provided in Figure 4.8.

Figure 4.7

Cloze Procedure: Instructions for Use and an Example

Directions
1. Select a passage. Type the passage omitting every fifth word except when
   the fifth word is the first word in a sentence. In this case omit the second
   word of the sentence and then begin omitting every fifth word from that
   point. Leave about 15 typed spaces for children to write in omitted words.

2. Scoring. Count as correct only words that.are *exactly the same* as those
   used in the original passage. Compute the percentage of correct words.
   This is accomplished by dividing the number of correct words by the total
   number of blanks in the passage. For example, in a 500-word passage with
   100 blanks, a youngster who had 71 words correct would receive a score
   of 71% (71 divided by 100 equals .71).

3. Decision Rules.
   a. If a student receives a score of 58% or higher, he is operating at the
      independent reading level with this material (Bormuth, 1968). That is,
      he should be able to read and learn from this material with minimal
      need for teacher assistance.
   b. If a student receives a score falling between 44-57% correct, he is
      operating at the *instructional* level with this material (Bormuth, 1968).
      That is, he should be able to read and learn from this material given
      teacher assistance with the difficult sections.
   c. If a student receives a score of 43% or below, he is operating at the
      frustrational level with this material (Bormuth, 1968). Because of
      difficulties such a youngster might encounter with this material, it is
      desirable that less difficult reading sources be found for him. When
      reading materials of a frustrational level of difficulty are used, it is
      impossible to separate problems with decoding from problems with new
      concepts as potential explanations for learners' difficulties.

Example of a Cloze Test (This abbreviated example, 250-words, of a Cloze
   Test, draws material from "The Peddler of Ballaghadereen," in Ruth
   Sawyer's *The Way of the Story Teller*, 1966, pp. 243-244.)

   Now it is more .... lucky that hungry men .... dream; and the peddler
   .... Ballaghadereen had a strange .... that night. He dreamed .... there
   came a sound .... knocking in the middle .... the night. Then the .... on
   the front door ...., the door opened without .... creak or a cringe, ...
   inside the cabin stepped .... Patrick. Standing in the .... the good man

Figure 4.7
(Continued)

pointed ....(14) finger; and he spoke ....(15) a voice tuned as ....(16) as the wind over ....(17) bogs. "Peddler, peddler of ....(18), take the road to ....(19) town. When you get ....(20) the bridge that spans ....(21) Liffey you will hear ....(22) you were meant to ....(23)"

On the morrow the ....(24) awoke and remembered the ....(25) He rubbed his stomach ....(26) found it mortal empty; ....(27) stood on his legs ....(28) found them trembling in ....(29) him; and he said ....(30) himself: "Faith, an empty ....(31) and weak legs are ....(32) worst traveling companions a ....(33) can have, and Dublin ....(34) a long way. I'll ....(35) where I am."

That ....(36) the peddler went hungrier ....(37) bed, and again came ....(38) dream. There came the ....(39) on the door, the ....(40) of the latch. The ....(41) opened and Saint Patrick ....(42) there, pointing the road: " ....(43), peddler of Ballaghadereen, take ....(44) road that leads to ....(45) Town. When you get ....(46) the bridge that spans ....(47) Liffey, you will hear ....(48) you were meant to ....(49)!"

The second day it ....(50) the same . . . .

Key

1. than
2. will
3. of
4. dream
5. that
6. of
7. of
8. latch
11. a
11. and
12. Saint
13. doorway
14. a
15. in
16. low
17. the
18. Ballaghadereen
19. Dublin
20. to
21. the
22. what
23. hear
24. peddler
25. dream
26. and
28. and
29. under
30. to
31. stomach
32. the
33. man
34. is
35. bide
36. night
37. to
38. the
39. knocking
40. lifing
41. door
42. stood
43. peddler
45. Dublin
46. to
47. the
48. what
49. hear
50. was

From an examination of strengths and weaknesses of individual diagnostic data-gathering techniques referenced to a given set of performance objectives, decisions can be made regarding the procedures that can meet identified information needs. A list of these "best choices" for the two sample performance objectives is provided in Figure 4.9.

Use of these "best choices" assures that needed information can be gathered reasonably efficiently. Prioritizing alternative procedures permits a tight focus on those techniques that can produce the most pertinent information in the shortest period of time. In short, this process acts to professionalize the entire diagnostic data-gathering activity.

Diagnostic Information as "Insurance" Against
Teaching Learners What They Already Know

Diagnostic techniques introduced to this point have been discussed in terms of helping teachers to achieve a better "fit" between individual students and proposed new learning experiences. Use of these procedures is predicated on the assumption that students do not already know what we wish them to learn.

Figure 4.8

Summary Chart: Strengths and Weaknesses of
Diagnostic Data-Gathering Techniques

	Prerequisite Knowledges 1 2 3 4	Prerequisiite Skills 1 2 3 4	Hoped-for Attitudes 1 2 3 4
Work Samples	C C C C	C A B B	B B C C
Anecdotal Records	C C C C	B C A C	B A C C
Conferences	C C C C	C C A B	B C B C
Checklists	C C C C	C C C C	A C A C
Interest Inventories	C C C C	C C C C	A C A A
Teacher-made Tests	A A A A	A A C A	C C C C

Key:
A = good source
B = fair source
C = poor source

Figure 4.9

Diagnostic Data-Gathering Techniques Most Suitable
for Providing Information to Meet Information Needs
Suggested by Two Sample Performance Objectives

Area	Best Technique
Prerequisite knowledge 1 ("figure of speech")	teacher test
Prerequisite knowledge 2 ("analogy")	teacher test
Prerequisite knowledge 3 ("literal")	teacher test
Prerequisite knowledge 4 ("denotation")	teacher test
Prerequisite skill 1 (grade seven or eight readability)	teacher test
Prerequisite skill 2 (error-free sentences)	work samples; teacher test
Prerequisite skill 3 (verbalize concerns)	anecdotal record
Prerequisite skill 4 (learn by listening)	teacher test
Hoped-for attitude 1 (increased enjoyment of reading)	checklist, interest inventory
Hoped-for attitude 2 (make personal, public decisions)	anecdotal record
Hoped-for attitude 3 (increased interest in folktales)	checklist, interest inventory
Hoped-for attitude 4 (increased interest in metaphors)	interest inventory

When teachers have worked with individuals in their classes over a period of time, usually their perceptions are valid with regard to new instructional materials truly being "new" for individuals in the class. But even experienced teachers make mistakes in failing to credit some students with knowing as much as they do. Most such errors in judgment occur at the beginning of the school year, when teachers are adjusting to strengths and weaknesses of individuals.

Even later in the year, teachers' instructional decisions may go awry. Frequently, this happens when learners have acquired certain knowledges and skills in settings unrelated to formal instruction in the school. Many a student, with no formal training in geometry, has learned to compute the length of the hypotenuse of a right triangle while helping a parent plan a lawn or a garden plot. Attitudinal problems may result when students are asked to sit through instructional experiences that present, as "new," material already known. Consequently, a diagnostic preassessment is desirable that provides assurances that any proposed new sequence of instruction will be more than a repetition of previous learnings.

Diagnostic pretests ought to be based on performance objectives selected to guide a proposed new learning sequence. Of the two sample performance objectives used for purposes of illustration throughout this chapter, one is a cognitive-dimension performance objective requiring learners to write sentences demonstrating the correct use of metaphors. A pretest for this ability that called upon learners only to demonstrate their grasp of the essential meaning of the concept "metaphor" would fall short of the demands of the performance objective. The performance objective requires that learners be able to "apply" knowledge as evidenced by the production of sentences illustrating the correct use of metaphors. Thus, an appropriate diagnostic pretest of this ability would require the learner to write sentences using metaphors properly. If learners can perform this application task successfully, their knowledge and understanding level comprehension of the concept "metaphor" can be inferred.

A pretest for this cognitive-dimension performance objective need not be complex in form. Each learner might be provided a sheet of paper and told to write 20 sentences, each of which includes a metaphor. Teachers can set the "test out" criterion at any level they deem appropriate. In pretests of this type, frequently a criterion-level of 80% is set. If this level were adopted for the pretest involving the production of 20 sentences illustrating the proper use of metaphors, learners who had 16 or more sentences correct (16 divided by 20 = .80) would be assumed to have mastered the performance objective. For such individuals, alternative instructional programs would be in order.

The second sample performance objective discussed throughout the chapter is an attitudinal objective relating to learners' feelings about folk tales. For a performance objective of this type, an interest inventory works well as a diagnostic pretest. The interest inventory is prepared in accordance with procedures introduced earlier in the chapter.

Data from pretests on attitudinal performance objectives are treated differently from those on cognitive performance objectives. For example, on a pretest developed from a cognitive-dimension performance objective, the proposed new instructional program can go forward as planned for learners scoring below the "test out" level. For those few achieving scores beyond this level, alternative learning experiences will need to be provided. But, because of their nature and the way they are tested, attitudinal dimension performance objectives do not lend themselves to pretesting that offers clear guidelines for teacher decisions.

Measurement in this area attempts to describe the relative importance at a given point in time of a particular feeling, value, or attitude as compared to others. Consequently, data that are gathered (using, for example, the interest inventory) do not lend themselves to discussion in terms of a criterion-level such as 80% or 90%. Rather, scores are reflected in a scaled array of preferences. (In an interest inventory, with eight options, this array would range from preference-level #1 to preference-level #8.) Thus, pretests on attitudinal-dimension performance objectives provide a baseline of information regarding the relative standing of certain feelings, values, or attitudes held by learners before a new unit of work is initiated.

When pretests on attitudinal objectives reveal low or mediocre ratings on areas teachers hold important, there is a clear hope that these ratings will be changed in a positive direction as a result of the learning experiences provided in the new instructional unit. Those learners who gave ratings to areas prized by their teachers on the pretest would be expected to give similarly high ratings should a preference scale be administered at the conclusion of the unit. Any drop in ratings would suggest that parts of the new program had resulted in the development of negative reactions toward feelings, attitudes, or values that the program designer had hoped to encourage. Comparison of ratings on attitude scales given before and after a unit of instruction can provide useful information as teachers attempt to analyze the impact of their program with a view to revising and refining their practices. Detailed procedures for performing these analyses will be introduced in Chapter 7, "Evaluating the Effectiveness of Instruction."

Developing Prescriptions from Diagnostic Data

After teachers analyze data they have gathered, and pinpoint youngsters who may experience difficulties with different components of the new instructional program, learning prescriptions must be prepared tailored to the needs of each of these learners. This process begins by a preparation of a catalog of potential prescriptions to be used when diagnosis reveals certain individuals to be weak in terms of any of the prerequisite knowledges or skills, or have a wide divergence from hoped-for attitudes. As an illustration, a catalog of prescriptions is presented below, based on the two sample performance objectives.

The sample catalog of prescriptions in Figure 4.10 includes no separate section for hoped-for attitudes. While teachers do gather information about attitudes before and, often, after instruction, these data function only to broaden understanding of individuals in their classrooms. Unlike knowledges and skills that are truly "prerequisite" to success on a new unit of work, attitudes are only "hoped-for." That is, it would be nice if attitudes teachers consider desirable were held by most of their learners, but these attitudes are not absolutely essential for mastery of the new material in the sense that prerequisite knowledges and skills are necessary. Thus, while teachers clearly are interested in the attitudes of their students, no special prescriptions need be prepared in this area that are independent of the instructional experiences built into the new unit itself.

Once the catalog of prescriptions has been prepared, the stage is set for developing prescriptions for individual learners. This process begins with a check of the personal folders of individual youngsters in the classroom. Notations in the folders will reflect the unique nature of prescriptions to be developed for each learner in need of special help. For example, a student named Warren Witte might have in his folder notations such as are shown in Figure 4.11.

Once specific needs are identified from a learner's folder, the catalog of prescriptions can be used to select an appropriate remedial program. With the information regarding Warren Witte,

Figure 4.10

A Sample Catalog of Prescriptions

Prerequisite Knowledge #1: "Figure of Speech"

Possible prescription(s):

a. read short handout, two paragraphs in length, grade four level of readability, in which term "figure of speech" is (1) defined and (2) illustrated in three sample sentences.

b. listen to short cassette containing (1) teacher definition of "figure of speech" and (2) three sentences illustrating use of term "figure of speech."

Prerequisite Knowledge #2: "Analogy"

Possible prescription(s);

a. read short handout, two paragraphs in length, grade four level of readability, in which term "analogy" is (1) defined and (2) illustrated in three sample sentences.

b. listen to short cassette containing (1) teacher definition of "analogy" and (2) three sentences illustrating use of term "analogy."

Prerequisite Knowledge #3: "Literal"

Possible prescription(s):

a. read short handout, two paragraphs in length, grade four level of readability, in which term "literal" is (1) defined and (2) illustrated in three sample sentences.

b. listen to short cassette containing (1) teacher definition of "literal" and (2) three sentences illustrating use of term "literal."

Prerequisite Knowledge #4: "Denotation"

Possible prescription(s):

a. read short handout, two paragraphs in length, grade four level of readability, in which term "denotation" is (1) defined and (2) illustrated in three sample sentences.

Figure 4.10
(Continued)

b. listen to short cassette containing (1) teacher definition of "denotation" and (2) three sentences illustrating use of term "denotation."

Prerequisite Skill #1: Ability to Read Prose at
Grade Seven or Eight Level of Readability

Possible prescription(s):

a. use *Dozens of Kittens*, primary level of readability, to teach use of metaphors in lieu of "The Peddler of Ballaghadereen."

b. use teacher lesson on tape to explain the concept "metaphor" and to illustrate use of metaphors.

Prerequisite Skill #2: Ability to Write
Sentences Free of Mechanical Errors

Possible prescription(s):

a. assign learner to complete short, programmed learning package focusing on development of writing skills.

Prerequisite Skill #3: Ability
to Verbalize Personal Concerns

Possible prescription(s):

a. at least twice daily, offer teacher praise to youngster when he makes a positive verbal self-reference. (See "b" if not feasible.)

b. if youngster makes no positive self-reference, twice daily praise any other worthy behaviors.

Prerequisite Skill #4: Ability to
Absorb Information Through Listening

Possible prescription(s):

a. record account of a sporting event or some other episode of high learner interest. Ask learner to listen for ten or fifteen minutes. Require him to develop and hand-in a short, accurate, written account of the specific things that took place.

Figure 4.11

Notations from a Sample Learner Folder

Witte, Warren

Prerequisite knowledge #2   . . . does not understand "analogy." Prepare prescription. 2/23

Prerequisite knowledge #4   . . . does not understand "denotation." Prepare prescription. 2/23

Prerequisite skill #2   . . . has difficulty writing grammatical sentences. Prepare prescription 2/23

(Figure 4.11) and the prescriptions described in Figure 4.10, a prescription might be developed as indicated in Figure 4.12. Note that this prescription is relatively limited in scope. Properly, a prescription attempts to focus only on a learner's major knowledge and skill deficiencies. For Warren Witte, then, this three-part prescription will suffice.

Figure 4.12

An Example of a Prescription for a Single Learner

Witte, Warren

Prescription for remediation

a. read short handout, two paragraphs in length, grade four level of readability, in which term "analogy" is (1) defined and (2) illustrated in three sample sentences.

b. read short handout, two paragraphs in length, grade four level of readability, in which term "denotation" is (1) defined and (2) illustrated in three sample sentences.

c. complete short, programmed learning package focusing on development of writing skills.

In addition to providing for the needs of individuals, teachers sometimes find it useful to develop a profile of their entire class from the diagnostic data they have gathered. It is possible to organize diagnostic information on a class in such a way that it will fit on a single sheet of paper. Not only does this procedure simplify quick identification of learners with problems, it also provides a view of how serious a given difficulty may be in the class as a whole. An example of how such a composite class data sheet might be organized is provided in Figure 4.13.

Once a composite class data sheet has been completed, there is no need to refer back to folders of individual learners regarding entry-level deficiencies. Additionally, the data sheet itself can be the source for pinpointing areas in which large numbers of youngsters are experiencing problems. This information can be useful as teachers plan the specifics of their day-to-day lessons during the new unit of instruction. An illustration of how the composite class data sheet can be used to develop class problem-area charts is provided in Figure 4.14. Numbers are taken from Figure 4.13.

An examination of the data displayed in Figure 4.14 reveals that few students in this class have serious problems in terms of deficiencies in prerequisite knowledges and skills. In the prerequisite knowledge area, two learners need help with the term "analogy" (relates to prerequisite knowledge #2). One learner needs assistance with the term "literal" (relates to prerequisite knowledge #3), and one other has failed to grasp the meaning of the term "denotation" (relates to prerequisite knowledge #4). No youngster in the class shows evidence of difficulty with the term "figure of speech" (relates to prerequisite knowledge #1).

In the skills area, several of these youngsters have reading difficulties that may interfere with their ability to deal with the intended focus selection, "The Peddler of Ballaghadereen." Five learners may have some reading related difficulties with this material (relates to prerequisite skill #1). In other skill areas, two youngsters need help in developing an ability to verbalize personal concerns (relates to prerequisite skill #3), and two show deficiencies in their abilities to compose sentences free of mechanical errors (relates to prerequisite skill #2). No student in this group seems to be having difficulty absorbing information through listening.

Figure 4.13

Example of a Composite Class Data Sheet

	Prerequisite knowledges				Prerequisite Skills				Hoped-for attitudes			
	1	2	3	4	1	2	3	4	1	2	3	4
Abrams					X	X						
Bentz						X			X		X	
Cole					X							
Denny												
Ender												
Fogg					X				X			
Gear			X									
Howar												
Islip												
Jensen												
Kent					X				X			
Lewing		X										
Muntz												
Newsome					X				X			
Ott												
Penda												
Quigley					X				X			
Ross												
Witte		X	X		X				X			
Xell												
Zack												

Key:

X in the prerequisite knowledge and prerequisite skills areas indicates an entry-level deficiency.

X in the hoped-for attitudes area represents an attitude that the teacher would like to see changed as a result of the learning experiences in the new unit or work.

Figure 4.14

Example of Class Problem-Area Charts

	Prerequisite knowledges			
	1	*2*	*3*	*4*
Learners with problems in category	0	2	1	1
Learners with no problems in category	21	19	20	20

————————

	Prerequisite skills			
	1	*2*	*3*	*4*
Learners with problems in category	5	2	2	0
Learners with no problems category	16	19	19	21

————————

	Hoped-for attitudes			
	1	*2*	*3*	*4*
Teacher would like to see changes here	6	0	11	0
Teacher is satisfied with these	15	21	20	21

In the hoped-for attitudes area, a number of learners show evidence of having only a marginal interest in reading (relates to hoped-for attitude #1). This finding suggests the necessity for seeking out reading materials of high interest and at a suitable level of reading difficulty.

Class problem-area charts can be an invaluable aid to teachers during the final planning phases preceding the beginning of a new instructional unit. A careful review of problem-area charts can provide a rationale for making selective instructional changes designed to compensate for deficiencies in prerequisite knowledges and skills that may be particularly widespread.

Summary

Diagnostic procedures introduced here promote professional instructional planning by giving teachers a means of identifying key learner needs. The value of decisions made on the basis of assessment of gathered diagnostic information relates directly to the degree to which data-gathering was guided by information needs stemming from relevant performance objectives. This practice protects teachers from the twin threats of (1) gathering too much diagnostic information, and (2) gathering inappropriate diagnostic information.

The following general sequence assures professionalism in diagnosing learners:

1. Derive specific information needs from performance objectives.
2. Determine which diagnostic data-gathering techniques can best provide responses to those information needs.
3. Gather, organize, and analyze data.
4. Administer "test out" procedures.
5. Develop a catalog of prescriptions for each identified potential entry-level deficiency.
6. Develop prescriptions for individual learners.
7. Develop and analyze class problem-area charts.

Once prescriptions have been made and implemented, it is necessary to look ahead to selection and implementation of strategies selected to facilitate mastery of the performance objectives guiding the new instructional unit. Procedures for making reasoned selections of instructional strategies will be introduced in the next chapter.

References

BORMUTH, John R. "The Cloze Readability Procedure." *Elementary English* (April 1968), 429-436.

FRY, Edward. "A Readability Formula that Saves Time." *Journal of Reading* (April 1968), 513+.

SAWYER, Ruth. *The Way of the Storyteller.* New York: The Viking Press, 1966.

TAYLOR, Wilson L. "Cloze Procedure: A New Tool for Measuring Readability." *Journalism Quarterly* (Fall 1953), 415-433.

Additional Professional Study

Books

BLAIR, Glenn M. *Diagnostic and Remedial Teaching: A Guide to Practice in Elementary and Secondary Schools* (Revised Edition). New York: Macmillan Publishing Co., Inc., 1956.

BRUECKNER, Leo J. *The Diagnosis and Treatment of Learning Difficulties.* New York: Appleton-Century-Crofts, Inc., 1955.

CARTER, Homer L.E. and Dorothy J. MC GINNIS. *Diagnosis and Treatment of the Disabled Reader.* New York: Macmillan Publishing Co., Inc., 1970.

DECHANT, Emerald V. *Diagnosis and Remediation of Reading Disability.* West Nyack, New York: Parker Publishing Company, Inc., 1968.

ELEMENTARY LANGUAGE ARTS CONFERENCE. *Diagnostic Teaching for Reading and Language.* Bloomington, Indiana: Indiana University School of Education, 1971.

GLENNON, Vincent J. and John W. WILSON. "Diagnostic-Prescriptive Teaching," in *National Council of Teachers of Mathematics Yearbook,* 1972.

GUSZAK, Frank J. *Diagnostic Reading Instruction in the Elementary School.* New York: Harper & Row Publishers, 1973, pp. 282-318.

LEE, Doris M. *Diagnostic Teaching.* Washington, D.C.: National Education Association, 1966.

LEIBERT, Robert E. (Ed). *Diagnostic Viewpoints in Reading.* Newark, Delaware: International Reading Association, 1971.

ROSENBERT, Marshall B. *Diagnostic Teaching.* Seattle, Wash.: Special Child Publications, 1968.

SAWYER, Ruth. *The Way of the Storyteller.* New York: The Viking Press, 1966.

SKARBEK, James F. "Diagnostic Analysis of Mathematical Skills." In *National Council of Teachers of Mathematics Yearbook,* 1972, pp. 513-516.

STRANG, Ruth M. *Diagnostic Teaching of Reading* (2nd Edition). New York: McGraw-Hill Book Co., 1971.

WILSON, John A.R. (Ed). *Diagnosis of Learning Difficulties.* New York: McGraw-Hill Book Co., 1971.

WILSON, Robert M. *Diagnostic and Remedial Reading for Classroom and Clinic* (2nd edition). Columbus, Ohio: Charles E. Merrill Books, Inc., 1972.

Periodicals

BESEL, Ronald. "Diagnosis-Prescription in the Context of Educational Management." *Educational Technology* (July 1973) 23-27.

BROWN, Thomas C. and Lloyd E. MCCLEARY. "Learner Performance Accounting." *Educational Technology* (May 1973) 17-18.

CLEMENTS, Zacharie J. "Taking All Students from Where They Really Are." *Bulletin of the National Association of Secondary School Principals* (April 1976) 104-108.

COX, L.S. "Diagnosing and Remediating Systematic Errors in Addition and Subtraction Computation." *Arithmetic Teacher* (February 1975), 151-157.

DODD, C.A. *et al.* "Diagnosis and Remediation of Pupil Errors: An Exploratory Study." *School Science and Mathematics* (March 1975), 270-276.

FRY, Edward. "A Readability Formula That Saves Time." *Journal of Reading* (April 1968), 513+.

HAKIM, Clifford C. "Task-Analysis: One Alternative: Diagnosis of a Mild Learning Disability." *Academic Therapy* (Winter 1974-1975), 201-209.

HAMBLETON, Ronald K. "Testing and Decision-Making Procedures for Selected Individualized Instructional Programs." *Review of Educational Research* (Fall 1974), 371-400.

HAMMILL, Donald D. "Evaluating Children for Instructional Purposes." *Academic Therapy* (Summer 1972) 469.

OZER, Mark N. and H. Burt RICHARDSON, JR. "Diagnostic Evaluation of Children with Learning Problems: A Communication Process." *Childhood Education* (February 1972) 244-247.

SALVIA, John and John CLARK. "Use of Deficits to Identify the Learning Disabled." *Exceptional Children* (January 1972), 305-308.

TAYLOR, Wilson L. "Cloze Procedure: A New Tool for Measuring Readability." *Journalism Quarterly* (Fall 1953) 415-433.

WOLOK, Rose S. "Let's Use Tests for Teaching." *Teacher* (October 1972), 62-64.

YSSELDYKE, James E. and John SALVIA. "Diagnostic-Prescriptive Teaching: Two Models." *Exceptional Children* (November 1974), 181-185.

ZEITZ, Frank. "What to Teach to Whom and When? Prescriptive Teaching of a Unit." *School and Community* (October 1974).

Chapter 5

Selecting Instructional Strategies

OBJECTIVES
This chapter provides information to help the reader to:

1. distinguish between instructional strategies that are "process-centered" and "content-centered."

2. categorize types of instructional strategies using the framework provided.

3. identify strengths and weaknesses of selected instructional strategies.

4. describe step-by-step procedures for implementing selected instructional strategies.

5. point out the function of instructional strategies in the total instructional process.

Instructional strategies are facilitating activities that are chosen to help learners achieve specified performance objectives. In addition to supporting the performance objectives selected to guide an instructional program, strategies must take into account diagnostic data that have been gathered relating to the capabilities of each learner. For example, it would be an exercise in futility to select a strategy requiring students to read materials written at a grade 12 level of difficulty if no individual was able at present to comprehend material written above a grade eight level of difficulty.

Through the years, many teachers have developed repertoires of strategies that have worked well. While every one savors memories of past successes, there is a need to guard against the temptation to label a given procedure as a universally "good" instructional strategy. Such labeling can interfere with attempts to evaluate dispassionately (1) the degree to which a given strategy might be expected to help learners master *present* performance objectives, and (2) the appropriateness of the proposed strategy for the particular group of youngsters to be served.

Individual instructional strategies, then, cannot be described as "good" or "bad," or "effective" or "ineffective." Such bipolar characterizations ignore the *function* of instructional strategies, which is the facilitation of learner achievement of specified performance objectives. Performance objectives vary from content-centered to process-centered to feeling-centered. Additionally, performance objectives vary widely in terms of the levels of conceptual thinking they require of learners. Considering the diverse nature of performance objectives, the likelihood of finding a single instructional strategy that is "universally effective" is remote indeed.

The issue reduces not to a question of "which instructional strategies are good?," but rather to a question of "which instructional strategies are good for *what*?" The "for what" component of the question demands analysis of the specific nature of the performance objectives selected to guide the instructional program.

Most performance objectives can be thought of as ranging along a theoretical continuum from 100 percent "content-centered" to 100 percent "process-centered." A 100 percent "content-centered" objective would be one in which the teacher had *total interest* in promoting learner mastery of a specific body of subject matter and *no interest* in promoting learner internalization of a content processing technique. Conversely, a 100 percent "process-centered" objective would be one in which the teacher had *total interest* in promoting learner mastery of a content processing technique and *no interest* in promoting learner mastery of a specific body of content.

One-hundred percent "content-centered" and 100 percent "process-centered" objectives do not exist in the "real world." All performance objectives, to some degree, are both "content-centered" and "process-centered." However, the two constructs are useful for purposes of analysis. Some performance objectives selected for inclusion in a program will tend more toward the "content-centered" end of the continuum. Others will tend more toward the "process-centered" end. The relative degree of "content-centeredness" or "process-centeredness" is a factor that must play a part in the decision to select or reject a given instructional strategy for use in a particular plan of instruction.

In addition to the content or process dimension of each performance objective, selection of an instructional strategy must also take into account the nature of the "flow of activity" characteristic of a given strategy. In general, two "flow of activity" types exist. Instructional strategies characterized by the first of these patterns are those in which talk and activities tend to be channeled through the teacher. Such strategies may include both highly controlled teacher activities, such as lecturing, and highly indirect teaching styles in which learners' verbal comments predominate, prompted only by an occasional teacher query or comment. The critical dimension of strategies where talk and activities are channeled through the teacher is that the "flow of activity" is to and through the teacher rather than directly from one learner to another (or from one learner to himself, as in the case of self-instructional materials).

The second general "flow of activity" pattern characterizes instructional strategies in which talk and activities are *not* channeled through the teacher once the strategy is underway. Instructional strategies of this variety involve direct teacher control only at the beginning, when ground rules are being explained. Once the activity has begun, primary patterns of communication flow *directly* from learner to learner and need not be channeled through the teacher. Brainstorming and role playing are examples of strategies of this type.

When selecting strategies for use with a given group of learners, teachers have to consider whether the performance objectives tend to be more "content-centered" or "process-centered," *and* how they wish the activity to flow. These considerations suggest the existence of four general types of instructional strategies: (1) "content-centered" strategies in which talk/activity is channeled through the teacher; (2) "content-centered" strategies in which talk/activity is *not* channeled through the teacher; (3) "process-centered" strategies in which talk/activity is channeled through the teacher; (4) "process-centered" strategies in which talk/activity is *not* channeled through the teacher. Figure 5.1 displays these relationships and includes listings of strategies that fit logically into each of the four major categories.

Instructional strategies included within each cell of the Figure 5.1 matrix will be described in the four sections of the chapter to follow.

Content-Centered—Talk/Activity Channeled Through the Teacher Strategies

The Lecture
Perhaps the most maligned of instructional strategies (particularly by proponents of inductive approaches), the lecture does serve a valuable instructional function. Problems with the approach result not from any inherent failings of the strategy, but

---

Figure 5.1

A Framework for Categorizing Instructional Strategies

	Content-Activity	Process-Centered
Talk/Activity Channeled Through the Teacher	Lecture Questioning Concept Attainment	Data-Retrieval Charts Suchman's Inquiry
Talk/Activity *not* Channeled Through the Teacher	Role Playing Simulations Games Team Learning Case Studies	Brainstorming Creative Thinking

rather from its misuse. Indeed, in certain respects, the lecture has strengths that are matched by few other approaches. For example, the lecture enables teachers to organize and make available to students a large volume of information in a relatively short time. Further, a good lecture can simplify and clarify material that might prove too difficult for learners if it were introduced only in the course textbook.

Paradoxically, strengths of the lecture are weaknesses of the strategy, when it is misapplied. The potential of the lecture for presenting a great deal of information carries within it the seeds for delivering entirely too much information too quickly. Further, in the hands of an unskilled teacher, a lecture can add unnecessary complexity, obfuscate issues, and undermine learners' abilities to distinguish between important and trivial material.

In planning an effective lecture, there is a need to consider *the nature of the audience* (the learners). In particular, diagnostic information needs to be reviewed in seeking assurances that, at a minimum, students have the verbal skills necessary for them to understand the vocabulary to be used in an intended lecture.

In addition to these more general verbal skills, learners will need to know certain things in advance if the lecture is to "make sense" to them. There is, then, a need to assess *the degree to which learners are familiar with fundamental concepts* they are assumed to know as "baseline" information. It is illogical to use a lecture to introduce material when learners have not mastered fundamental understandings prerequisite to that material.

Once information about learners is in hand, careful attention must be given to *planning and organization of the lecture.* A logical framework must be developed according to which ideas build systematically one upon the other. A simple framework developed for use by instructors in the military services involves a three-step process in which the lecturer (1) "tells them what he is going to tell them," (2) "tells them," and (3) "tells them what he has told them." In more familiar terms, a good lecture needs a logical *introduction* to focus attention on central issues, a *main body* where ideas are expanded and presented in depth, and a *conclusion* where a recapitulation of important points is provided.

In addition to developing a sequence of presentation for their own use, many teachers find it useful to *provide a general topic*

Figure 5.2

Illustration of a Lecture Outline
Designed for Learner Use

Topic: Fencing and the Great Plains

  1.   Differences in native vegetation patterns in the East and in the Great
       Plains.

  2.   Attempts to grow hedge fences on the plains.

  3.   Opposing views of farmers and cattlemen about fencing.
       3a. The argument for fencing farms.
       3b. The argument for fencing cattle.

  4.   The invention of barbed wire.

  5.   Reactions to barbed wire.

  6.   Spread of barbed wire, and the results.

---

outline for their learners. Such outlines serve as organizers that
help youngsters to separate key points and to distinguish critical
information from background material. Figure 5.2 illustrates such
an outline.

During a lecture, teachers need to *use a variety of stimuli.* More
specifically, changes in volume, rate of delivery, inflection, and
supporting physical gestures ought to be incorporated as safe-
guards against monotony.

Finally, the lecture *should be kept short.* This consideration is
particularly critical when the audience consists of younger
children. Even with classes of highly motivated eleventh- and
twelfth-graders, lectures lasting more than about half an hour
begin to decline rapidly as effective facilitators of learning.

Summarizing, a good lecture is characterized by:
  1. Responsiveness to the needs of the audience.
  2. Careful planning and organization.
  3. Inclusion of a variety of stimuli.
  4. Brevity.

Questioning

The revelation that teachers ask learners a good many questions may be an observation that is tediously obvious. However, it is less well known that there are ways to organize and order questions in a way that prompts learners to engage in increasingly demanding thought processes.

Hunkins (1972) cites "centering" and "expansion" as two important functions of teachers' questions. "Centering questions" help learners establish a tighter focus on the topic under consideration. Some examples of centering questions are:

- What did we conclude yesterday about the identifying characteristics of the halogen family?
- Who will review for us the steps a bill goes through before becoming a law?
- Joey, will you tell us the names of the days of the week?
- What major themes appear in *East of Eden*?
- If someone asked you to find the area of this irregular polygon, where would you begin?

"Expansion," a second function of questioning, involves questions that require learners to increase the range and sophistication of their thinking. "Expansion questions" require learners to move beyond simple knowledge and understanding to apply previously-learned information and to make inferences about new situations.

Expansion questions can be sequenced in such a way that they demand increasingly sophisticated levels of learner thinking. A systematic strategy for utilizing expansion has been developed by Hunkins (1972) from the earlier work on cognitive thinking by Bloom *et al.* (1956). According to this procedure, learners build a base of information as a consequence of being asked "knowledge" and "comprehension" questions. If the students respond correctly to these questions, teachers can move on to ask more challenging questions, requiring learners to "apply" what they have learned to new contexts. Next, in an attempt to push learners to still more sophisticated levels, "analysis" and then "synthesis" level questions can be asked. Should learners still continue to respond well, the sequence can be capped by asking questions at the "evaluation" level. Some examples of teacher questions at each cognitive level follow:

- **Knowledge**
  What is the capitol of Vermont?
  Who was our 18th President?
  How many sides does a tetrahedron have?

- **Comprehension**
  How can litmus paper be used to identify an acid or a base?
  What must be done to center a piece of typewriter paper.
  How is natural rubber made?

- **Application**
  Can you solve for the hypotenuse using the Pythagorean theorem and a right triangle with legs of five and seven inches respectively?
  Given that on this map one inch equals 50 miles, can you tell me how far it is from Houston to Minneapolis?
  If we know that 1 meter equals 100 centimeters, how many meters are there in one kilometer?

- **Analysis**
  What elements are contained in this unknown solution?
  What caused the disappearance of smelt from Monterey Bay?
  Why did Seattle rather than Port Townsend develop as the major port on Puget Sound?

- **Synthesis**
  Which port, New Orleans, San Francisco, or Seattle, is likely to serve the largest net tonnage in the year 1990?
  What were the primary causes leading to the massive U.S. military involvement in South Vietnam in the 1960's?
  What contrary arguments might be posed to the continental drift theory?

- **Evaluation**
  Who is likely to be the best Republican choice for President in 1988 and why do you make that choice?
  Supporting your selections with evidence, can you name

the five individuals who have made the greatest con-
tributions to chemistry in the past two hundred years?
Why do you consider this painting technically superior to
that one?

Hunkins (1972) suggests that, in an instructional sequence,
teachers systematically ought to demand more of students by
asking questions at increasingly higher cognitive levels. This should
not be, however, a simple "by the numbers" process according to
which there is an automatic move from knowledge, to comprehension, to application, to analysis, to synthesis, and, finally, to
evaluation questions. The rule for moving to a question of a higher
order is learner success in responding to a question asked at the
cognitive level immediately below.

For example, if learners are asked knowledge level questions to
which they respond appropriately, comprehension level questions
should follow. Further, if those comprehension level questions are
handled adequately, teachers should feel free to ask application
level questions. If, in asking application level questions, learners
experience difficulty, it would be a serious mistake to ask even
more demanding questions at, for example, the analysis or
synthesis levels.

When, by increasing systematically the cognitive difficulty of
questions, there comes a point where learners are unable to
generate adequate responses, the tactic is to begin building a
broader base of information by asking questions involving a level
of cognitive difficulty one step lower. For example, if there is
difficulty with application level questions, an attempt should be
made to build a deeper reservoir of understanding by asking
comprehension level questions. Once this has been accomplished,
then a new attempt can be made to move students to higher levels
of cognitive functioning by asking questions at the application
level and higher.

In utilizing a questioning strategy, a beginning is made by asking
several "centering" questions to establish the focus for the lesson.
Once this has been established, then there can be movement to the
complex process of sequencing "expansion" questions in a
systematic response to learner answers.

This questioning strategy does not accommodate itself easily to a teaching repertoire. The difficulty lies in the necessity, at first, to attend carefully both to the substance of a learner's answer and to the cognitive levels of the questions asked and about to be asked. Given practice, however, use of the strategy can become a comfortable and familiar instructional procedure. Once mastered, the questioning strategy introduced here can serve as a powerful tool to promote the development of learners' higher level thinking abilities.

Concept Attainment Strategy

Concepts are the basic building blocks of the curriculum. Attempts to describe the characteristics of a concept have been legion. For the purposes of this strategy, a concept will be defined as a "term that applies a common label to a class of phenomena sharing certain characteristics." "War," "revolution," "catalytic reaction," "community property," "inelastic demand," and "democracy" all are examples of concepts.

Concepts are mental constructs used to organize and categorize phenomena encountered in the "real world." Concepts vary in power and inclusiveness. The concept "three-toed sloth," for example, is highly restrictive and narrow in that it includes a very limited number of examples (e.g., a sluggish, arboreal edentate of the family *Bradypodiae* of tropical America having three toes on the front foot.) On the other hand, a concept such as "democracy" is incredibly powerful and inclusive in that it encompasses a host of examples and is defined by a complex assortment of interacting subordinate concepts.

For teachers, there is a dilemma resulting from the fact that concepts which are very complex tend to crop up again and again in the learning materials available for use in the classroom. Indeed, because of the descriptive power of such concepts, there appears to be a direct relationship between concept difficulty and frequency of occurrence. This reality necessitates the development of procedures that provide learners with clear operational understandings of those powerful and inclusive concepts that will appear often throughout the course of study. Learners lacking such understandings will not possess the fundamentals necessary for growth in a subject area.

Taba and her associates (Taba *et al.*, 1971), consistent with the work of Gagné (1970), have suggested a strategy designed to help learners internalize certain important concepts. This systematic approach consists of a structured set of teacher questions designed to (1) familiarize the learner with the name or label given the concept, (2) enable the learner to recognize the defining characteristics of the concept, and (3) distinguish between examples and non-examples of the concept.

The sequence used teaching a new concept is as follows:

The teacher says,

1. Say this new term after me. (Learner says name of concept.)
2. This is a (an) . . . . (Teacher points to an example of concept, reads a description of concept, or describes an example of a concept.)
3. This is also a (an) . . . . (Teacher points to a second example of concept, reads a description of a second example of a concept, or describes a second example of a concept.)
4. This is *not* a (an) . . . . (Teacher points to a *non-example* of a concept, or describes a *non-example* of a concept.)
5. From these examples and non-examples of . . . (names concept), I would like you to point out the examples of the new term (concept).
6. How would you define this new term (concept) in your own words?

An example with content provided follows.

1. *Teacher*: Say the term "arachnid."
   Students: "Arachnid" (Teacher listens.)
   Teacher: John, I don't think you've quite got it. Will you repeat "arachnid."
   John: "Arachnid"
   Teacher: Fine. That's right.
2. *Teacher*: This is an "arachnid." (Shows picture of a black widow.)
3. *Teacher*: This is also an "arachnid." (Shows picture of a small brown spider.)
4. *Teacher*: This is not an "arachnid." (Shows picture of a blue bottle fly.)
5. *Teacher*: Tell me, which ones are "arachnids?" (Shows

picture depicting spiders, earthworms, centi-
pedes, bees, mosquitoes, house flies.)

Students: That one, that one, and that one. (Points out spiders in picture.)

Teacher: That's right.

6. *Teacher*: Who will give me a definition of an "arachnid?"

Student: (gives definition)

Use of this concept attainment strategy provides a system for developing learners' understanding of concepts they will need to organize the information. Time spent in insuring that learners adequately grasp basic terminology pays off handsomely later when teachers attempt to add more sophisticated understandings to this base of fundamental concept knowledge.

Content-Centered—Talk/Activity *NOT* Channeled Through the Teacher Strategies

Role Playing

Role playing engages learners psychologically with the perspectives of others. The technique demands intense personal and emotional involvement in activities in which the "role player" attempts to react to a situation as he believes some "real" person might react (or, in case of a historical situation, might have reacted).

Role playing has a mission in both attitudinal and cognitive learning. Often teachers use the procedure to help learners get "inside someone else's head." To prepare students for realistic involvement in these feelings-oriented experiences, teachers need to provide them with a broad base of information that can be used to develop a tie to reality as their interpretations of roles unfold. The process of acquiring this base of information comprises the cognitive learning component of role playing.

The first step in preparing for a role playing exercise involves *developing the scenario*. The scenario consists of a general description of a given incident, situation, or set of circumstances. In developing scenarios, there is a need to provide sufficient detail for learners without overloading them with so much information that they are unable to distinguish between significant and trivial aspects of the situation.

The scenario may be presented in written or oral form. If a decision is made to provide a written scenario, diagnostic data must be examined that relates to each learner's relative development in terms of such factors as levels of conceptual function and general reading ability. In oral presentations of scenarios, there is a need to check frequently on learners' grasp of the basic outline of the described situation.

In many role playing situations, particularly those that are somewhat complex in nature, it is desirable to follow scenario preparation with a tightly focused *role description* for each character. Role descriptions, which again may be introduced either orally or in written form, sketch the background of individual characters in some detail. Role descriptions focus on general world views of characters and on decisions they have made in the past that reflect their values.

Having established scenarios and, possibly, role descriptions, the role playing exercise next moves to a *role assignment and role internalization phase.* Specific role assignments are made. Learners are urged to "get into the character" as deeply as possible to understand how the portrayed individual reacts to situations and to certain other people. At this point, learners need to be reminded to react to a situation as they think the character they are playing would react. They need to understand that the reactions of their portrayed characters may be quite different from the reactions they, themselves, would have in similar circumstances.

The *activity phase* of the role playing strategy occurs when learners have a clear idea of the nature of the situation and of the characters they have been assigned to play. Usually, a role playing session will involve no more than six or seven individuals. Class members without roles can observe the development of dialogue carefully for the purposes of participating in the debriefing session.

When it is time for the activity phase to commence, "players" can be asked to come to a part of the room where their actions can be viewed and heard easily by others. Chairs and other necessary props should be arranged.

Once the activity phase has begun, characters are permitted to follow their own instincts in responding to statements of other characters. Hopefully, they will have internalized the viewpoint of the individual whose identity they are assuming well enough to react more or less as that individual might have acted in similar circumstances. There are, however, no "consequences" built in to the activity phase of a role playing exercise when a given player strays from the sort of responses that logically would follow from his character. The emphasis in the activity phase is on interactive communication processes. For this reason, no constraints are put on players in terms of limiting the range of their responses.

In terms of length, the activity phase may last from five to fifteen minutes. Shorter sessions do not give players time for sufficient interaction. Activity phases lasting much longer than fifteen minutes frequently result in characters rehashing positions established earlier in the exercise.

Perhaps the most important component of the role playing activity is *the debriefing session* that follows the activity phase. During the debriefing session, observers as well as role players participate in a guided discussion focusing on what took place during the activity phase. In debriefing, teachers ought to utilize increasingly narrow questions beginning with the general, continuing to the specifc, and concluding with the personal. An example of a sequence of debriefing questions follows:

1. General questions
   a. What caused the situation?
   b. What happened during the actual role playing?

2. Specific questions
   a. What character worked hardest to achieve a solution to the problem?
   b. Did our players respond as the "real life" person they were portraying would have responded?
   c. What criticisms would you make about how the players reacted to this situation?

3. Personal Questions
   a. How do you personally feel about the actions of Mr. B. . . (or other characters)?
   b. Why do you feel that way?

    c. Have you ever been in a situation similar to the one depicted here?

    d. How did you feel about that?

    e. How were your feelings similar to and different from those of others in the same predicament?

Topics for role playing exercises may range from school ground incidents (a fight over who is going to get the jump ropes . . . an argument over use of a swing . . . a hair pulling incident . . . etc.) to relatively sophisticated adaptations of formal subject matter content (Galileo's confrontation with authorities charged with protecting the conventional "wisdom" . . . Wolfe and Montcalm at the Battle of Quebec . . . A debate between "Adam Smith" and "John Maynard Keynes" on the economic efficacy of *laissez faire* . . . etc.).

In summary, role playing provides learners with opportunities to become acquainted with the perceptions of people other than themselves. This process involves both cognitive and attitudinal learnings. Role playing promotes tolerance and acceptance of diverse viewpoints by requiring learners to become thoroughly immersed in viewpoints likely to differ from their own. Additionally, because of the active participation demanded of learners in role playing, the strategy frequently is highly motivating for learners.

Summarizing, the role playing strategy develops according to the following sequence of events:

1. Develop the scenario.
2. Learn role descriptions (may be omitted when scenarios are very simple).
3. Assign roles and assure internalization.
4. Conduct activity phase.
5. Conduct debriefing session.

Simulation

Simulations, while relatively new to public school classrooms, have had a long history of use by the military and by business. "War games" have been used to familiarize generations of soldiers with the "feel" of battlefield conditions. Similarly, the United States' space program developed incredibly sophisticated pieces of apparatus designed to replicate conditions astronauts would encounter in space. Large corporations frequently have developed programs requiring junior managers to engage in simulated decision-making activities.

While simulations designed for use in industry and in the military are too complex for the classroom, basic design features from these models have been borrowed and incorporated into simulations that have proved successful with learners in schools. Simulations have proved to be useful vehicles for providing learning experiences requiring learners to engage in decision-making. Decision-making requires learners to apply, analyze, synthesize, and evaluate previously learned knowledge. These higher level cognitive activities frequently have not been well served by many less personally-involving instructional strategies.

Basically, simulations present participants with opportunities to focus on selected features of a "real world" situation. The purpose of this effort is for learners to learn about features of the "real world" that cannot be transported intact into the classroom. For example, the United States Senate cannot be brought into a classroom and, even more obviously, learners cannot become real Senators. But certain activities typical of the Senate's operations can be brought into the classroom using a well designed simulation as a vehicle.

Simulation as a strategy has been widely promoted as a learner motivator. Because simulations reflect "real world" situations, youngsters initially may think of them as more relevant than other classroom learning experiences. This motivational advantage may be short-lived if the simulation proves to be poorly designed. It is particularly important that issues simulated be considered important by learners.

Simulations most frequently focus on the teaching of processes rather than of isolated facts. They can help clarify complex problems and relationships that are not taught easily via a book or lecture.

A representative simulation emphasizing process is the *Game of Democracy,* distributed by Coleman Associates. In *Democracy,* participants assume roles of legislative assembly members who must bargain with one another to gain support or opposition for certain pieces of legislation. A goal for each participant is to be reelected to the legislature by gaining passage of bills favored by constituents. The game focuses heavily on the process of "logrolling" to secure support for specific bills. It is true that many texts deal with "logrolling," but there is evidence that learners may better come to understand the practice by directly confronting the process in an active, involving simulation such as *Democracy.*

Many excellent simulations are available from commercial sources. But when budget restrictions have prevented consideration of commercial products, many teachers have found that simulations of their own design have worked well.

In designing a simulation, there is a need to begin by carefully delimiting the scope of the process to be taught. It is well to identify a general area of conern and restrict the focus to one simple event or process. It is much easier to *add* detail than *delete* it later on.

The design of a simulation begins by *defining the objectives.* Anticipated learnings need to be described as specifically as possible. In addition to the statement of objectives, a general statement about possible places the simulation could be used ought to be included. This information is useful when a teacher other than the developer considers the simulation for use in his classroom.

Next, *the target population and necessary prerequisite knowledge* need to be described. This information ought to be as specific as possible, again considering the possibility that the simulation may be used by someone other than the developer.

Following this step, it is necessary to *identify the event to be simulated and develop a model.* This model will include all significant events and personages to be included in the simulation. Specifically, the model may describe (1) the geographical setting, (2) the principal participants, (3) the constraints on the actions of the participants, (4) the psychological mood of the participants, (5) the historical setting, (6) the interactions among the participants, and (7) anything else that might influence the flow of events or the outcomes of the simulation.

Next, the *key roles must be identified.* Key players, groups, institutions, or other forces must be described. Roles that individuals will assume and resources they will have at their disposal should be developed in outline form. At this point there is a need to consider how many students will be involved at one time. Will half the class participate? All?

Following role identification, *the goals and objectives for each participant* must be specified. Clear descriptions need to be provided concerning what each participant should accomplish as the simulation unfolds. For example, are participants to accumulate power, wealth, or other forms of rewards? Decisions must be made regarding how accomplishment of objectives will be determined.

Our next task is to *write role profiles for each participant.* Role profiles tell each participant (1) how he is to react in different situations, (2) what his obligations are, (3) what he can or cannot do, and (4) any other information that will be helpful to him in understanding how the role is to be played. Brevity in the role profile is important. Participants must not be overwhelmed with too much information.

The next step is to *specify the interaction sequence.* It is necessary to describe how the simulation is to begin and which participants will be interacting. Possible consequences of alternative courses of action that participants might select should be described. The manner in which the simulation will progress and be terminated ought to be included in this point in the planning process.

Next, there is a need to *develop support materials* that will be required. These include such items as score sheets, play money, record-keeping systems, and other material needs.

Finally, the *debriefing session must be outlined.* The debriefing session should be designed so the focusing objectives of the simulation are brought to light and reinforced. It is at this point that teachers can underscore important points and probe carefully for any misconceptions learners may have taken away from the simulation experience. The debriefing session can give learners an opportunity to reflect on decisions made and to discuss any issues not resolved at the time the simulation terminated.

Teacher-prepared simulations require careful development. Without a tight organizational structure resulting from careful preplanning, simulations are likely to result in large numbers of student questions that teachers are going to be poorly prepared to answer. Such experiences are likely to be frustrating for both teacher and learners. Productive learning cannot result in such a circumstance. If teachers are unwilling to commit the time to do a careful job of planning a simulation, they are better advised to select a commercially-prepared product or to adopt an alternative strategy.

Summarizing, the steps required in preparing a teacher-made simulation are:

1. Define objectives.
2. Define target population and prerequisite knowledges.
3. Identify the event to be simulated and develop a model.
4. Identify the key roles.
5. Specify the goals and objectives for each participant.
6. Write role profiles for each participant.
7. Specify the interaction sequence.
8. Develop support materials.
9. Outline the debriefing session.

Games

Educational games have been confused frequently with simulations. Indeed, simulations and games do share many common elements. But there are sufficient differences in structure and purpose for games and simulations to be categorized as separate and independent instructional strategies.

Games usually involve highly competitive relationships. Unlike simulations, games tend to be structured in such a way that there is always a clear "winner" and "loser." While the expectation is that the player using the most appropriate strategy will "win," because games, unlike simulations are only loosely tied to the real world, there is a possibility that the element of chance may play a role in determining the outcome.

Designers of games, as opposed to designers of simulations, make no conscious attempts to represent "reality." Games usually focus on teaching and reinforcing skills or lower level cognitive knowledges. Only infrequently do games demand players to engage in higher level thinking processes such as many simulations require.

Games tend to be formatted differently than simulations. In general, instructional games make much more frequent use of such devices as playing boards, dice, spinners, tokens, and other pieces of equipment familiar to all who have played commercially-prepared entertainment games. Educational games tend to be less complex than simulations. Consequently, commercial versions often are less expensive than commercial simulations, and teacher-prepared games are easier to construct than teacher-prepared simulations.

Games frequently work well as motivating devices used in preparation for study of a new unit of work. An example of a commercial game that is fairly simple and highly motivating is *Raid,* distributed by Abt Associates, Inc. This game features interactions among a team of policemen, some racketeers, and groups representing different city blocks. Use of *Raid* might be an appropriate beginning to social studies units focusing on urban crime.

If a game such as *Raid* cannot be found, teachers can construct their own games without great difficulty. As a first step, there is a need to *state the purposes and objectives of the game.* A decision must be made regarding whether the game will teach new content, reinforce a skill, motivate learners, or fulfill some other function.

Next, it is necessary to *define the target population and describe any prerequisite skills or knowledges.* Careful attention to these matters will help identify information that must be presented in advance of the game so that learners will have adequate background to do those things demanded of them as the interaction unfolds.

The third step involves preparation of a *tentative layout or design.* A preliminary design must be developed that identifies how the game will be played. Such issues as materials needed and number of players that can participate at one time need to be addressed here. Some teachers, at this stage of development, have found it profitable to brainstorm several design possibilities. When several options are before them, then they select the strongest elements of each in putting together the final design.

Once the game design is in hand, it is necessary to *provide objectives for each player.* Each player must know exactly what he is to accomplish. Resources to be distributed to each player at the beginning of the game need to be described.

Next, it is necessary to *list rules and outline the playing process.* Procedures for beginning the game and going ahead with interactions among players must be made clear. Constraints on actions of any of the players should be described. In general, the flow of the game from beginning to end needs to be described.

At this point in the development of a game, it is critically important that potential player questions be anticipated. If alternative ways of playing are to be open to players, they need to be made explicit in the rules. Every effort should be made to eliminate ambiguity in terms of what players are to do.

The final step is designing a game that requires *identification of the "win" criteria.* Designers must establish how the game will be terminated and how the winner will be determined. One of the procedures that will have to be worked out concerns deciding how scores will be kept. Once the decision has been made, it will be necessary to provide score sheets, tokens, and any other needed score-keeping materials.

If the game is designed carefully, it can provide a valuable learning experience. Teacher-made games enjoy the advantages of being designed to fit a specific curricular or instructional need. Successful games have been constructed by teachers using an incredibly diverse array of materials for game components. Among them are such items as: bottle caps, index cards, poker chips, play money, jacks, rubber bands, stick-on labels, shoe boxes, tag board, graph paper, paper clips, spinners, corks, and tongue depressors.

Summarizing, the steps in constructing a teacher-made game are the following:

1. State the purposes and objectives of the game.
2. Define the target population and describe any prerequisite skills or knowledges.
3. Prepare a tentative layout or design.
4. State objectives for each player.
5. List rules and outline the playing process.
6. Identify the "win" criteria.

Team Learning

The need to provide learners with certain basic information required as a foundation for future learning sometimes seems to conflict with teachers' desires to provide more activity-oriented learning experiences. Dunn and Dunn (1972) have suggested a team learning strategy that combines active learner involvement in small groups with exercises designed to build learners' stores of basic information.

A first step in a team learning exercise is writing several paragraphs containing the substance of the new material. These paragraphs are reproduced and distributed to learners along with questions centering on the material in the paragraphs. Questions vary in complexity from simple factual recall queries to those demanding inferences that go beyond information provided in the paragraphs.

Once paragraphs and questions have been distributed, learners are divided into small groups of from five to eight individuals each. Each group is asked to select a recorder. Students in each group are asked to answer the questions. Group recorders write down responses. Teachers need to emphasize that anyone *within* a group may help another group member, but that no one from one group is to help someone from another group. This feature of the team learning procedure promotes relatively quiet discussion within individual groups.

Typically, groups begin by quietly reading the prose passages. Next, individuals attempt to answer questions by themselves. Soon, occasional questions about the material in the paragraphs or about the written questions themselves begin to be exchanged among group members. As group cohesiveness builds, there is an increase in questions and general give-and-take among group members.

When most groups appear to have completed their work, the class is called together. (It is not necessary for learners to move physically out of their group areas. Learners from this point on will be acting, however, as a single class unit.) The teacher begins by asking the first question on the list. One of the group recorders responds. Other recorders are advised to cross their group's response to the question off their list if it corresponds to the answer given by the recorder responding to the teacher's question.

This procedure is followed (teacher asking questions and calling for answers from representatives of different groups) until all questions have been dealt with. When there is a lack of consensus on answers to a given question, the teacher can list all responses on the chalkboard and engage the group in a discussion leading either to a consensus on a single response or to a realization that several "correct" answers are possible.

A modification of the team learning strategy requires the teacher to list names of individual groups on the chalkboard. As group answers are provided, scores are kept for each group in terms of how many questions are answered correctly. This modification adds a competitive dimension that can prove to be motivating to learners under certain circumstances. It depends heavily, however, on the teacher providing rather low level questions to which very specific answers are the only ones that can be accepted as "correct."

Team learning represents an approach in which specific necessary subject matter information can be transmitted to learners without resorting to silent reading, lecture, or other more passive activities. Properly handled, team learning can be a highly involving and motivating experience for learners.

In summation, the procedures for conducting a team learning activity are:

1. Write out several paragraphs including basic information learners are to acquire. Some questions refer to specific factual information in paragraphs. Others require students to make inferences going beyond provided information.
2. Divide learners into groups consisting of five to eight individuals.
3. Appoint a recorder for each group.
4. Advise learners that anyone *within* a group may help anyone else within a group and that no one in one group may help someone in another group.
5. Call groups together.
6. Ask recorders or other group representatives to respond to every question.
7. Achieve group consensus on questions.

The Case Study

The case study is an instructional strategy that seeks to promote close learner involvement with a specific situation by presenting that situation in such a way that learners identify closely with it. Instead of presenting elements of a situation as separate pieces of information that the learner himself must synthesize, the developer of the case study synthesizes these data to produce a vivid description of a single incident or episode that is intended to illustrate the situation of interest. Case studies, then, focus on a single incident, and they typically describe interaction patterns of human beings. Many case studies include bits of dialogue among the characters. In a few case studies, characters even speak in the present tense.

Learners tend to identify much more readily with characters in a case study than they do with situations described in textbooks. Much less of an intellectual leap is required for a learner to sense the "reality" of a situation transmitted through the words and actions of a character in a case study than from a textbook dissection of the causes of a particular phenomenon.

The strength of the case study—its ability to evoke a close personal identification from learners—is at the same time the weakness of the method, or at least the potential weakness. By their nature, case studies center on only a single incident, a small happening, a thin slice of life. From intensive examination of these microcosms, learners are encouraged to infer characteristics of a much larger universe of events. The potential danger, then, is that the case study may inaccurately reflect the dimensions of this larger reality.

When carefully prepared, case studies prove to be highly motivating experiences for learners. Many outstanding case studies developed by distinguished professionals in many fields are, with some adaptation, well suited for use in classrooms.

Teachers' preparation of their own case studies frequently can provide outstanding learning experiences in areas where suitable commercial materials are lacking. As a first step, it is necessary to *develop a rationale* for the general topic that is to be illuminated by the case study. As professionals, teachers will wish to develop a connection between the proposed case study and the major objectives of their instructional program.

The second step requires a *description of the specific incident* that will provide the focus for the case study. Care must be taken to assure that this incident description includes all critical elements.

The third step in developing a case study is the actual *writing of the scenario*. It is necessary to check diagnostic data on learners' reading levels to be sure that prose does not soar to heights beyond students' level of understanding. The scenario needs to be long enough to develop fully the focus situation and characters' response to that situation. It must be short enough to maintain interest. When there is an opportunity to choose either dialogue or descriptive prose, it is better to choose dialogue. Discussions among characters tend to motivate learners. If there are students in the class who have been particularly difficult to involve, it is desirable to write dialogue in the present tense (there is less of an intellectual leap required to identify with immediate than with past action).

The final feature that must be planned is the *debriefing session.* Case studies provide opportunities for analytical thinking. Such an outcome, however, is doubtful unless some general questions are developed for use with learners when they have completed their work with the materials.

The precise nature of the questions will vary in accordance with the actual incident selected. The following sample questions will provide a general idea of the questioning sequence that might be followed:

1. What was the general nature of the situation described?
2. What specific roles did each character play?
3. Were the actions of the characters the "right" actions? Why?
4. Have you ever been involved in a similar situation?
5. How was it similar? How did you react?

The carefully designed case study can be a strategy that motivates learners to identify closely with situations that otherwise might hold little inherent interest. The following steps should be followed to assure that all necessary details have received attention:

1. Develop a rationale.
2. Prepare a description of the specific incident.
3. Write a scenario.
4. Plan a debriefing session.

Process-Centered—Talk/Activity
Channeled Through the Teacher Strategies

The Data Retrieval Chart
The use of data retrieval charts, a procedure suggested by Hilda

Taba and her associates (Taba *et al.*, 1971), is directed toward enhancing learners' analytical skills. This strategy encourages students to compare and contrast elements of situations and to derive generalizations as a result of their analyses.

Data retrieval charts help learners to organize large quantities of information in a systematic fashion. A particular strength of this strategy is its versatility. Modified according to the needs of each group, the strategy can be used with persons of varying ages and abilities.

Typically, in the middle grades learners spend some time studying the American states. Data retrieval charts are useful devices at times when youngsters must attempt to make sense out of a confusing multitude of specific pieces of information such as confronts them when the 50 states are considered individually. A data retrieval framework such as shown in Figure 5.3 might prove helpful in such a situation.

This chart reveals the basic characteristics of a framework for a data retrieval chart. More specifically, those characteristics include category names laid out either horizontally or vertically. In preparing these frameworks, teachers may select any category names that are appropriate for the material with which they are dealing.

Figure 5.3

Data Retrieval Chart Format

	Major Farm Products	Largest Industry	Pop. per sq. mile	Total Area
Florida				
Minnesota				
Texas				
Washington				

The next step requires learners to gather specific information that can be fitted logically into each cell of the retrieval chart framework. This phase of the exercise might be handled by assigning a single learner or group of learners to gather data that would fit into a particular cell. For example, one individual or one group could be assigned specifically to find out which major farm products were grown in Florida. An alternative arrangement might involve individuals or groups getting information for several of the cells.

Once learners have their information in hand, data can be filled into the appropriate cells.

Data retrieval charts have the advantage of engaging collective attention on topics that traditionally have been fragmented. Consider, for example, the frequent practice of asking youngsters in the sixth grade to each become an "expert" on a single Latin American country. This assignment quite often culminates in an oral report which may prove highly to mildly stimulating to the student giving the report, wearisomely reminiscent of dozens of previous such efforts to the teacher, and mortally dull to the rest of the class. Basically, the deficiency of this procedure results from the complete isolation of one student's report from that of every other student. Using a data retrieval chart framework to guide preparation might result in a more meaningful learning experience for all.

Summarizing, retrieval charts represent vehicles that teachers can use to (1) help learners organize large amounts of information in a systematic way, and (2) prompt learners to engage in higher level thinking by providing opportunities to infer generalizations from data they have gathered, organized, and analyzed. To promote efficient use of data collected and categorized in data retrieval charts, a sequence of teacher questions similar to the following is suggested:

1. What similarities among data in various categories do you see?
2. What differences do you see?
3. How do you explain these similarities and differences?
4. Can you make some general statements that might explain some of the things you see?

Suchman Inquiry

J. Richard Suchman (1966) has formulated a strategy designed to promote active student involvement in the process of generating and testing their own hypotheses. The Suchman strategy is unique among inquiry approaches in that the teacher himself functions as an information source that learners must interrogate as they attempt to formulate and test hypotheses. Learners ask questions that are categorized as *verification questions, experimentation questions, necessity questions,* or *hypothesis checking questions.*

"Verification questions" concern efforts to determine the existence or non-existence of a certain piece of information. "Experimentation questions" attempt to determine the consequence of some change described by the questioner on a given phenomenon. "Necessity questions" attempt to get answers relating to what conditions may or may not be present for a given phenomenon to exist. "Hypothesis checking questions" are questions designed to obtain a verification of a hypothesis suggested by the questioner.

Basically, the Suchman strategy proceeds in a fashion reminiscent of the old parlor game of "20 Questions." An inquiry session begins with the teacher presenting a stimulus to his learners of a type that Suchman describes as a "discrepant event." A discrepant event is an incident, episode, artifact, representation, or something else that does not quite "fit" with the learner's general conception of how the world is put together. An example of a discrepant event from a commercially distributed science program based on Suchman's approach is a man wearing asbestos gloves who (1) removes a large glass cover from the top of a vigorously boiling beaker of water, (2) puts the glass cover down and gingerly picks the beaker up with his gloved hands, (3) carries the beaker to his mouth, and, in a flash, (4) gulps down the steaming liquid with no apparent ill effects. The teacher's focus question: "How was he able to do it?" (for the reader who cannot wait, the glass cover originally over the beaker was there because a vacuum was needed—created by pumping air out through holes in the platform on which the beaker rested—to "boil" the liquid in the beaker at a temperature sufficiently low that the man experiences no discomfort whatever in gulping it down.)

Having presented the discrepant event and asking the focus

question, the next step is for the teacher to provide general operating guidelines to the class. The rules for a Suchman inquiry session are that (1) the teacher will answer any learner question about the discrepant event that can be answered with a "yes" or a "no" *provided that* (2) the question is not a "hypothesis-checking question." If the learner attempts to get a "yes" or a "no" to a "hypothesis-checking question," the teacher should turn it aside with a comment such as "that's an interesting hypothesis you've come up with. I can't give you a 'yes' or 'no' answer. If your hypothesis is true, what other things must also be true? Why don't you ask me about those things?"

Suchman inquiry techniques have been broadly applied, particularly in the physical sciences and in the social studies. The strategy works well with learners of all age groups. (With very young children, one needs to check carefully to ascertain that conceptual development is sufficiently advanced so these youngsters will see the "discrepancy" in the stimulus event.) A wide variety of stimuli have served as discrepant events. A much used example in the social studies has been a photograph of a crumbling Rocky Mountain community with a train speeding through. The focus question is a simple "What happened to this town?" This photographic stimulus and question have been used successfully in Suchman inquiry sessions with groups as disparate as second graders and university graduate students.

Suchman inquiry proceeds on the assumption that all knowledge is tentative. This explains the ground rule forbidding "yes" or "no" answers to "hypothesis-checking questions." According to this view, the educated man is engaged in a never-ending quest for truth that he pursues by testing the value of promising explanations of reality against selective elements of that reality.

In addition to its emphasis on the tentativeness of knowledge and on the philosophical necessity for seeking rather than finding "truth," the Suchman strategy presumes that the learner's basic problem is not absence of information but rather presence of too much information. According to this perspective, learners are adrift in a sea of information so vast that they are unable to discriminate between helpful and unhelpful information. The Suchman strategy proposes to remedy this situation by teaching individuals to ask potent questions that enable them to distinguish quickly relevant information from the irrelevant.

Summarizing, the Suchman Inquiry strategy consists of three basic elements: (1) a "discrepant event," (2) a focus question, and (3) learner questions to the teacher. The ground rules are that the teacher will respond to any question to which he can answer "yes" or "no" except for "hypothesis-checking questions" to which he will refuse to provide "yes" or "no" answers.

Process-Centered—Talk/Activity *NOT*
Channeled Through the Teacher Strategies

Brainstorming

The strategy of brainstorming, originally developed as an aid to creative problem solving among management teams in corporations, attempts to unleash learners' untapped reservoirs of thinking talents by encouraging them to pour forth as many ideas as possible that relate to a defined situation. An important emphasis in brainstorming is the encouragement of *quantity* rather than *quality* of participants' responses.

Brainstorming evolved because of a realization that people many times fail to tap their creative resources to make public a truly creative response to a problem situation. Their failure to do so results from a fear that a response that represents a dramatic break from the ordinary may be held up to ridicule. Consequently, most tentative solutions tend to reflect a conservative, cautious bias that may result in their falling well short of what is needed to resolve a given problem of interest.

Brainstorming attempts to break through inhibitions by encouraging public commitment of *all* ideas. This is accomplished by establishing a rigidly-enforced ground rule of no public comment or reaction to *any* idea put forward. More specifically, the brainstorming strategy moves forward after the teacher has made *each* of the following points:

1. Learners are asked to focus only on the problem situation (e.g., what can be done to reduce the dropout rate from this school?).
2. Once the session begins, each learner is to call out his suggestion as soon as an opening occurs (that is, a time when no other learner is calling out *his* suggestion).
3. No verbal or facial reactions to *any* suggestion are permitted.

4. Every suggestion, no matter how "wild," will be written down by the teacher for the group to see.

During the brainstorming session, ideas will pour forth. As the teacher records responses, he may have to ask the group to slow down to allow him to catch up with the flow of ideas being suggested. Ordinarily a time limit, perhaps two to four minutes, is imposed. Knowledge of the time limit prompts learners to call out responses more quickly. Additionally, the time limit saves the teacher from writing down more information than can possibly be processed in a debriefing session.

Dunn and Dunn (1972) suggest a series of five short two-minute brainstorming sessions in which a progressive analytic structure is built into the attempt to solve a problem. A sequence of three positive and two negative focus questions is used as learners work toward ever more precise solutions. An example of such a sequence of focus questions follows:

+ 1. To prevent a recurrence of the 1974-1975 recession, the United States Government should. . .?
- 2. What situations are likely to occur that would prevent these things from taking place?
+ 3. What might *we* do to remedy these situations?
- 4. What might prevent the success of our remedies?
+ 5. What should our next steps be?

Once the final brainstorming session (based on focus question #5) has been completed, the teacher and the class can conclude the exercise by establishing priorities for suggestions called out and written down. A variety of possibilities for accomplishing this task exist. A simple response involves a debriefing process during which learners and teacher exchange ideas that result in each suggestion being placed in a "high priority," "intermediate priority," or "low priority" category. These prioritized suggestions offer possibilities for organizing additional learning experiences. For example, lessons might be built around the political, social, and economic costs of implementing each of the "high priority" suggestions.

The specific nature of the product of a given brainstorming session is not nearly so important as the process learners go though in generating that product. The strategy promotes creative thinking by calling forth innovative responses at no psychological cost to the participant. Brainstorming, unlike many other instructional strategies, provides learners with a "pay off" for the sorts of creative, divergent thinking teachers often say they want but which tend to be discouraged by learning experiences that most frequently reward the "conventional wisdom."

Summarizing, the following are the basic steps in a brainstorming strategy.

1. Identify a specific focus problem.
2. Explain the rules for participation.
3. Conduct brief sessions to encourage "explosions" of learner ideas (written down by the teacher).
4. Conduct debriefing session.

A Creative Thinking Strategy

For years, conference speakers have encouraged teachers to promote creative thinking abilities of students. Proponents of creative thinking point to the transitory nature of subject matter learning.

Creative thinking is directed toward prompting learners to respond to problems in unconventional ways. A basic premise is that most problems would not *be* problems if familiar and available solutions were applicable. It must be recognized, then, that creative solutions do not spring automatically from the breasts of learners when they are confronted with the necessity of resolving difficult problems.

Our learners' patterns of behavior are conditioned by responses of the external environment of previous manifestations of those patterns. A creative response, by definition, is a response that is not typical of the behavioral repertoire of learners. Therefore, it is unlikely that creative responses will evolve without teachers arranging circumstances that in fact train and reward youngsters for creative responses.

A variety of approaches have been used by teachers to stimulate creative thinking behaviors. One simple procedure involves the use of 3" x 5" note cards and paper clips. This activity begins when each student is given one note card and one paper clip. The teacher provides instructions as follows: "Take your note card and paper clip. Make something creative using only these items. You have five minutes. Begin."

At the end of the five-minute period, learners are asked to bring their creations to the front of the room, where they can be lined up on tables or, possibly, on the floor next to the wall. Next, the teacher places a label with a number next to each "creation." For example, if there are 25 "creations," they will be placed by numbered labels running from 1 through 25.

Next, members of the class are asked to rate each "creation" using a scale from 5 to 1, with *5 being awarded to highly creative works, 4 to moderately creative works, 3 to slightly creative works, 2 to barely creative works,* and *1 to uncreative works.* Ratings for each "creation" should be written on a piece of paper ("creations" are identified by label number).

The next step involves collection of the ratings. On the board the teacher tallies the rating for each "creation." When this task has been completed, all of the creations are removed except for those *three* having the highest numerical ratings (indicating mostly 5's and 4's). At this point the class should be ready for the crux of the lesson. The teacher asks, "What makes these three creations creative?"

In response to the question, learners generate responses that the teacher writes on the board. Referrring to these responses, the teacher should make the point that the class has generated *criteria* for creativity. The exercise helps learners recognize that something is not simply creative because someone *says* it is, and that creativity is a label that results when judgments have been made in the light of some sort of a standard (for example, "bending" some defining attribute of a concept in an unexpected way). There is a need to emphasize that criteria for creativity do exist, but that they are not always made public. The observer of a creative work, thus, has the responsibility for generating criteria of his own that can be used as the basis of judgment.

Exercises such as the one described help to develop a fuller understanding of what is implied by creative thinking. Further, there is psychological "pay off" for the "most creative" efforts because those "creations" are singled out for special attention by the whole class. This "reward" for creative production can prompt future instances of creative thinking on the part of the youngsters involved.

In sum, creative thinking helps learners break loose from the conceptual frameworks within which they typically view reality. Such creative thinking skills are unlikely to flourish unless systematic attention is given to developing and reinforcing them. Because persistent problems do not yield easily to conventional procedures, strategies designed to foster creative thinking constitute an important addition to the instructional repertoire of the professional teacher.

Summary

The strategies introduced here represent only a sample of those that are available. The intent has been to provide some useful exemplars of strategies rather than to present an exhaustive treatment of all instructional strategies. References cited at the end of this chapter will suggest sources of information regarding additional strategies as well as more detailed descriptions of those discussed here.

As a final consideration, the authors wish to reiterate the importance of selecting a strategy only after a careful consideration of instructional purposes. The framework for categorizing strategies used in this chapter will be a helpful tool in this regard.

Prior even to a consideration of strategies in regard to their placement within this framework, teachers ought to look very carefully at their performance objectives and at available diagnostic information. Strategies selected without consideration for planned instructional outcomes or for characteristics of students may result in learning that is marginally effective (at best) in promoting learner mastery of objectives. When consideration of these matters *does* precede strategy selection, strategies can become very effective aids to learners.

Selection of strategies, following specification of performance objectives and diagnosis of learners, completes the "pre-implementation" phase of introduction. The next chapter will focus on procedures for putting these plans into operation and interacting with learners.

References

BLOOM, Benjamin S. (Ed.). *Taxonomy of Educational Objectives: Handbook I: Cognitive Domain.* New York: David McKay Company, 1956.
DUNN, Rita and Kenneth DUNN. *Practical Approaches to Individualizing*

Instruction: Contracts and Other Effective Teaching Strategies. West Nyack, New York: Parker Publishing Company, Inc., 1972.

GAGNE, Robert M. *The Conditions of Learning.* 2nd Edition. New York: Holt, Rinehart, and Winston, Inc., 1970.

HUNKINS, Frances P. *Questioning Strategies and Techniques.* Boston: Allyn and Bacon, Inc., 1972.

SUCHMAN, J. Richard. *Developing Inquiry.* Chicago: Science Research Associates, Inc., 1966.

TABA, Hilda, Mary C. DURKIN, Jack R. FRAENKEL, and Anthony H. MC NAUGHTON. *A Teacher's Handbook to Elementary Social Studies: An Inductive Approach.* 2nd Edition. Reading, Mass.: Addison-Wesley Publishing Co., Inc., 1971.

Additional Professional Study

Books

BOOCOCK, Sarane S. and E.O. SCHILD (Eds.). *Simulation Games in Learning.* Beverly Hills, Calif.: Sage Publications, 1968.

CHESLER, Mark and Robert FOX. *Role-Playing Methods in the Classroom.* Chicago, Ill.: Science Research Associates, Inc., 1966.

DUNN, Rita and Kenneth DUNN. *Practical Approaches to Individualizing Instruction: Contracts and Other Effective Teaching Strategies.* West Nyack, New York: Parker Publishing Company, Inc., 1972.

GAGNE, Robert M. *The Conditions of Learning.* 2nd Edition. New York: Holt, Rinehart, and Winston, Inc., 1970.

GORDON, Alice Kaplan. *Games for Growth: Educational Games in the Classroom.* Chicago, Ill.: Science Research Associates, Inc., 1970.

HUNKINS, Francis P. *Questioning Strategies and Techniques.* Boston, Mass.: Allyn and Bacon, Inc., 1972.

HYMAN, Ronald T. *Ways of Teaching* (2nd edition). New York: J.B. Lippincott Company, 1974.

JOYCE, Bruce and Marsha WEIL. *Models of Teaching.* Englewood Cliffs, N.J.: Prentice-Hall, Inc., 1972.

MERRILL, M. David and Robert D. TENNYSON. *Teaching Concepts: An Instructional Design Guide.* Englewood Cliffs, N.J.: Educational Technology Publications, 1977.

PIGORS, Paul J.W. *Case-Method in Human Relations: The Incident Process.* New York: McGraw-Hill Book Co., 1961.

POPHAM, W. James and Eva BAKER. *Planning an Instructional Sequence.* Englewood Cliffs, N.J.: Prentice-Hall, Inc., 1970.

RATHS, James, John R. PANCELLA, and James S. VAN NESS. *Studying Teaching* (2nd edition). Englewood Cliffs, N.J.: Prentice-Hall, Inc., 1971.

RATHS, Louis E., Merrill HARMIN, and Sidney B. SIMON. *Values and Teaching.* Columbus, Ohio: Charles E. Merrill Publishing Co., 1966.

SANDERS, Norris M. *Classroom Questions: What Kinds?* New York: Harper and Row, Publishers, 1966.

SAVAGE, Tom V. Jr., "Games and Simulations for Teachers." Unpublished paper, Bellingham, Washington, Western Washington State College, 1975.
SCHMUCK, Richard, Mark CHESLER, and Ronald LIPPITT. *Problem Solving to Improve Classroom Learning.* Chicago, Ill.: Science Research Associates, Inc., 1966.
SHAFTEL, Fannie R. and George SHAFTEL. *Role Playing for Social Values.* Englewood Cliffs, N.J.: Prentice-Hall, Inc., 1967.
SIMON, Sidney B., Leland W. HOWE, and Howard KIRSCHENBAUM. *Values Clarification.* New York: Hart Publishing Company, Inc., 1972.
STRASSER, Ben B. *Components in Teaching Strategy.* San Anselmo, Calif: Search Models Unlimited, 1967.
SUCHMAN, J. Richard. *Developing Inquiry.* Chicago, Ill.: Science Research Associates, Inc., 1966.
TABA, Hilda, Mary C. DURKIN, Jack R. FRAENKEL, and Anthony H. MC NAUGHTON. *A Teacher's Handbook to Elementary Social Studies: An Inductive Approach.* 2nd Edition. Reading Mass.: Addison-Wesley Publishing Co., Inc., 1971.
TAYLOR, John and Rex WALFORD. *Simulation in the Classroom.* Baltimore, Md.: Penguin Books Inc., 1974.
WILLIAMS, Frank. *A Total Creativity Program for Individualizing and Humanizing the Learning Process.* Books, posters, cards, cassettes. Englewood Cliffs, N.J.: Educational Technology Publications, 1972.

Periodicals

BALL, Daniel W. "Brainstorming." *School and Child* (December 1973), 14-15.
BILLS, Frank L. "Developing Creativity Through Inquiry." *Peabody Journal of Education* (July 1973), 298-201.
D'ANGELO, Gary and Jody NYQUIST. "Teaching Strategies for Large Lecture Groups: Use of Multi-Media and Discussion Groups." *The Speech Teacher* (November 1973) 310-317.
EGELSTON, Judy C. "Inductive vs. Traditional Methods of Teaching High School Biology Laboratory Experiments." *Science Education* (October 1973) 467-477.
EHRLICH, Harriet W. "Creative Dramatics As a Classroom Teaching Technique." *Elementary English* (January 1974), 75-80.
KOURILSKY, Marilyn. "Anatomy of a Dead Lecture." *The Clearing House* (September 1971), 20-26.
NELSON, William *et al.* "Revised Strategy for Idea Generation in Small Group Decision-Making." *The Speech Teacher* (September 1973), 191-196.
PALOMARES, Uvaldo, H. "Key to Understanding Self and Others; Magic Circle, Human Development Program." *Educational Leadership* (October 1974), 19-21.
SARTAIN, Harold D. "Emphasis on Learning Packages for Developmental and Supplemental Instruction." *Audiovisual Instruction* (November 1973), 12-13.

SMITH, Bruce D. and Ronald L. VAN SICKLE. "Focusing on Inquiry Teaching Behaviors." *The High School Journal* (April 1975), 285-294.

TAYLOR, A.J.R. "Developing Your Own Simulation for Teaching Social Studies." *Clearing House* (November 1976), 104-107.

TITUS, Charles. "Uses of the Lecture." *Clearing House* (February 1974), 383-384.

TORRANCE, E. Paul. "Interscholastic Brainstorming and Creative Problem Solving Competition for the Creatively Gifted." *Gifted Child Quarterly* (Spring 1974), 3-7.

TRAUGH, Cecilia E. "Evaluating Inquiry Procedures." *The Social Studies* (October 1974), 201-202.

URANECK, William O. "Creativity into Action: A Creative Problem Solving Course." *Journal of Creative Behavior* (First Quarter 1974), 69-74.

VICTOR, Edward. "Inquiry Approaches to Teaching and Learning: A Primer for Teachers." *Science and Children* (October 1974), 23-26.

WATSON, Patricia J. "Discovery and Inquiry: Techniques of the New Breed of Learner." *Music Educators Journal* (January 1975), 50-53.

WRIGHT, Lin. "Creative Dramatics and the Development of Role-Taking in the Elementary Classroom." *Elementary English* (January 1974), 89-934.

Chapter 6

Interacting with Learners

OBJECTIVES
This chapter provides information to help the reader to:

1. specify procedures for working with large groups of learners.

2. distinguish among teacher responsibilities in task choice groups, tutorial groups, research groups, and predetermined role groups.

3. describe general procedures for preparing class ground rules.

4. point out techniques that can be used to assure clarity when assignments are made.

5. suggest general principles to observe during lesson sessions to minimize classroom control problems.

6. describe elements of procedures that may be used in dealing with severe behavior problems.

_____

Interacting with learners is an instructional skill that might be characterized as the "doing" phase of instruction. Performance objectives have been established, learners' characteristics have been identified, and appropriate strategies have been selected. In short, an instructional sequence has been planned using the best professional information available. The time has come to try out this plan with learners in a real classroom situation.

Beginning teachers, who may have experienced little difficulty in mastering the mechanics of writing performance objectives, diagnosing learners, and selecting strategies, frequently are frustrated when well conceived plans sometimes fail to "click" with learners. This frustration arises from a mistaken assumption that careful planning in and of itself will assure flawlessly delivered and enthusiastically received lessons. Unfortunately, there is much more to effective teaching than careful attention to the planning phases of instruction.

It should not be surprising that mastery of the teacher-learner interaction dimension of the instructional process comes much more slowly than mastery of procedures associated with development of performance objectives, diagnosis of learners, and selection of strategies. These latter competencies can be acquired and demonstrated largely in isolation from direct contact with learners. Only rarely do teachers find themselves pressed to make important decisions about these matters when students or pupils are gathered around the desk clamoring for attention. On the other hand, many decisions relating to the teacher-learner interaction dimension must take place as the actual instruction unfolds. Dozens of unforeseen contingencies may arise demanding immediate teacher decisions. Given these conditions, it is understandable that teachers require some seasoning to become truly proficient in this area.

In considering this dimension of instruction, it is necessary, as a first step, to decide what the interaction should be about. To be certain that planned interactions are supportive of the intended program outcomes, it makes sense to keep program objectives guiding a given program well in mind. Teachers who do not have a clear sense of program direction may find that their learners are able to subvert the intended program aims by leading teachers into discussions of highly peripheral issues.

One of the authors recalls being party, in his high school days, to maneuvers directed at getting his English teacher to recount personal experiences from his island-hopping adventures in the Pacific during World War II. These tactics frequently led to discussions that were highly interesting to the learners (and inordinately satisfying to the "old warrior."). Indeed, these class sessions met many criteria of an effective teacher-learner interaction pattern, with one glaring exception: they did nothing to facilitate learners' attainment of the English objectives that were central to the course.

In making decisions relating to teacher-learner interaction patterns, a very important consideration is the size of the instructional group. Of course, groups may vary enormously in size from the proverbial one teacher and one student seated at opposite ends of a log, to auditoriums filled with hundreds of students who are addressed by a teacher at a podium. For purposes of dealing with this issue here, the discussion of group size will focus on two very general categories, large groups and small groups. Large groups will be considered to be groups of 25 to 40 learners, such as might be encountered in traditional self-contained classrooms. Small groups will be considered any grouping arrangements in which these large groups have been broken down for the purpose of providing more than a single instructional experience at a time to all students in a given classroom.

Interacting with Learners in Large Group Settings

In large group instructional settings, teachers deal with classes of learners as single units. Learning experiences may be varied slightly to meet peculiar needs of selected students, but, for the most part, activities center around a common program instead of being diffused among groups pursuing different ends.

Teachers' verbal behavior with learners in large group settings is critically important. A basic aspect of verbal communication when working with large numbers of learners involves nothing more sophisticated than volume. Voices must be projected so that learners in all parts of the classroom can hear. Attention will be short-lived from youngsters who have to strain to hear instructions.

A second difficulty associated with learners' verbal behavior concerns difficulties some students experience in understanding the *substance* of what has been said. This problem frequently arises when instructions lack a logical sequence. Consider, for example, the following set of instructions that were transcribed from an audio tape of an actual class session:

> Let's take a different approach today. Forget about the map, O.K.? That is, forget about it just for now—maybe we'll get back to it tomorrow. Instead of checking out all the maps—one at a time I mean—how about just one map at a time, just for today, I

mean. Can we say something about this map, and maybe about this one, I mean as it compares to these two on the green wall here. Remember that inferencing session, you know where you came up with all those different ideas? Well, we're not going to do anything like that—what a relief for you, Ralph—ha! ha! Well anyway, when we did do that inferencing, you know a few of you said we skipped around—or some of us did—from subject to subject too much. Get that pencil later, Eunice. OK Ralph, put the PTA notices on my desk and close the door. Well, now let's all try to listen to one another—maybe we'll even hear something we don't know. Don't jump in all at once. Wave your little pinky. If I don't see it right away, don't worry, you'll have your say. Let's have some quick thinking today. OK, Rosemarie, you be first . . . .

What *was* the intent of these instructions? Whatever the intent was, surely at the conclusion of this teacher's rambling discourse, members of the class must have been hopelessly confused and at the point of crying "Uncle!" Instructions delivered according to a poorly focused "stream of consciousness" model can undermine learners' self-confidence when they are chided for not performing up to the teacher's expectations—a state of affairs likely to have resulted as much from a misunderstanding of the instructions as from a lack of ability or motivation.

To diagnose problems or potential problems in the area of communicating expectations to learners, audio recordings, made during representative class periods, are useful. When instructions are delivered properly, a transcript taken from the recording will reveal a logical progression from point "a" to point "b" to point "c." The flow of words need not be as mechanically perfect as a set of prose instructions, but still elements of logical point-by-point development should be clearly in evidence.

When analyses of recordings reveal problems in delivering instructions clearly, one suitable remedy involves writing out proposed instructions in longhand before class begins. This exercise helps pinpoint possible areas of confusion and prompts a rethinking of how instructions that might mislead learners could be rephrased to communicate more clearly. There is no need for these written instructions to be read verbatim to a class, but when they are kept close at hand, an occasional glance at the writing will help keep the explanation on track. Quite frequently teachers report that the process of writing out instructions in advance results in such a thorough "internalization" of the sequence of points to be made that they have no need to look at these notes when giving the instructions orally to the class.

In addition to the issue of clarity, the variety of words chosen by teachers to express themselves merits consideration. In a given teaching day, there are many occasions for teachers to call students' attention to something they have done. For example, there are needs to praise learners for good work, to draw the focus of everybody in the class to a laboratory experiment being conducted at a side table, or to put a stop to some potentially disruptive behavior. Words and phrases selected to affect specific learner behaviors lose their emotive force with overuse. If certain words or phrases are used *every* time a given situation arises, they will lose whatever impact they once had and will have an influence on learner behavior only slightly more significant than sounds made by expanding radiator pipes when the steam goes on. Consider, for example, the attempts of the following teacher to get the class to settle down:

Time	Teacher's words
9.06	1. Let's quiet down.
	2. John, QUIT TALKING!
	3. Now I want it quiet.
	4. Quiet.
	5. Now quiet. Quiet, I have your tests!
	6. I said be quiet!
9.11	7. Please. Quiet. QUIET!
	8. Donna, be quiet!
	9. Quiet! If you want your tests, quiet!
	10. Albert, Quiet.
	11. Now, you just be quiet.
	12. Joanna. Quiet, please.
9.16	13. Quiet please.
	14. Jack, Paul, Bill—You boys be quiet.
	15. Goodness sakes! QUIET!
	16. You, too, Jennie, Quiet.
	17. Quiet. Everybody, please be quiet.
	18. That' enough, Paul!
	19. QUIET!

This unhappy pattern illustrates the futility of staying relentlessly with a given verbal strategy. The word "quiet" had no emotive force for these youngsters or, perhaps more accurately, the emotive force operated at such a low level of intensity that there were no noticeable changes in learners' behaviors.

In this situation, a change in the teacher's verbal tactics might have resulted in a desirable change in the behavior of the youngsters in this class. Teachers who are particularly strong in the instructional skill of interacting with learners tend to use a rich vocabulary when commenting on students' behaviors. Consider the relative impact on a learner of a teacher who responds regularly to quality work with a predictable "very good" or "fine" to that of a teacher who responds variously with "fantastic," "outstanding," "a professional effort," "fabulous," "*very* creative," "superlative," "I'm in awe," "first rate," or any one of a dozen other possibilities. As teachers grow in their ability to use naturally a wider variety of verbal responses, they make their verbal communication much more personal by selecting words that a learner perceives as "meant just for me" rather than as something that "they always tell everybody."

In working with large groups, there is a need to be particularly alert to the possibility that some student may get "lost in the crowd." Educational psychologists suggest that learners prefer even teachers who give them mostly negative comments to those who give them no recognition at all. Considering that many classes have more than 30 learners enrolled, teachers frequently find it difficult to recall the number of verbal interactions they have had with each learner. To provide specific information related to this issue, it sometimes is desirable to ask an observer to use one of a number of available classroom observation techniques that can provide insights related to teacher-learner interaction patterns.

In addition to developing plans to increase the frequency and contexts of verbal interactions, another important dimension needs to be considered in helping learners develop a sense of "belonging." This dimension has to do with the physical distance between teachers and students in their classrooms. Evidence exists of a direct relationship between the physical distance separating a teacher and learner and the learner's perception of the teacher's respect for him. Closer physical distances are thought to imply to the learner higher levels of teacher esteem.

Additionally, Sommer (1969) reports that increasing distances between a speaker and a listener tends to inhibit the desire of the speaker to talk. Increasing space seems to pose a threat to comfortable conversation. An implication of this finding for classroom teachers is that, with certain individuals at least, attempts to seek verbal responses from a learner seated at some distance from the front of the room might make that individual feel very uncomfortable. This especially is likely to be true when the learner is unsure of the teacher's feelings toward him. To promote comfortable verbal rapport with someone whose commitment to the instructional program seems marginal, it is a good idea for the teacher to move fairly close to the student involved before initiating a conversation.

Many teachers take time during the day to circulate among students in their classes to check on individual progress and to provide opportunities for more personal teacher-learner interactions. In such circumstances, teachers' intentions ordinarily are to spend some time in each part of the classroom to provide equal "access" for all learners. To check on whether these good intentions are being carried out, it is desirable to utilize periodically an observational instrument that can provide precise information regarding the actual location of the teacher in the classroom at various times during an instructional session. When such information is available, teachers can compare *intended* patterns of movement with their *actual* patterns of movement with a view to making adjustments, when desirable, during subsequent class sessions.

In general, interacting with learners in large groups requires teachers to develop procedures directed toward communicating their expectations clearly and to deal with learners' potential feelings of being "lost in the crowd." The dynamics of teacher-learner interactions in large groups are complex. Possibilities for fast-developing novel situations abound, and teachers rarely have the luxury of being able to back off and study a situation before a decision must be made. The immediacy with which responses must be made to developing situations almost assures an occasional mistake in judgment.

The instructional skill of interacting with learners requires a longer "percolation time" in beginning teachers than other elements of the instructional process. Beginners must realize that seasoned teachers have "seen much of it before." Patterns of learner behavior that may be disconcerting to the novice often prove to be neither disconcerting, novel, nor even very challenging to the experienced teacher. With attention to planning in the area of interacting with learners and recognition that there will be some eminently forgettable days, less experienced teachers can begin developing a professional competence in the area of interacting with learners. They should be heartened by the knowledge that the skill is complex, and that even teachers who have had years of experience continue to learn in this important instructional area.

Interacting with Learners in Small Groups
   A combination of high enthusiasm for individualized instruction and the development of learning resources unknown a generation ago have led to great interest in developing programs centered around small group learning. The small group mode facilitates instruction that is differentiated to meet the special needs of individuals.

   The strength of small group instruction—the possibility for different groups to pursue alternative learning activities—presents certain problems in planning for teacher-learner interaction. Because a number of learning groups may be working on different tasks during a given class hour, teachers cannot plan to interact with the entire class at the same time. Since learners are pursuing different ends, it is not feasible to provide a common set of instructions to the class as a whole.

   In making decisions relating to interacting with students organized into small groups, a first consideration is the size of the groups into which learners are clustered. In a study of the size of groups into which people organize themselves in casual, unstructured social situations, James (1952) found that 71 percent of observed conversational groups consisted of only two people, 21 percent consisted of three people, 6 percent consisted of four people, and only 2 percent consisted of five or more individuals. Initially, these figures seem surprising. But with the number of new communications channels that become available with the addition of each new member to a group, there is little to be wondered at the heavy preference for two-person conversational groups. For example, in a two-person conversation, there are but two channels of communication possible: (1) from person "A" to person "B," and (2) from person "B" to person "A." In a four-person group there are 12 possible communications channels. Clearly the difficulty of maintaining a coherent conversation is much more serious in the four-person than in the two-person group.

The finding that there is a preference for two-person conversational groups has implications for teacher planning for small group activities. When possible, it is wise to organize learners into groups of the smallest size feasible. But extremely small groups, however sound in terms of the research evidence, simply are not practical in many instructional settings. Typically, teachers find it difficult to reduce group sizes much below four, five, six, or even seven members. Because there is little natural cohesion to groups of these sizes (particularly those having more than five members), teachers must provide clear directions that enable each group member to understand the specific role he is to play. Without attention to these details, groups, once the activity has started, may "fragment" into more natural conversational clusters of two or three individuals each.

In addition to their utility as builders of cohesion, clear instructions for each small group help teachers to make the most effective use of their time once activities are under way. Properly understood directions and role responsibilities enable learners to go forward with only a minimal necessity to seek out the teacher for clarification. This permits the teacher to move freely from group to group to monitor activities and to make suggestions.

One consideration that might be included in planning the nature of instructions and directions for each group has to do with what might be called "group geography." This concerns the actual physical location of a given individual within a group *vis a vis* other group members. For example, a teacher may be interested in providing certain students with some leadership experience. A general rule of "group geography" is that leadership roles tend to be exercised by individuals seated at a "point" or at an "apex" within a group configuration. This principle is illustrated in Figure 6.1.

Figure 6.1

*Positions of Leadership in a Small Group
(leadership positions are circled)*

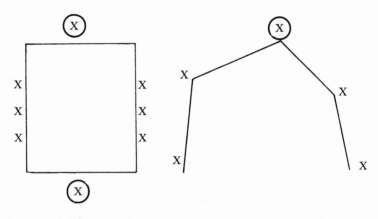

Note the individuals seated at the circled points in Figure 6.1. Individuals at these locations would be well positioned to exercise leadership roles within their respective groups. Teachers can use this principle to increase the probability that certain individuals will be asked by other group members to assume leadership responsibilities. Students identified as in need of leadership experiences can be asked by their teachers to sit in "apex" positions similar to those circled in Figure 6.1. In a high percentage of cases, this manipulation of seating arrangements will result in leadership roles for those selected.

On other occasions, the lesson may be of a nature that it is desirable that no single individual consistently assume a leadership role. In such a situation, it is a good practice to begin group work by asking learners to seat themselves in a circular fashion. In this arragement, all group members enjoy equivalent visual and spatial access to one another.

The nature of teachers' roles in working with small groups depends to a great degree on the specific purpose of the groups. To illustrate this point, subsequent sections will discuss four kinds of small groups, (1) task choice groups, (2) tutorial groups, (3) research groups, and (4) predetermined role groups. These group types, extensions of categories identified by Glatthorn (1968), all require different patterns of teacher-learner interaction.

Task Choice Groups

Task Choice Groups are used frequently in instructional programs built around classroom learning centers. Learning centers are areas, usually five to ten in number, where learners go to receive written or recorded instructions and to pursue learning activities. Each center has a different focus. A single Task Choice Group consists simply of those individuals who have elected to work at a given learning center at a certain point in time. Membership of each Task Choice Group is not static. Indeed, there may be different persons at a single learning station (and, hence, in a single Task Choice Group) even within a single class period.

Task Choice Groups are learner-developed groups organized on the basis of a common interest at a given learning station at a particular time. The teacher's role in working with Task Choice Groups, beyond the development of learning activities for each learning station, revolves around development of patterns of systematic visitation to each working group. Further, the teacher must check to see that general operating rules are understood before learners are released to work at the learning stations. Finally, the teacher's role involves a continual appraisal of which students are working at which learning stations in order to spot the occasional individual who has made a hopelessly inappropriate choice.

There are times when, in working with Task Choice Groups, the teacher must become a supportive learning activities counselor to help students make choices that are consistent with their real interests and abilities and not based simply on a desire to work with friends. Perhaps the greatest pitfall teachers face in working with Task Choice Groups is the tendency to spend too much time at three or four learning centers and to rush through conferences with learners at other centers to "beat the bell" at the end of the period. Care must be taken to allocate time fairly among all groups.

Tutorial Groups

Each Tutorial Group can be thought of as a miniaturized large group. In Tutorial Groups, teachers call a small group of youngsters together and go over content, much as they might do with a large group. Frequently, Tutorial Groups are used to provide help for students experiencing special problems. A Tutorial Group enjoys a great advantage over a large group instructional setting in that the teacher can soon ascertain the level of understanding of *each* person in the group. Further, because of the small size of Tutorial Groups, individuals frequently pay closer attention than in large groups because (1) they are physically closer to the teacher, and (2) any unusual behavior is certain to be noticed.

A semi-circle of chairs around the teacher seems to work well for instruction with a small Tutorial Group. The teacher assumes a role of directive leadership. But, because of the small size of the group, responses directed to the needs of individuals are possible. The Tutorial Group setting provides teachers with opportunities to make supportive statements to those students who hesitate to participate in discussions when larger numbers of learners are involved.

Research Group

A Research Group consists of a small number of learners who have been brought together for the purpose of developing their problem-solving skills. Typically, such groups are provided with opportunities to apply step-by-step decision-making procedures as members attempt to make inferences about novel situations. Many Research Groups follow a decision-making sequence similar to the following:
(1) identification of the problem;
(2) development of tentative hypotheses;
(3) collection of data to test tentative hypotheses;
(4) interpretation of collected data; and
(5) synthesis of gathered data and revision of tentative hypotheses.

Learners function more effectively in Research Groups when each individual is given a specific responsibility. A "group leader" should be appointed to coordinate work and help promote a sense of unity. A "group secretary" can maintain data and organize information that group members decide tends to either support or not support tentative hypotheses. A "group contrary-interpreta-tions-advocate" may be chosen to challenge the logic of group members who wish to use specific pieces of evidence to support or refute the validity of tentative hypotheses. This individual attempts to keep the group from coming to a premature consensus. Finally, a "group disseminator" can be asked to see that every member of the group obtains each piece of information uncovered by any one individual. These roles suggest that each member of a Research Group has a specific responsibility. Assignment of these roles assures a careful assessment of evidence and a careful drawing of conclusions.

Teachers' responsibilities with Research Groups begin with clear explanations to participants of the step-by-step decision-making sequence that is to be followed. There may be a need to list problem areas for groups to use as foci for their investigations. This is particularly necessary when learners are new to the Research Group mode of classroom organization. Once topics have been assigned, teachers must assure adequate resources are available to provide students with data they will need to make reasonable judgments and interpretations.

Once individual groups begin work, there is a need for the teacher to circulate from group to group to determine that all individuals understand what they are to be doing. It is particularly desirable to spend time with individuals selected as "group leaders" to help them build their confidence and skills as they work with others in their groups. When each Research Group has completed its task and is prepared to report final conclusions, the teacher can assume the role of a sympathetic "devil's advocate." This involves challenging conclusions, questioning interpretations of evidence, and probing to determine the extent to which a proper step-by-step sequence preceded decision-making. There is a need to be sensitive with verbal responses because these interpreta-tions represent students' tentative attempts at "new learning" or syntheses that have required them to move beyond the security of dealing with "facts." Learners are likely to feel ill at ease, initially, in their unfamiliar roles as producers of synthetic knowledge. Teachers must be judicious in their choice of comments and should seek to build the confidence of learners who are much more familiar with tasks demanding them to operate at less challenging cognitive levels.

Predetermined Role Groups

Predetermined Role Groups are designed to provide learners with opportunities to view a common situation from several perspectives. Learning experiences seek to help individuals understand that only rarely are there positions on complex problems that are "right" or "wrong" in any absolute sense. In Predetermined Role Groups, learners have opportunities to recognize that frequently determinations of "right" or "wrong" are conditioned by orientations unique to those who have made the judgment.

In the Predetermined Role Group, each person is charged with reacting to a particular situation as a given character might be expected to react. Once roles have been assigned, each group member prepares to react to the described situation in accordance with the role he has been asked to play. For example, a situation might be described as follows:

> Troops of the government of Lebanon have surrounded an encampment of the Palestine Liberation Organization in hill country about 50 miles from Beirut. Food supplies, water, and electricity have been cut off. Yesterday, a group of PLO soldiers attempted to break out. Lebanese forces killed 20 people. Today, there will be a debate on the issue in the United Nations on a motion by Syria to condemn the government of Lebanon for allowing the PLO troops to be killed. (*To the Class*: Each of you will be assigned a role in this United Nations debate.)

Among roles that might be developed and assigned to individual students are:

1. A representative from Syria
2. A representative from Israel
3. A representative from Lebanon
4. A representative from the Palestine Liberation Organization
5. A representative from the United States
6. A representative from the Soviet Union

Once roles have been identified and assigned, the teacher must make certain that sufficient learning resources are available to permit students to acquire an adequate grasp of the positions of the characters they are to portray. As the exercise unfolds, learners must be reminded that the positions they espouse may well not be positions they hold personally. They should be asked to make every effort to keep personal feelings from coloring the nature of the responses they make as they play out their assigned roles.

After the exercise, the teacher needs to lead a group debriefing session focusing on the degree to which each individual succeeded in accurately presenting the views of his assigned character. This discussion might well be extended to include a consideration of the reasons educated people often come to different conclusions after examining the same situation. In the debriefing phase, the teacher's role is a supportive one directed toward helping learners move beyond themselves to develop a greater sensitivity for how others see the world.

With the Predetermined Role Group, as with all small groups, clarity of instructions is essential. When groups understand what they are to do, teachers may move from group to group at will. Under these conditions, teachers can establish close personal contacts with students that can result in improved understandings of the interests and capacities of each individual learner. This freedom to move easily from one group to another and to engage in conversation with those in need of direction are hallmarks of a professionally planned and executed small group learning program.

High time "costs" may be exacted when teachers plan for several small groups rather than for a single large group of students, but "benefits," in terms of increased participation by learners who do not function well in instructional programs designed for 30 or 35 persons, suggest that these "costs" may well be justified. Few would argue that *all* instruction should occur in small group settings, but there is good logic supporting the inclusion of some small group learning experiences in the instructional program.

Whether small groups or large groups are being utilized, teachers have to face certain problems having to do with classroom management. The next section provides information designed to help teachers cope with this important dimension of classroom life.

Classroom Management*
Many behavioral problems in school result from learners'

*Material in this section is extracted from David G. Armstrong. "Equipping feelings that, for one reason or another, their human dignity has been diminished. Numerous school practices have the potential to turn into psychologically demeaning experiences. Many of these are associated with classroom tasks that learners find too frustrating and which leave them with a sense of personal inadequacy.

For example, students whose grades have never been high or who for years have observed teachers praising learners with better grades may see the school as a conspiracy directed toward institutionalizing their second rate status ("second rate," at least, in terms of how they believe themselves to be viewed by teachers). Those who find themselves in this unhappy situation may have skill deficiencies, perceptual problems, or other difficulties that make it all but impossible for them to "come up winners." From a long history of unrewarding school experiences, these individuals may be seen as behavioral problems by teachers unresponsive to their needs.

As a beginning step in dealing with such learners, operating guidelines must be established that are stated clearly and enforced consistently and impartially. (If Joannie B., the pert cheerleader with the B+ average shouts across the room in a disruptive manner, the teacher must respond to her behavior exactly as he would had the offending learner been Joey C., the unwashed, uninvolved D-scholar who lives only for his Saturday nights at the drag races.) Three general types of operating guidelines are useful in attempting to organize in advance some sound responses to problems that may arise during a day's teaching. These categories are: (1) General Ground Rules; (2) Making Assignments; and (3) Planning and Monitoring Classroom Activities.

General Ground Rules

General Ground Rules may be developed jointly by teacher and learners or by the teacher alone. Generally, the first procedure is preferred in that it tends to result in more learner commitment to

Student Teachers to Deal with Classroom Control Problems." *The High School Journal* (October 1976), *60*, 1-9. Copyright © 1976 The University of North Carolina Press.

the adopted procedures. However, there are situations in which cooperative planning is not feasible. Whether prepared jointly or by the teacher alone, these ground rules must be made specific and public. They should be broad enough in scope to deal with all major issues relating to general classroom operating procedures. Once developed, the teacher needs to undertake specific actions to assure that the rules are distributed and understood. A procedure many have found effective involves a distribution of a printed list of rules to learners in the class. Such a list might focus on issues suggested by the following questions:

1. What are learners to do when they come into the classroom?
2. What teacher behavior signals the beginning of the instructional phase of the class? (Teacher places attendance slips on the door clip and turns around. Teacher closes grade book. Teacher looks up and stares out at class. Teacher walks to the front of the desk, etc.)
3. What are the rules for talking during discussions?
4. What should a learner do if he has to leave the room?
5. At what time during the period should a learner with a personal problem make his need known to the teacher?

Certainly the ground rules may address many questions other than those included in the sample list. The number, nature, and range of the ground rules is not nearly so important as the decision to specify, reduce to writing, and distribute whatever rules are adopted. A class period spent discussing ground rules with learners will prove to be a useful follow-up to the distribution of the printed list.

Time spent preparing and discussing ground rules can pay off handsomely in terms of smooth classroom operation. The procedure adds an enormous element of psychological security for learners. Expectations are clear. The learners need not approach the class with anxieties arising from unclear understandings about what behaviors are and are not acceptable. When a problem arises involving a clear breach of a listed ground rule, the teacher is free to act without fear that he is responding in an arbitrary fashion or in support of a rule that learners may not understand.

Formulation of ground rules is particularly important for student teachers. Learners with whom they are working will have been accustomed to attending classes taught by the regular teacher. The student teacher needs to make his ground rules clear so learners will understand how they vary from and how they are similar to procedures followed by their own teacher. A day spent dealing with this issue will ensure a vastly diminished number of those annoying "But Mr. Smith never said we had to do . . . " comments.

Making Assignments

Many classroom problems stem from learner misunderstandings about assignments. Specific strategies for assuring that each learner knows (1) what he is to do, and (2) what will constitute successful completion of his task are prerequisite to any attempt to assess learner achievement. Without such assurances, measures of achievement may yield scores that reflect the degree of confusion about the nature of the assignment rather than the degree of mastery of the material.

In dealing with this issue, clarity must be assured (1) before an assignment is made, and (2) while an assignment is being made. A check of diagnostic information available on learners in the class is essential as a preparation to making assignments. Are there, for example, learners with hearing or sight problems? If so, can seating arrangements be modified so that physical deficits will not impair understanding of the assignment?

Additional information needs to be gathered concerning whether learners in the class have the prerequisite knowledges and skills necessary for the completion of the proposed task. Learners who do not have an adequate background are placed in a "fail-certain" category when given an inappropriate assignment. Requiring learners to attempt tasks clearly beyond their capabilities undermines self-confidence. Further, lack of success can generate control problems directed at the teacher who arranged for what learners may see as a "no-win" situation.

When diagnostic data reveal a wide divergence within a class in terms of prerequisite skills and knowledges, the logical solution is to develop alternatives within the general assignment to ensure that all learners have the potential for success when they begin work on their assigned tasks.

Several matters require attention *while* the assignment is being given to the class. If part of the teacher's explanation of what is to be done requires him to write on the chalkboard, potential visual barriers need to be checked. To get a feel for the nature of this problem, many teachers take time to sit at a learner's desk at the rear of the room for a moment or two for the purpose of trying to read something they have written on the chalkboard. A frequent comment is: "All those heads really get in the way." To avoid this difficulty, nothing should be written on the *lower one-third* of the boards. Writing below this level tends to result in straining learner necks, comments of frustration, standing, and other behaviors that can lead to classroom control problems.

After an assignment has been made, a "communication check" is desirable to ensure that learners understand what they are to do. Many student teachers make the mistake of asking a very general question such as "Does everybody understand?" As a "communication check," this question is a failure. When it is asked, typically all heads nod an affirmative "yes, I understand." When assignments come in, the student teacher is perplexed when large numbers of learners obviously failed to follow instructions. The problem results from the unreliable responses inevitable in a school classroom when the "does everybody understand?" question (or others like it) is asked.

Students are endowed with a healthy measure of personal pride. Certainly they have no inclination whatever to expose themselves as dense and unperceptive . . . the very impression classmates might get were they to answer "no" to a "does everybody understand?" question. Not wishing to appear the dunce, those who have no idea about what they are to do are quite likely to nod an affirmative "yes" to the question along with those who really know exactly what is to be done.

To obtain more accurate information about how well instructions have been understood, teacher questions ought to be directed to specific learners. Questions can be phrased in such a way that they prompt more than a "yes" or "no" answer. For example: "John, I want to be sure I covered all the points about the assignment. As a check to help me out, could you tell me what it is you're to do for tomorrow?"

A random pattern of calling on learners can be adopted so that, over the period of several weeks, each learner might have an opportunity to relate the specifics of the assignment to the class. This procedure can yield information about how well learners understand what they are to do. Further, learners, knowing they may be called upon to explain assignments, will tend to pay more attention when the teacher explains what is to be done.

Planning and Monitoring Classroom Activities

Careful planning and monitoring of classroom activities tend to reduce the incidence of learner behaviors that, unattended, might escalate into seriously disruptive problems. Most class sessions have an "activity profile" characterized by high percentages of task-oriented learner activities in the middle of the period and dramatically-reduced percentages of task-oriented learner activities at the beginning and at the end of the period. An implication of this profile is that teachers need to plan specific activities for use at the beginning and at the end of the class period, the times when most potential control problems are likely to arise.

To deal with boisterous incoming learners, an initial activity that dampens the noise level and quickly involves learners in a purposeful task is in order. One possibility may be an assignment written on the chalkboard, to be completed and turned in for evaluation ten minutes after the official beginning time of the period. A teacher adopting such a procedure might stand near the door, direct incoming learners' attention to the board, and provide the inevitable equipment-shy learner with what he needs to get started.

Generally, end of the period strategies focusing on silent seat work are ineffective. By this time, frustrations resulting from physical inactivity have begun to mount. As a remedy, an activity calling for lively verbal interaction during the final five to ten minutes may rekindle interest in the day's lesson. With middle school and junior high school youngsters, a quick game at this time is often a huge success: ("You people on the right are the Aardvarks. You on the left are the Hairy Anteaters. I'll award a point to the team whose member first gives me the right factors to these flash card equations. No shouting out. Hands only. Here's the first one. Joe. X-1 and X+4 you say? That's right. There's a quick point for the Hairy Anteaters . . . ")

In planning for classroom activities, control problems will be diminished if the teacher takes into consideration that (1) learners like to talk, and (2) learners get tired of sitting. (College students who complain vociferously when they have more than three classes during a single day should have no trouble empathizing with high school students who may sit five or six hours in classrooms every day of the week.) If some learning activities are built around small group work in which learners are encouraged to exchange ideas, they are more likely to develop positive feelings toward the class than if reading or listening to lectures are the modes through which they are expected to get all of their information. Similarly, activities permitting learners to get out of their seats, when carefully planned, meet the need for physical activity and help reduce the potential for control problems.

The suggestion that *some* activities permit learners to talk and to move about does not reduce the necessity for learning experiences that do require learners to work relatively quietly. Beginning teachers, after making an assignment requiring silent seat work, often are lulled into a perilous inattention when, as a first reaction, an entire class seems to get right to work. Initial purposeful activity, punctuated only by an occasional learner comment, in a matter of minutes can explode into a cacophony of loud chatter.

Teachers need to attend to subtle changes in noise levels. It is time to act when there is a slight change from an initial pattern. In many cases, teachers find that simply standing up and staring out across the room stems the tide when the occasional learner remark begins to escalate to two or three hushed mini-conversations. A reminder of the ground rules, if a pertinent rule exists, is another option that may prove effective. The particular response is not so crucial as is the decision to act quickly and to act in response to a minor change. Once "the dam has burst" and conversations are going on everywhere at the same time, it is very difficult to bring a group of youngsters back to a quiet, "at task" behavior pattern.

By attending to practices associated with making ground rules, communicating assignments, and monitoring classroom activities, teachers attempt to prevent classroom control problems. Advance planning in each of these areas enhances day-to-day "survival" capabilities. However, suggestions regarding classroom management are not designed to change undesirable learner behavior patterns of long standing. To achieve this end, it is necessary to apply tested behavioral change procedures. A consideration of techniques that teachers can use to cope with these more serious problems will be included in the next section.

Changing "Problem Behavior" of Learners

In the previous section, several techniques designed to prevent the occurrence of disruptive learner behaviors were presented. Implementation of these procedures tends to reduce the rate of incidence of disruptive behaviors, but these techniques, alone, will not eliminate them entirely from classrooms. To remediate behavior problems of a more persistent nature, it will be necessary to move beyond "preventive maintenance" strategies to more rigorous and sophisticated behavioral change techniques.

In this section, two general sets of procedures for dealing systematically with dysfunctional learner behaviors will be introduced. The first of these, a *behavior modification* approach, derives from the work of B.F. Skinner (1959). Behavior modification assumes that behavior results neither from internal psychological constructs (the *id,* the *ego,* the *superego,* and other elements from the lexicon of the Freudian psychologists) nor from an interaction between internal factors and the external environment (a positon of Gestalt/field theory psychology). Indeed, behavior modification stems from a view of human behavior that denies even the existence of internal factors. According to Skinner and his followers, *all* behavior results from reinforcement by elements in the external environment. According to this logic, then, one has only to rearrange reinforcers to modify or change a given behavior.

Another approach, called *reality therapy,* has been formulated by William Glasser (1965). Glasser, unlike the proponents of behavior modification, suggests that external environmental factors, alone, are not sufficient to explain human behavior. Reality therapy proceeds on the assumption that behavior results from conscious thought about the possible consequences of a given action. Behavior, then, does take environmental factors into account; its direction is shaped not by external environmental factors alone—instead, by thought about these external environmental factors.

Behavior Modification

Behavior modification assumes that human behaviors result as a consequence of their being reinforced by certain features of the external environment. By definition, *all* behaviors are reinforced, regardless of whether they are considered "good," "indifferent," or "bad" behaviors. Many beginning students of behavior modification, once they have accepted the idea that all behaviors are reinforced, make the mistake of assuming that all teachers have to do is reinforce "good" behaviors and stop reinforcing "bad" behaviors to eliminate problems in the classroom. At a very superficial level this conclusion is logical. But the rub comes in the disheartening reality that an environmental event that is reinforcing for one person may not be reinforcing for another.

By definition, a reinforcer is an environmental event that increases the probability of recurrence of the behavior it follows. Because people differ, it is logical that an environmental event that acts as a reinforcer for one person may not act as a reinforcer for another. Take, for example, two high school sophomores, one of them a follower of the country western music scene, the other an *afficianado* of symphonic works. Five minutes of listening to recordings of Beethoven's Fifth Symphony following successful solution of five algebra problems would be unlikely to function as a reinforcer for the country music fan. Similarly, five minutes of listening to "Grand Old Opry" broadcasts would be a doubtful reinforcer for the classical music lover.

The definition of a reinforcer is, then, situational. If an environmental event does act to increase the probability of recurrence of the behavior it follows, it is a reinforcer. If it does not, then that very same environmental event is not a reinforcer. Certainly, for large numbers of people, many of the same environmental events will prove to be reinforcers. But, there is no environmental event that is a reinforcer for *all* people. This reality implies that, as part of the behavior modification strategy, there is a need to determine exactly which environmental events serve as reinforcers for the individuals targeted for behavior change. Before presenting some procedures for obtaining this information, it will be useful to examine some general procedures for (1) identifying behaviors in need of change, and (2) identifying possible teacher options.

Behavior modification demands a precise focus on the behavior to be changed. Because of personality, cultural and economic differences, and other factors, a teacher occasionally gets a student with whom he simply does not get along. When pressed for an explanation, teachers may avoid precise explanations of the difficulty with statements such as: "He gets in my hair all the time!" "She has such a negative attitude!" "She just doesn't like me!"

There is a need to move beyond such global characterizations to narrower, more observable descriptions of the objectionable behavior. A useful procedure for accomplishing this end involves focusing only on behaviors that can be clearly identified as being disruptive of the instructional process. Such behaviors are usually observable, and they tend to go well beyond actions that may be annoying, but that fall short of being truly disruptive. Once these behaviors have been identified, several options are available.

One possibility is a strategy designed to eliminate the offensive behavior through *punishment.* Punishment consists of either (1) the imposition of an environmental event the learner views as negative, or (2) the removal of an environmental event the learner views as positive. For example, with a child who dislikes washing desks and who enjoys watching self-contained film loops, punishments might take the form of (1) requiring him to wash desks, or (2) denying him the privilege of watching film loops.

There are several difficulties with punishment as a response to an undesirable behavior. While punishment may suppress behaviors that are believed to be interfering with the instructional program, there is a possibility that the learner may also develop negative responses toward other aspects of the school program. Further, while punishment suppresses a given behavior, there is not ordinarily a parallel reinforcement of a desirable behavior the learner can substitute for the one that got him in difficulty. New behavior, then, is likely to be undirected by the teacher and may take a form that is as disruptive as the behavior suppressed.

Finally, unless great care is taken in their selection, punishments which teachers believe to be unpleasant experiences for the learner may actually be reinforcers and encourage additional outbreaks of the undesirable behavior. For instance, punishment involving sending a youngster out into the hall might prove to be a rewarding experience for him because of the opportunity to chat pleasantly with custodians and others. Such a learner might increase the rate of his disruptive behavior to win more of this delightful "punishment."

Should punishment be rejected as an option, teachers might consider *extinction.* Recall that reinforcers increase the rate of recurrence of preceding behaviors. Logically, then, the absence of reinforcers following behaviors results in a decrease in the rate of recurrence of preceding behaviors. This gradual decrement in rate, resulting ultimately in disappearance of a behavior, is referred to as the process of extinction. In practice, this means that many undesirable behaviors can be eliminated by teachers who (1) determine which environmental events are reinforcing undesirable behaviors, and (2) take action to eliminate these environmental events. For example, when a teacher suspects that disruptive behavior may be reinforced by an increase in personal attention given to the offender, he often can extinguish the undesirable behavior by refusing any personal contact with the youngster when his behavior is undesirable.

On many occasions, it turns out that undesirable behavior is being reinforced not by the teacher but by other members of the class. When this occurs, teachers need to take steps to prevent other students from reinforcing the disruptive behavior (remember the "class clown" from junior high school days?). Usually such problems can be resolved by reinforcing behaviors of youngsters that do *not*, in turn, reinforce undesirable behavior patterns of one or two individuals.

Manipulation of reinforcers constitutes another option on the list of possible responses to disruptive behaviors. As noted previously, reinforcers tend to increase the likelihood of recurrence of a preceding behavior. Frequently, reinforcers are subdivided into *positive reinforcers* and *negative reinforcers.* A positive reinforcer is an environmental event whose occurrence results in an increase in frequency of the behavior it follows. For youngsters who like baseball, the opportunity to watch the World Series after solving correctly 15 of 20 math problems would tend to be a positive reinforcer promoting an increase in proficiency in math problem-solving behavior.

A negative reinforcer is an environmental event that, when

removed, prompts an increase in frequency of the behavior preceding that removal. The threat of "no recess" removed when quiet "at task" behavior resulted would be an example of a negative reinforcement being used to increase the frequency of quiet, task-oriented behavior. (If the threat of "no recess" were carried out, and youngsters were actually kept in, that would be an example of *punishment.*)

Ordinarily, positive reinforcement is preferred over negative reinforcement. A difficulty with negative reinforcement is that, to be effective, learners must believe that what is being threatened (for example, "no recess") may actually be carried out. If, in every case, only a threat is made, the removal of the threat loses its value as a reinforcer because learners from the beginning see the threat only as idle verbiage. Consequently, to be effective, threats must occasionally be carried out if their removal is expected to function as negative reinforcement. A carried-out threat consitutes punishment, and punishment has potentially undesirable side effects. For this reason, given a choice between selecting a positive reinforcer or a negative reinforcer, it makes more sense to choose the positive reinforcer.

There are three general categories or types of environmental events that may function as reinforcers: (1) *physical objects*; (2) *visible, audible, or visible and audible social praise*; and (3) *preferred behaviors from the individual's own repertoire.* Physical objects used as reinforcers may be "consumable" or "symbolic." Examples of consumable objects used as reinforcers would include such practices as giving a peanut to each youngster who remembers to raise his hand before speaking, or providing popcorn to individuals getting at least 15 of 20 spelling words correct. Symbolic physical objects functioning as reinforcers include such items as tickets given to youngsters for every 15 minutes of quiet behavior, to be exchanged for certain privileges. In general, physical objects tend to be most frequently used to reinforce behavior of younger learners. Certainly, older youngsters are reinforced by physical objects, but practically speaking, it is much easier for school budgets to find monies for the lollipops, popcorn, and tickets that reinforce many second graders than to find funds for stereo tapes, mag wheels, and other expensive items that would reinforce eleventh graders.

Social praise tends to reinforce behaviors of youngsters of all ages. A problem for teachers is that as youngsters progress through school, the sources of social praise that function as reinforcers tend to broaden to include many individuals other than teachers. Indeed, some secondary school youngsters may not be reinforced by teacher praise at all. On the other hand, a large majority of children in the lower elementary grades are highly reinforced by teachers' praise.

A third reinforcer was initially described by Premack (1965). According to the "Premack Principle," behaviors with a high frequency can be used to reinforce behaviors with a low frequency. Thus, if it is noted that a youngster enjoys playing "Monopoly" (a high frequency behavior), opportunities to play the game can be used to reinforce accurate completion of mapping assignments (a low frequency behavior). Use of high frequency behaviors to reinforce and, thus, increase the rate of incidence of low frequency behaviors, works well with youngsters of all ages.

Before attempting to use a given environmental event to initiate a change in the behavior of a given learner, teachers must determine that the selected environmental event is, indeed, a reinforcer for the learner whose behaviors are to be modified. Once the offending individual has been identified, there is a need to engage in a diagnostic process directed toward pointing out the nature of environmental events likely to serve as reinforcers. Sources of this information include individual conferences, anecdotal records, and personal interest inventory data. Sometimes simply asking the youngster what he would choose to do if he had ten minutes of class time to pursue an activity of high personal interest brings forth a number of possibilities for suitable reinforcers.

Once individuals and reinforcing environmental events have been matched, there is a need to determine the initial rate of incidence of the identified problem behaviors. It is useful, too, to note the types of teacher responses that are being made when these behaviors occur. If, for example, three problem students, Paul, Sarah, and Joanne, have a history of responding well to the teacher's social praise, it might be desirable to note the relative frequency of positive and negative teacher comments.

In determining frequencies of both learner and teacher behav-

Figure 6.2

Learner and Teacher Behaviors: Baseline Information

Date: October 2nd

Elapsed Time: 50 minutes

	Out of Seat	Teacher Positive Comments	Teacher Negative Comments
Paul	12	1	25
Sarah	7	2	15
Joanne	15	0	18

iors, it is convenient to determine rates of behavior occurrence within a given period of time, perhaps during a 50-minute class session. This original "baseline" information might be gathered and organized into a format something like that shown in Figure 6.2.

These baseline data provide entry rate information about both learner and teacher behavior. Once a systematic behavior modification strategy begins, there is an expectation that the rate of incidence of "out of seat" behavior will decrease. Since it has been determined that social praise acts as a reinforcer for each of these youngsters, and since baseline data reveal that the teacher has used very few praise statements with these individuals, it is logical to conclude that use of teacher praise to reinforce "in seat" behavior might be appropriate. Since new learning, in this instance, "in seat" behavior, occurs most efficiently when reinforcement occurs every time a desired behavior is emitted, there is a need to establish an identifiable unit of correct behavior and to reinforce that behavior each time it occurs. For example, three minutes of in-seat behavior might be designated as one unit of appropriate behavior. In such a case, each youngster would be praised by the teacher after every three minutes of "in seat" behavior.

A second part of this change strategy might involve a reduction in the incidence of negative statements made by the teacher to these youngsters. Note in Figure 6.2 that, initially, there is a high frequency of negative statements by the teacher to these individuals. Though probably intended to be corrective in nature, these negative statements may actually be reinforcing "out of seat" behavior by drawing the teacher's attention to these youngsters mainly when they are behaving in this inappropriate way. The hope is that by encouraging the teacher to reinforce "in seat"

Figure 6.3

Learner and Teacher Behaviors:
Intervention Day One

Date: October 3rd

Elapsed time: 50 minutes

	Out of Seat	Teacher Positive Comments	Teacher Negative Comments
Paul	5	13	5
Sarah	1	15	2
Joanne	2	16	1

behavior with positive comments while extinguishing negative comments following "out of seat" behavior, there will be an increasing incidence of "in seat" behavior (paralleled, of course, by a decrease in "out of seat" behavior). Look at the chart in Figure 6.3, taken on the first day such a change strategy was put into operation.

Note that there has been a tremendous decrease in the incidence of "out of seat" behavior as compared with the baseline frequencey (see Figure 6.2). This decrease has been accompanied by a decrease in the number of negative teacher comments and an increase in the number of positive teacher comments. Encouraged by these results, the teacher of these youngsters resolved on the subsequent day to work even harder at reducing negative comments and increasing the number of praise statements. The results of that effort are reflected in the chart in Figure 6.4.

Figure 6.4

Learner and Teacher Behaviors:
Intervention Day Two

Date: October 4th

Elapsed time: 50 minutes

	Out of Seat	Teacher Positive Comments	Teacher Negative Comments
Paul	2	16	2
Sarah	0	16	1
Joanne	0	16	1

By the end of this second day of intervention, there was a tremendous decrease in "out of seat" behavior as compared with data on the baseline chart (see Figure 6.2). Indeed, two of these youngsters, Sarah and Joanne, were not out of their seats all period long. Once such evidence of a desired behavioral change is in hand, the stability of this new behavior pattern can be enhanced by changing from a continuous to an interval schedule of reinforcement. This means that, whereas initially each unit of appropriate behavior was reinforced, now it is desirable to provide reinforcement after several units of appropriate behavior have been observed. A progressively decreasing frequency of reinforcement schedule might be instituted. For example, an initial reinforcement (praise statement) could be given after a three-minute period of "in seat" behavior, a second after a seven-minute interval, a third after a twelve-minute interval, and so on, successively requiring longer periods of appropriate behavior before providing reinforcements. This practice gradually weans learners from a dependence on teacher praise and toward a state where they are reinforced by the new behavior itself.

In summary, behavior modification demands a very precise identification of the behavior to be changed. Once identified, baseline data are gathered with respect to the frequency of occurrence of that behavior. An increase in frequency of preferred behaviors is sought by presentation of reinforcers after preferred behaviors occur. Frequency of occurrence data are kept both for the behavior to be changed and for the reinforcers designed to increase the frequency of alternative desirable behaviors. Evidence of success is taken to be a reduction in the frequency of undesirable behaviors as compared to the frequency of desirable behaviors. In terms of its sequence, a behavior modification strategy follows these steps:

1. Precise identification of behavior to be changed.
2. Precise identification of environmental events that serve as reinforcers for targeted individuals.
3. Gathering baseline data with respect to initial rate of occurrence of undesirable behaviors.
4. Implementing appropriate intervention strategy.
5. Gathering data to determine whether a reduction in frequency of occurrence of undesirable behaviors has been achieved.

Reality Therapy

Reality Therapy, developed by William Glasser (1965), is designed to help learners to identify and remediate their own behavioral problems. According to proponents of reality therapy, teachers often err in assuming that behaviors they view as inappropriate are also viewed as inappropriate by learners. Reality therapists argue that a learner, himself, must identify a behavior as inappropriate and cite probable consequences of that continued behavior before a change to a more appropriate pattern can be expected.

Reality therapy focuses on the present and the future rather than the past. There *is* a recognition that a student's past history may have helped to shape present patterns of behavior. For example, there may have been squabbling between parents at home, inadequate prior preparation in selected school subjects, peer adulation after bloodying a nose of an opponent in a playground brawl, and a host of other antecedents to present behavioral patterns of a given individual. But, reality therapists argue, most people one must work with in life will have no knowledge of these matters. Consequently, reactions people have to behaviors of youngsters (and adults, too) tend to be determined by the nature of the behaviors themselves rather than by any understandings of the historical underpinnings of those behaviors. In response to this "reality," reality therapy focuses only on present and future learner behaviors.

In approaching a student whose present behavior is unacceptable, teachers are advised to express warm, but purposeful, concern. That concern ought not to be judgmental (it is not the teacher, after all, who needs to see the inappropriate nature of the behavior, but rather the learner). The teacher's initial purpose should be to encourage the learner to identify the specific nature of the behavior that is of concern.

Teacher: Paula, what do you have in the bottom of your lunch box?
Paula: Just some pencils.
Teacher: How many pencils are there?
Paula: Well, about forty or fifty I guess.
Teacher: How did you happen to get so many?
Paula: Well, actually, I just kind of picked them up.
Teacher: Where did you "just kind of pick them up?"
Paula: Er . . . ah . . . well, from the supply room. (Learner begins to identify behavior.)

Teacher:	Did anybody tell you you could take the pencils?
Paula:	No, not really.
Teacher:	What do we call something like that?
Paula:	Ah. I'd guess it would be stealing or robbery or something like that. (Learner identified behavior.)

After a youngster has identified a behavior and labeled it *himself* as an example of an unacceptable action), the next step is to ask him to make a value judgment about that behavior.

Teacher:	Do you think you should be stealing or robbing?
Paula:	Well, we don't have much money to buy school supplies and things.
Teacher:	Would you say you are the only one in that situation?
Paula:	No.
Teacher:	Then let me ask again what you personally think about stealing and robbing.
Paula:	Well. I really don't feel good about it. I don't think it's right. (Learner make value judgment about behavior.)

After a youngster has made a value judgment about an identified behavior, he needs to be encouraged to identify the personal consequences of continuing that behavior. Once these consequences have been pinpointed, the learner needs to make value judgments about them.

Teacher:	What sorts of things happen to people who steal or rob?
Paula:	Well, they can get into trouble.
Teacher:	What kind of trouble can they get into?
Paula:	Well . . . some people lose their jobs . . . maybe go to jail.
Teacher:	What else?
Paula:	Well, I suppose a kid could get kicked out of school. That's what might happen to someone like me, I suppose. (Learner identified consequences of behavior.)
Teacher:	What can happen to someone who loses his job, or goes to prison, or gets kicked out of school?
Paula:	Well, I suppose people aren't going to trust them very much anymore.
Teacher:	How would you feel if you thought people didn't trust you?
Paula:	I guess I wouldn't like that very much at all. (Learner makes value judgment about consequences of behavior.)

After a learner has reached the point of making a personal value judgment indicating unhappiness with possible consequences of his behavior, he needs to be helped to formulate a plan of action. If the plan of action the learner suggests is unacceptable, he must be told that his plan will not do and that he should select another.

The teacher may have to suggest alternatives.

Teacher: Well, Paula, what do you think you might do about this pencil business?

Paula: Maybe we could just not do anything, and they'd never be missed from the supply room.

Teacher: Would that be right?

Paula: No. Not really.

Teacher: Then, what else might you do?

Paula: Well, I'm sort of scared to, but maybe I could take them back to the supply room. (Learner formulates a plan.)

Teacher: How might I help?

Paula: Could you come with me . . . that supply room lady will really let me have it. (Learner refines plan.)

Teacher: Fine. Shall we go now?

Paula: OK

In summary, the steps followed in a reality therapy program are:

1. Learner identifies his behavior.
2. Learner makes a value judgment about his behavior.
3. Learner identifies consequences of his behavior and makes a value judgment about those consequences.
4. Learner identifies a specific plan for action.

Reality therapy focuses on learner specification of behavior and identification of consequences of behavior. It is designed to prevent learners from dwelling on causes of behavior. By following the sequence listed above, teachers can avoid the temptation of asking a person an inappropriate question of the sort that enables him to develop a rationale for a behavior that clearly is going to have negative consequences. Note the following incorrect and correct applications of a reality therapy approach.

Teacher: It's 20 minutes after eight Paula. Why are you late? (Incorrect. This question invites the learner to build a rationale for an inappropriate behavior.)

Paula: I stayed up until two this morning because I wanted to do a really good job on the paper I'm writing for you.

Teacher: It's 20 minutes after eight, Paula. What does that mean? (Correct. The focus is on the *behavior*. No teacher judgment is made.)

Paula: I'm late to class.

Teacher: What might happen if you come to class late? (Correct. Again, there is no teacher judgment. The effort is to encourage the learner to look at and evaluate the con-

sequences of the behavior as she sees them.)
Paula: I might miss part of the lesson . . . etc.

Reality therapy does not presume that antecedent causes of behavior are unimportant. Clearly, many students do have serious problems that may contribute to undesirable behavior patterns they exhibit at school. The world, however, is largely ignorant of the individual histories of its people. What tends to count, what tends to be rewarded or punished, is *present* behavior. Since humans are social creatures living in a group culture that responds in relatively predictable ways, reality therapists contend that the humane approach to behavior problems involves providing individuals with opportunities to think about, make value judgments about, and alter behaviors in the light of how those behaviors are likely to be viewed by others. Valid and compelling as the causes for inappropriate behavior may be, the fundamental truth remains that behavior that *is* inappropriate will be so regarded in the "real" world. Reality therapy attempts to help people perceive this truth and to change their behaviors to acceptable patterns, even when those patterns have not been well nurtured by antecedent conditions.

The description of reality therapy provided here is very brief. Those interested in the approach are directed to William Glasser's book, *Reality Therapy* (New York: Harper and Row, 1965).

Summary

This chapter has provided guidelines for working with large and small groups of learners. Specific characteristics of several types of small groups were described. A section on classroom management introduced a number of "preventive maintenance" techniques focusing on planning for instruction, monitoring classroom activities, and making assignments. Procedures for dealing with more persistent behavioral problems through the use of behavior modification techniques and reality therapy were discussed.

To conclude this chapter, the authors would caution that these techniques ought to be viewed as guidelines, not mechanistic approaches to be followed in lockstep fashion with every group. Each class represents a unique constellation of personal histories. To suggest that a single set of classroom organization and management procedures will meet universal success is to profess ignorance of this truth. However, with judicious selection of procedures from among those suggested here, and others, workable combinations can be developed that can contribute significantly to improved patterns of interacting with learners.

References

ARMSTRONG, David G. "Equipping Student Teachers to Deal with Classroom Control Problems." *The High School Journal* (October 1976), 1-9.
GLASSER, William. *Reality Therapy: A New Approach to Psychiatry.* New York: Harper and Row Publishers, 1965.
GLATTHORN, Allan A. *Learning in Small Groups.* Dayton, Ohio: I/D/E/A - Kettering Foundation, 1968.
JAMES, John. "A Preliminary Study of the Size Determinant in Small Group Interaction." *American Sociological Review*, 1952, 474-477.
PREMACK, David. "Reinforcement Theory." In *Nebraska Symposium on Motivation*, D. Levine (Ed.). Lincoln, Nebraska: University of Nebraska Press, 1965.
SKINNER, Benjamin F. *Cumulative Record.* New York: Appleton-Century-Crofts, 1959.
SOMMER, Robert. Personal Space: *The Behavioral Basis of Design.* Englewood Cliffs, N.J.: Prentice-Hall, Inc., 1969.

Additional Professional Study

Books
AMOS, William E. *Managing Student Behavior.* St. Louis: W.H. Green, Co., 1967.
CROSBIE, Paul V., Ed. *Interaction in Small Groups.* New York: Macmillan Publishing Co., Inc., 1975.
DAVIE, Jean E. *Coping with Disruptive Behavior.* Washington, D.C.: National Education Association, 1974.
DRIEKURS, Rudolf, Bernice B. GRUNWALD and Floyd C. PEPPER. *Maintaining Sanity in the Classroom: Illustrated Teaching Techniques.* New York: Harper and Row, Publishers, 1971.
DYER, William G. *The Sensitive Manipulator.* Provo, Utah: Brigham Young University Press, 1972.
GLASSER, William. *Reality Therapy: A New Approach to Psychiatry.* New York: Harper and Row, Publishers, 1965.
GLATTHRON, Allan A. *Learning in Small Groups.* Dayton, Ohio: I/D/E/A— Kettering Foundation 1968.
GLAVIN, John P. *Behavioral Strategies for Classroom Management.* Columbus, Ohio: Charles E. Merrill Publishing Co., 1974.

GNAGNEY, William J. *Maintaining Discipline in Classroom Instruction.* New York: Macmillan Publishing Co., Inc., 1975.

GOOD, Thomas L. and Jere E. BROPHY. *Looking in Classrooms.* New York: Harper and Row Publishers, 1973.

GORDON, Thomas. *T.E.T.: Teacher Effectiveness Training.* New York: P.N. Wyden, 1974.

HALL, Edward T. *The Hidden Dimension.* Garden City, New York: Doubleday and Company, Inc., 1966.

HALL, Edward T. *The Silent Language.* Garden City, New York: Doubleday and Company, Inc., 1959.

LA MANCUSA, Katherine C. *We Do Not Throw Rocks at the Teacher.* Scranton, Penn.: International Textbook Company, 1966.

MACHT, Joel. *Teaching Our Children.* New York: John Wiley and Sons, Inc., 1975.

MC LEISH, John *et al. The Psychology of the Learning Group.* London: Hutchinson, 1973.

MEACHAM, Merle L. and Allen WIESEN. *Changing Classroom Behavior: A Manual for Precision Teaching.* Scranton, Penn.: International Textbook Company, 1969.

PHILLIPS, Gerald M. *Communication and the Small Group.* Indianapolis, Ind.: Bobbs-Merrill Publishing Co., 1973.

PIPER, Terrence. *Classroom Management and Behavioral Objectives: Application of Behavior Modification.* Belmont, Calif: Fearon Publishing Co., 1974.

POPHAM, W. James and Eva BAKER. *Classroom Instructional Tactics.* Englewood Cliffs, N.J.: Prentice-Hall, Inc., 1973.

PREMACK, David. "Reinforcement Theory." In *Nebraska Symposium on Motivation,* D. Levine (Ed.). Lincoln, Nebraska: University of Nebraska Press, 1965.

SARASON, Irwin G., Edward M. GLASER and George A. FARGO. *Teacher's Guide to Behavior Modification.* New York: Behavioral Publications, 1972.

SHARAN, Shlomo and Yael SHARAN. *Small Group Teaching.* Englewood Cliffs, N.J.: Educational Technology Publications, 1976.

SKINNER, Benjamin F. *Cumulative Record.* New York: Appleton-Century-Crofts, 1959.

SOMMER, Robert. *Personal Space: The Behavioral Basis of Design.* Englewood Cliffs, N.J.: Prentice-Hall, Inc., 1969.

SULLIVAN, Edward A. *The Future: Human Ecology and Education.* Homewood, Ill.: ETC Publications, 1975.

WIENER, Daniel N. *Classroom Management and Discipline.* Itasca, Ill.: F.E. Peacock Publishers, Inc., 1972.

Periodicals

BENNETT, Roger V. "Curricular Organizing Strategies, Classroom Interaction Patterns and Pupil Affect." *The Journal of Educational Research* (May 1973) 398-393.

DODGE, Emelie R. "High School Classroom Control." *School and Community* (March 1975), 58-60.

HANSEN, J. Merrell. "Discipline: A Whole New Bag." *The High School Journal* (February 1974) 172-181.

HAVIS, Andrew L. "Alternatives for Breaking the Discipline Barrier in Our Schools." *Education* (Winter 1975), 124-128.

HEARN, Gordon. "Leadership and the Spatial Factor in Small Groups." *Journal of Abnormal and Social Psychology* (March 1957), 269-272.

JAMES, John. "A Preliminary Study of the Size Determinant in Small Group Interaction." *American Sociological Review* (August 1951).

KELLEY, Eugene W. JR. "Classroom Discussions for Personal Growth and Democratic Problem-Solving." *The Elementary School Journal* (October 1974) 11-15.

KOCH, Robert. "Nonverbal Observables." *Theory into Practice* (October 1971), 288-294.

LANDRETH, Garry L. "Dynamics of Group Discussion." *The Clearing House* (October 1973), 127-128.

MILLER, Harry G. and John BEASLEY. "Seven Ways to Get a Discussion Going." *Teacher* (November 1973).

Chapter 7

Evaluating the Effectiveness
of Instruction

OBJECTIVES
This chapter provides information to help the reader to:

1. distinguish between criterion-referenced and norm-referenced tests.

2. identify the functions of pretests, progress tests, and final posttests.

3. prepare exemplary test items in accordance with item construction conventions.

4. determine whether a given set of test items adequately measures a targeted behavior.

5. explain differences between "relative" and "absolute" grading systems.

6. describe the use of pupil achievement scores in assessing instructional programs.

_____

Building a test in a hurry for tomorrow's quiz is a situation in which many teachers find themselves from time to time. Results of such a rushed effort can be damaging both to learners and to the instructional program. Items developed under the press of time often are ambiguous, stress factual recall at the expense of higher order thought, seek answers only tangentially related to performance objectives, and disregard simple test construction rules.

Such tests often turn out to be composed of a series of short-answer questions in which youngsters are asked to list, identify, or describe something. Looked at superficially, tests of this type appear to conserve teachers' time and creative talents. But usually they contain deficiencies that more than compensate for any apparent time-saving advantage. A particularly important problem with many of these tests has to do with the tendency of many hastily-prepared test items to demand from learners only relatively low level cognitive thinking, most frequently at the knowledge and understanding level.

Since testing practices telegraph teachers' expectations to learners, it is important that test items demand sophisticated thinking competencies if learners are going to undertake to prepare themselves to operate at these higher levels of cognitive functioning. It is a mistake to assume that performance objectives and instructional strategies designed to promote higher level thinking will result in those behaviors unless tests given in the program also demand higher level thinking. Learners are quick to "see through" a teacher who *talks* about wanting them to be able to analyze and evaluate problems but who demands only knowledge and understanding level functioning on weekly true-false tests. Given this situation, learners are quick to conclude that the teacher's "real interest" is in how well they can deal with factual recall questions. Once they have arrived at this conclusion, members of a class become extremely reluctant to push themselves to the point at which they can deal with new material in a sophisticated manner.

The production of tests that do challenge learners to engage in higher level thinking is no simple task. For example, it is difficult to produce a test to measure the thinking processes of analyzing and synthesizing that is both reliable and valid. *Reliability* refers to the consistency of scores a student would receive if he was retested using the same test on different occasions. *Validity* of a test is concerned with whether the test measures what it purports to measure. Reliability and validity of tests are more easily established when lower level thinking processes are being assessed. This is true because information relevant to each item is very specific, and there tends to be a single "right" answer for each question. For example, the range of acceptable answers to the knowledge and understanding item, *on what date was the Declaration of Independence signed?* is much more restricted than the range of acceptable answers to the analysis level question, *describe factors contributing to the outbreak of the Revolutionary War.*

Further, learners often urge teachers to administer familiar types of tests. Since most students have a history of having had mostly knowledge and understanding level test items, they are most comfortable in preparing for tests of this type. When teachers do require them to take tests demanding higher order thinking abilities, many students do poorly. Such circumstances frequently result in a campaign to urge the teacher to return to more familiar testing procedures. Pressures on the teacher can be considerable.

Types of tests individual teachers give are also influenced by their beliefs about the distribution of academic talent in their classrooms. For example, many teachers have assumed that the distribution of ability within their classrooms parallels the distribution of ability among the general population of the age group of learners with whom they are working. The general distribution of abilities is usually depicted by a bell-shaped "normal curve." An example of the "normal curve" is provided in Figure 7.1.

Figure 7.1

Population Distribution Assuming Normal Distribution of Ability

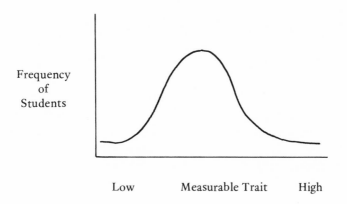

Frequency
of
Students

Low   Measurable Trait   High

While this "normal curve" does accurately describe the distribution of abilities among *very large groups* of learners of a given type, when a group as small as that found in a single classroom is considered, the distribution of any human trait cannot be considered to be "normally" distributed. This finding has profound implications for classroom teachers as they think about their testing programs.

For example, the logic of the "normal curve" suggests that the abilities of any given individual will always be relatively the same *vis-a-vis* the abilities of other people in the group. This phenomenon is observed when the groups are very large. But, again, given a unit as small as a classroom, an individual's position *vis-a-vis* his classmates is not nearly so stable. Indeed, teachers who subscribe to the idea of unchanging relative abilities seem to be suggesting that it is futile to adjust instructional practices to meet individual differences. For example, if the "normal curve" ordains that Johnny is at the bottom of the class, the best individualized program in the world will not change that "reality." Of course, such an assumption is nonsense, and teachers who have analyzed the "normal curve" and recognized its limitations reject the idea that their programs must result in a mechanistic allotment of a given percentage of A's, B's, C's, D's, and F's in every classroom. When there is a realization that every "Johnny" will go as far as his personal background and inclinations will take him, teachers reject the quick development of test items designed to generate scores that can be used to separate students according to the mandates of a "normal curve." Once there is a belief that every learner has the potential for success, test items can be developed that are designed to let teachers know how well their programs are helping each person to "come up a winner."

How can such tests be prepared? Clearly, tests built on the assumption of the normal curve, *norm-referenced* tests, are not the answer. A test is needed that focuses not on Johnny's score as compared to scores of others, but on how Johnny's work compares to some standard of excellence. Tests of this kind are referred to as *criterion-referenced* tests. A criterion-referenced test is designed to determine an individual's status with respect to a well-defined set of behaviors. In terms of the instructional model used for planning instructional practices described in this book, those behaviors are described by the performance objectives.

Historically, tests of this type date back to B.F. Skinner's operant conditioning theory of learning and programmed instruction. Because of the success of programmed sequences at imparting knowledge, the idea of total mastery of content (i.e., nearly every student can attain 100 percent mastery of any objective given appropriate instruction and time) seemed plausible to many educators for the first time. This astounding claim forced teachers to re-evaluate the instructional setting when learners failed to reach mastery. The instructional system rather than the learner's shortcomings were finally considered to be the source of dysfunction in the learning experience. Finally, the idea that instruction merely developed the native intelligence with which each youngster was born was struck a shattering blow. Mastery learning suggests that every youngster can learn, regardless of innate intelligence.

With the advent of well established instructional systems, instructional developers have begun to insist on tests which are designed to measure whether knowledges and skills related to a specific unit of instruction have been mastered by the learners experiencing the instruction. In other words, tests are needed that allow the instructional specialist to determine whether individuals, after experiencing a set of instructional experiences, have learned the material successfully.

If instruction is effective in meeting the individual needs of learners, the distribution of criterion-referenced test scores should be a negatively skewed distribution such as illustrated in Figure 7.2.

Tests needed for assessing group achievement, then, should contain items that allow the instructional specialist to determine the status of each individual with respect to well-defined instructional outcomes. Criterion-referenced tests are especially well-suited for this purpose. In the next section, a number of types of criterion-referenced tests will be introduced.

What Kinds of Tests Can Be Used?

Three varieties of criterion-referenced tests—(1) pretests, (2) progress tests, and (3) final posttests—are of interest to teachers. Each of these sub-types will be discussed in some detail.

Figure 7.2

*Population Distribution of Criterion-Referenced
Tests Assuming Instructional Needs of
Learners Are Being Met*

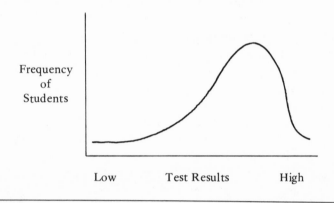

Frequency
of
Students

Low   Test Results   High

Pretests

Since the topic of pretesting was treated in Chapter 4, "Diagnosing Learners," little will be added here about the functions of a pretest. It will be sufficient to note observations by Glaser (1968) that pretests usually answer questions such as: (1) How much does the learner already know about this new information and task? (2) What are his strengths and weaknesses that should be considered in setting up his learning plan? (3) What materials and resources would best assist the learner to achieve the objectives? As these questions suggest, the pretest serves two primary functions, namely, (1) the diagnosis of entering prerequisite skills and knowledge, and (2) the opportunity for "testing-out" of the objectives in the unit and thus skipping that instruction.

Diagnosing entering knowledge and skills is addressed to the three questions cited by Glaser. Certain skills and information may be essential prerequisites a learner must have before he should begin an instructional unit. Typically, prerequisite concepts and skills may include: (1) definitions of important terms, (2) abilities to discriminate examples from non-examples of a concept, (3) equations for basic principles and laws, and (4) abilities to perform certain subskills and activities.

Simple, direct questions may be used to determine the presence of these behaviors. Further performance trials may be required as learners attempt to demonstrate psychomotor and cognitive skills. The use of objective test items such as multiple-choice, matching, and true-false, is recommended for the diagnostic sections of the pretests. Such questions require a minimal amount of time for administering and may provide nearly instant feedback if an answer key is available. The following examples have been drawn from several subject areas to illustrate both the nature of the measurement and the type of test items that may be used for diagnostic purposes.

Science

Performance Objective: All general chemistry students will develop and submit a position paper on recycling laboratory precipitates (inorganic) occurring from experiments conducted during freshman chemistry. The paper shall. . .

Prerequisite Knowledge (examples)
(a)   definition of Molar concentration of aqueous solutions
(b)   definition of solubility products and solubility constants
(c)   solubility constants for $AgCl$, $CuBr$, $PbSO_4$, $Ca(OH)_2$, Hg_2Cl_2
(d)   calculation of solubility products

Prerequisite Skills (examples)
(e)   ability to use the reference systems available in the school's library
(f)   ability to document important procedures with citations
(g)   ability to construct a bibliography

Representative Diagnostic Test Items
1.   A molar solution is a solution that contains:
     a.   one gram molecular weight of solute per liter of solution
     b.   one gram-equivalent weight of solute per liter of solution
     c.   weight of solute in 100 weight units of solution
     d.   one hundred grams of solute in one liter of solvent
2.   The mathematical expression for the solubility product constant of silver chloride is:
     a. $[Ag+]\ [Cl-]\ /\ [AgC] = Ksp$
     b. $[Ag+]\ [Cl-]\ [AgCl] = Ksp$
     c. $[AgCl] = Ksp$
     d. $[Ag+]\ [Cl-] = Ksp$
3.   When equal volumes of .02M $CaCl_2$ and, .0004M Na_2SO_4 are mixed together will a precipitate form? Ksp of $CaSO_4 = 2.4\ 10^{-5}$

Show your calculations.

    4.   References of current science periodicals by topic and author can be found in . . . .
        a.   *Abridged Reader's Guide*
        b.   *Current Index to Journals in Education*
        c.   *Review of Periodicals*
        d.   *Articles Unlimited*

The above items measure but a few of the potential prerequisite knowledges and skills that could be measured to determine learners' entry level into the general topic of solubility equilibria.

Mathematics

Performance Objective: Seventh grade mathematics students will be able to perform prime factorization of any three digit number by repeated division. This objective will be. . .

Prerequisite Knowledges (examples)
(a)   definition of commutative property of multiplication
(b)   definition of factor
(c)   square of a number exceeding number to be factored represents the largest number that needs to be divided into the number to identify all factors of that number
(d)   definition of multiples
(e)   definiton of prime numbers
(f)   the only even number that is a prime number is *two*

Prerequisite Skills (examples)
(g)   carry out long division on a three digit dividend with a one digit divisor
(h)   distinguish prime numbers from a series of examples and non-examples

Representative Diagnostic Test Items
    5.   The commutative property of multiplication states that the order of the factors does not affect the product.
            True   False
    6.   A factor is a number that is added to another number to name a sum. In the equation $4 + 3 = 7$, 4 and 3 are factors.
            True   False
    7.   A prime number is a number with only 2 factors, itself and 1.
            True   False

8. Indicate whether the following numbers are prime numbers.

    | 2 | yes | no |
    | 3 | yes | no |
    | 4 | yes | no |

Language Arts

Performance Objectives: Each student in eighth grade English will create metaphors with words used in the story "The Peddler of Bellaghadereen." This objective will be achieved. . .

Prerequisite Knowledge (examples)

(a-d) identify examples of the following terms used in defining a metaphor:

(a)   figure of speech
(b)   analogy
(c)   literal
(d)   denotation

Prerequisite Skillls (examples)

(e)   ability to read material written at a grade seven or eight level of readability
(f)   ability to write sentences free from mechanical errors

Representative Diagnostic Test Items

9. Select the choice which most correctly delineates the figure or figures of speech in the following statement:

    The tiny vessel plowed the sea as it moved relentlessly eastward toward Liverpool.

    a.   both "tiny vessel" and "plowed the sea"
    b.   "tiny vessel" alone
    c.   "plowed the sea" alone
    d.   both "plowed the sea" and "eastward toward Liverpool."

10. One of the following four sentences represents an example of an *analogy* that is superior to the other three possibilities. Select the *best* example of an analogy by encircling the letter preceding the statement.

    a.   In terms of food value, pole beans and bush beans are identical in every respect.
    b.   There are no parallels between the operation of the legislative assembly in Ghana and that in France.
    c.   A neurosurgeon's training bears little in common with a greenhouse attendant's training.
    d.   The Maine State Education Department resembles, to a degree, the Texas Education Agency.

11. The following passage describes a *literal* event. Select from among the four answers which best describes what literally happened:

Pierre pushed open the door, shuddered, and forced himself out to face the howling Montana January wind. He was gone not ten minutes. When he returned stomping his feet, clapping his hands, and hooting in discomfort, we could see that the cold had literally frozen the tips of his ears.

What happened to his ears?
a. they only seemed frozen
b. they were really frozen
c. he pretended they were frozen
d. they weren't frozen, but just felt as if they were

12. The following brief phrase is followed by four possible examples of *denotation*. Select the best example of denotation.

Stabbed in the back.

a. a knife really in the back
b. done "wrong" by friends
c. done "wrong" by enemies
d. done "wrong" by either "friends" or "enemies"

Social Studies

Performance Objective: Eleventh grade students in U.S. government class will be able to analyze the formal and informal structure and powers of Congress. This objective will be achieved by...

Prerequisite Knowledge (examples)
(a) functions of Congress
(b) definition of seniority
(c) selection of committee chairmen in Congress
(d) party affiliation and background of committee chairmen
(e) powers of committee chairmen
(f) autonomy of standing committees

Prerequisite Skills (examples)
(g) ability to read and comprehend the textbook, *Official Makers of Public Policy: Congress and the President*

Representative Diagnostic Test Items
13. The term "seniority" in Congress refers to the ....
a. chronological age of a member of Congress
b. number of consecutive terms of service in Congress

   c.   total number of years of service in Congress
   d.   influence wielded by a member of Congress

14.   The chairman of a Congressional committee quite often is the committee member of the majority party who has:
   a.   the longest number of unbroken years of service in Congress
   b.   served the greatest number of years in Congress
   c.   the most influence with the party power structure
   d.   the most support and respect of colleagues on the committee

15.   Chairmen of Congressional committees often come from rural areas because:
   a.   until recently, the United States has been primarily agrarian with respect to population distribution
   b.   farmers have held the balance of power in Congress in conflicts between business and labor
   c.   these areas have tended to be one-party areas with little chance of ousting incumbents
   d.   the Constitution was drawn up to favor agricultural interests

16.   Which of the following men would probably be selected as the chairman of a Congressional committee?
   a.   a moderate fellow who has just won his eleventh consecutive Congressional election
   b.   a popular middle-aged man on the committee
   c.   a close friend of the President elected to Congress for the first time
   d.   a young man who has just won a landslide victory for his second term to Congress

While the preceding examples have been provided to illustrate the types of questions that may be appropriate for a diagnostic test, they certainly are not comprehensive in the sense they measure all of the significant prerequisite knowledge and skills associated with each performance objective. The format of listing the objective, and the prerequisite knowledge and skills related to the objective, suggest a thought process that can be used to develop the test items. The challenging tasks are to determine knowledge and skills that are really prerequisite to instruction. If teachers are not careful, enabling information, namely, information to be acquired while accomplishing the objective, will be classified as prerequisite. A negative side effect of an inappropriate classification of this nature is that activities designed for remediation of prerequisite deficiencies are likely to become necessary components of the instructional program. Further discussion of how to use the data obtained from the administration of diagnostic pretests will not be undertaken here, since a substantial portion of Chapter 4, "Diagnosing Learners," dealt with establishing prescriptions based on receiving various diagnostic data.

A second distinct function of pretests is the "test-out" component. Test-out used here means the option of the learner to demonstrate proficiency in the skills or levels of knowledge stated in the performance objectives for the instructional unit before the instructional activities begin. An initial consideration that needs to be taken into account in constructing the test-out portion of a pretest is to examine the performance objectives to decide which objectives lend themselves to the test-out option. For example, if a given performance objective requests each learner to apply leadership skills in directing a group discussion on a social issue, the test-out option for the objective might prevent one individual or possibly an entire group of individuals from developing the social skills involved in this group exercise. In contrast to this example, if another performance objective in the same unit stated that each learner should identify and describe the "types of group members" in typical groups or committees, the test-out option would permit a knowledgeable learner to skip this activity and concentrate on other aspects of the instructional unit. Pretests can be so constructed that it is possible for a learner to test out of a portion of the unit by satisfying the requirements of selected performance objectives without completely bypassing the entire instructional unit.

Another consideration in constructing the test-out is the type of item to use. Factors such as guessing and superficial knowledge of a topic may certainly affect the learner's score or "proficiency" if a limited number of true-false and matching items is used to measure the learner's knowledge and skills. Written discussion questions and actual demonstrations of skills may be better alternatives for test-out questions. Generating discussion questions based on the performance objectives requires a minimum of time and practically eliminates guessing. Although more time would be required to administer skill tests to individual learners, only those students with some previous training and knowledge would likely attempt to test out of the related performance objectives.

Progress Tests

Progress tests constitute a second type of evaluation in a systematic instructional program. A few years ago Scriven (1967) suggested an evaluation procedure called *formative testing,* which provides for the systematic evaluation of curriculum development, teaching, and learning. In this type of testing, special emphasis is placed on assessing learners' progress periodically while instruction is "in progress." Because this testing occurs while instruction is "in progress" rather than at the conclusion of an instructional unit, the term *progress test* will be used here to describe these kinds of assessment instruments.

One of the most fundamental issues in developing progress tests is the selection of a unit of instruction. The scope of an instructional unit varies. Consequently, some units require more teaching time than others. Regardless of its length, each instructional unit contains subject matter to be learned by the student. To develop progress tests and final posttests for a unit, it is necessary to analyze the structure of content in the unit. This task can be accomplished through the development of a *set* of specifications which outlines the content to be taught, the performance objectives to be achieved, and the various cognitive levels of learning that are sought (e.g., knowing and understanding, applying, analyzing, synthesizing, and evaluating). Classifying the proposed content with respect to the cognitive learning categories is more difficult than merely identifying the content. However, with practice, teachers are able to categorize content they teach.

The process of analyzing the structure of content in an instructional unit is facilitated through the use of a table containing the content classified by cognitive level. Figure 7.3 illustrates a table of specifications for a unit on elementary dynamics in secondary school physics.

A table of specifications is a valuable planning aid to assure that the relationships among program elements are seen clearly. This visual summary provides direction as teachers attempt to identify kinds of assessment needed and relationships among assessment techniques. It is necessary that testing procedures be devised for each of the behavioral elements in Figure 7.3, since these represent performance objectives in the instructional program. The following sample items referenced to each element in the table of

Figure 7.3

Table of Specifications for Elementary Dynamics in General Physics

A. Knowing and Understanding	B. Applying	C. Analyzing	D. Synthesizing	E. Evaluating
1. Principle of inertia →		8. force diagram to initiate motion compared with force diagram on same object in constant motion		
2. Kinematics →	7. apply these equations: $a=\Delta V/\Delta K$, $d=Vot + \frac{1}{2} at^2$, $Vf^2 = Vo^2 + 2as$ in the resolution of unbalanced force problems.			
3. Dynamics →				
4. Inertial Mass →		9. Distinguish the similar and dissimilar characteristics of gravitational and inertial mass		
5. Gravitational Mass →				
6. Newton's Law and the unit of force →			→	10. Compare the solution of dynamics problems using vector addition compared to algebraic solution

specifications have been developed to illustrate appropriate progress test items. Although the majority of these items are multiple choice, it is possible to use other testing formats in progress tests.

Test Items for Knowing and Understanding

A-1 The property of matter which requires the application of a force on a body to change its positon or motion is a definition of:
    a.   force
    b.   rectilinear
    c.   inertia
    d.   momentum

A-2 The science which treats motion as a study unto itself is called:
    a.   dynamics
    b.   kinematics
    c.   mechanics
    d.   thermodynamics

A-4 Which of the following answers best describes the differences between inertial and gravitational mass:
    a.   they are inversely proportional
    b.   they are measured differently
    c.   the units of mass are different
    d.   all of the above

A-6 The unit of force in the English system of measurement is:
    a.   pounds
    b.   dynes
    c.   newtons
    d.   kilograms

B-7 A car that has a mass of 2000 kg is moving with a velocity of 15m/s in an easterly direction. If a force of 1000 newtons is briefly applied (3s) in a direction opposite to the direction of the car's motion, what will happen to the car's motion?
    a.   the car will speed up
    b.   the car will slow down
    c.   the car will stop
    d.   the car will reverse directions

C-8 Diagram the force vectors acting on a .1 kg cue ball to initiate motion, assuming it is struck by a cue stick with 5 nt of force. In a second illustration diagram the forces acting on the cue-ball in constant motion.

C-9 In making a determination of the mass of moon rock during blast-off from the moon's surface with a 2 pan balance, what is being compared?
    a.   the gravitational attraction between the rocks and the weights

    b.   the gravitational attraction of the rocket for the rocks and
for the weights

    c.   the resistance to a change in velocity of the rocks and of
the weights

    d.   the number of molecules in the rock and in the weights

    e.   the density of the weights to the density of the rocks

E-10 If several forces of different magnitude and directions act on an
object in what direction will the object accelerate? If you were to
solve this problem, which method of solution (vector additon or
algebraic solution) would you use? Discuss and defend your
answer.

The preceding examples illustrate the relationship of each test item to a behavioral element in the table of specifications in Figure 7.3. In this abbreviated illustration, only a single test item is provided for each behavioral element. In an actual unit, anywhere from eight to two dozen test items would be developed for each performance objective. This progress test should be administered to the learners at the conclusion of the instructional activities for the unit. Student performance with respect to each performance objective can then be recorded. This achievement information can be employed in assigning grades based on the number of performance objectives attained. A more extensive discussion of the role of progress test performance data in determining grades is provided in a later section of this chapter.

The most important information provided by progress testing is feedback concerning each learner's academic development. Results of progress testing let learners know if they are succeeding. If performance objectives are being achieved, the feedback serves as positive reinforcement. Evidence of success is a powerful motivator that keeps learners "at task." Given an indication of success, learners become increasingly willing to invest time, effort, and interest in the subject. Conversely, when learners do not answer enough test items correctly to achieve certain performance objectives, knowledge of these deficiencies points out to learners the specific parts of the unit to which they need to devote more attention. Given this information and provided with a variety of materials and review activities, hopefully these learners will achieve these missed performance objectives. When retesting opportunities are provided, learners' anxieties are reduced because the first administration of the progress test is not viewed as rendering a heavy-handed "final judgment."

Another function of progress tests is to provide information regarding the value of the instructional materials and activities selected to teach the behaviors listed in the table of specifications. By reviewing class performance on the items related to each performance objective, teachers can identify potential "soft spots" in the instructional program. As a rule of thumb, errors on a progress test made by a few learners in class likely reflect individual learner difficulties with the material and should be attended to on an individual basis (i.e., specific feedback and remediation). On the other hand, errors made by a majority of students on the same performance objective suggest a deficiency in the instructional program.

Final Posttests

Progress tests are criterion-referenced achievement tests over a *single unit* of instruction. Final posttests, on the other hand, are criterion-referenced achievement tests over a *number of units.* In terms of the kinds of test items they contain, progress tests and final posttests are quite similar. But there is a difference in the number of items provided to test each performance objective. Progress tests require sufficient test items for each performance objective to provide convincing evidence that a specified level of learning has occurred. Authorities in measurement agree that the more items provided per objective the better. Obviously, though, cost and time factors limit the number of items that can be included in a given progress test. Sound judgments about learners can be made when eight to ten items are provided for each performance objective. Thus, a progress test over a unit with six guiding performance objectives might consist of 48 to 60 test items.

Final posttests are designed to assess learners' academic growth over several units. For example, a final posttest might be given after five units had been completed. If each of these units had six guiding performance objectives, the final posttest would sample learner behavior over a total of 30 performance objectives (five units times six performance objectives equals 30 performance objectives). Obviously, it is not feasible to ask eight to ten questions about each performance objective on a final posttest. (In this instance, such a decision would result in a test with between 240 and 300 items!) Therefore, the final posttest must include a much smaller number of items per performance objective. Given the illustrated example, a final posttest with 30 items (one for each performance objective covered in the five units) would make sense.

One expects, of course, to see a relation between progress test results and final posttest results. This relationship does obtain when posttest items are selected with care. Those learners who scored high on individual unit tests are found to score high on final posttests as well. This suggests that competence, as measured by progress tests, provides a stable indication of learners' cognitive ability. In other words, high scores on progress tests will be followed by high scores on final posttests. These high scores may be taken as evidence of a positive influence of the instructional program on learners.

Scores on the final posttest provide data that may be averaged along with results obtained from progress tests to determine learners' grades. As an alternative, the authors suggest that grades be made contingent only on progress test scores. Student achievement scores on final posttests can be reserved for use in evaluating the instructional program rather than in assigning grades to individuals. This reduces the "final judgment syndrome" often associated with posttesting and provides end-of-course retention data relating to the quality of the instructional program components.

In summary, progress tests and final posttests are similar with respect to item format, but they differ with respect to the number of test items per objective as well as the frequency of administration of the tests. Further progress tests and final posttests serve different functions. Progress tests provide reinforced learners' progress and give information to teachers for grading and program monitoring. Final posttests, on the other hand, provide important information for assessing the impact of the various components of the instructional program.

The Construction of Tests

Whether progress tests or final posttests are being constructed, it is wise to follow a systematic plan. The following general steps apply to any teacher-made tests:

1. Establish a table of specifications for the subject matter in the instructional unit. Then select or develop appropriate test items which assess the cells in the table. (See Figure 7.3.)

2. Assemble the test items in groups according to the performance objective being tested. If different types are used (multiple choice, true-false, matching) to assess a single objective, it is useful to group common types together.

3. Develop a scoring scheme consistent with the criterion levels provided in the unit's performance objectives.

4. Develop directions for the test which cover such matters as: (1) whether the learner is to answer every question on an answer sheet or on the test; (2) whether he has some options on which questions to answer, a suggested time limit for each set of questions; and (3) whether he will be graded on an essay item for punctuation, spelling, and grammar as well as substance.

Material in the following sections will elaborate on these steps. Specific considerations relating to different types of test items will be described.

Essay Items

Discussion questions or short essays are used liberally on teacher-made tests. One reason for the popularity of discussion questions is the relative ease of constructing this type of item. Unfortunately, this apparent advantage is deceptive. Hastily constructed discussion questions tend to demand little more of learners than recall of specific content. This "knowing and understanding" information ought not to be tested with an essay item. Rather, test items that can be objectively scored—for example, true-false, matching, and multiple-choice items—are more appropriate choices. The development of challenging discussion questions is demanding and time consuming, especially if the items are designed to measure higher cognitive levels such as analyzing, synethesizing, and evaluating.

Consider the following items to illustrate the preceding remarks:

1. Define the word "hypothesis" and provide an example.
2. Cite an example of how man has upset the balance of nature.
3. In two handwritten pages, evaluate the utility and generalizability of F = ma as a basis for comparing the molecular motion of hydrogen gas with the motion of planets around the sun.

The first item exemplifies what frequently happens when test items are developed in haste. A definition is called for, but the learner is at a loss whether to supply a brief, concise answer or to provide an extensive commentary several pages in length. Since this item does not really demand cognitive thinking beyond the level of knowledge and understanding, the essay format is inappropriate. A much more suitable alternative would be a classification item containing both examples and non-examples of hypotheses and requesting the learner to identify the examples of hypotheses from the list of choices.

The *intent* of the second item may be to determine learners' ability to "discover" and analyze a man-made ecology crisis. However, the question as cited certainly does not prevent a learner from simply reporting an example covered in class or in his reading. When this occurs, learners are operating not at the levels of analysis or synthesis, but at that of knowledge and understanding. By adding qualifiers to the item (e.g., "No examples discussed in class or in the test are to be cited."), learners' cognitive functioning is much more likely to be at the target levels of analysis or synthesis.

The complexity of the third item helps clarify what the learner is expected to do. For example, the phrase "in two handwritten pages" tells learners that a somewhat detailed analysis of the utility of Newton's Second Law of Motion is expected. Given these specific instructions, a two sentence explanation of the equation of F = ma using examples of mass of a molecule of hydrogen and a planet will hardly suffice. The real substance of the question "evaluate the utility and generalizability of F = ma" is placed in the context (hopefully) of motions not compared previously (comparing the motion of a molecule with that of a planet). If, in fact, these motions have not been discussed previously, the learner responding to the item may indeed be providing an answer indicative of higher order thinking.

In preparing essay items, a number of considerations must be kept in mind. First, these items must be used judiciously. That is, the essay should be reserved for the measurement of higher levels of cognitive thinking. It makes little sense to use essay items to test student mastery of recall material. Multiple-choice, true-false, and matching tests are better suited for assessing knowledge and understanding. Second, it is necessary to provide enough information in the essay question to enable the learner to know the degree of detail and analysis expected (i.e., number of pages or words, time to spend on the item). Third, essay items ought to create situations that will require the learner to break *new* ground with respect to the issue being examined; otherwise, the question becomes a mere recall item.

Another issue that must be addressed concerns scoring the essay item. As a beginning, criteria must be determined that will be used to judge merits of the answers. Specifically, a decision must be made regarding whether substance alone will be the basis for evaluation or whether spelling, grammar, word usage, and sentence structure will play a part in determining the acceptability of the written responses. Regardless of the criteria used, learners must be apprised of standards to be used in determining the quality of the responses.

Care must be taken during the actual grading process. It is a good idea to score the same item on all papers before going to another question. This practice tends to reduce the possibility of allowing a learner's response on an initial question affect judgment of the quality of responses on ensuing items. Related to this suggestion is the idea of scoring the papers without referring to the learner's name. Although teachers try to be unbiased individuals, preferences may be given to some "favorites" when names are known. The practice of grading the papers "blind" tends to reduce the charge that grading essay items is very subjective and unreliable.

Multiple-Choice Items

Multiple-choice items are perhaps the best of those that can be scored objectively. An item with a series of possible responses increases the potential for a varied response, thereby enhancing the test's reliability. Further, presented with a number of options, the learner who tries to guess works against greater odds when there are four choices rather than two as with true-false items. However, appropriate multiple-choice items are time-consuming to construct, since each question roughly is equivalent in length to four or five true-false items. It is not surprising that teachers often elect to save time by constructing a number of true-false items rather than developing multiple-choice questions. Tempting as this option is, it makes better sense to use multiple-choice rather than true-false items. This is so because there are characteristics of multiple-choice items that tend to compensate for the length of time necessary to build good items. The most significant advantage of multiple-choice items is their capacity for measuring higher order learning.

Diagrams, pictures, and figures can be adapted readily to the multiple-choice format. The interpretation of a political cartoon, graph, or figure can be sought through a series of higher order cognitive questions directed at the application or analysis levels of thinking. The capability of well constructed multiple-choice items to measure higher cognitive levels is a characteristic not shared with other types of items that can be objectively scored. The following examples have been provided to illustrate this latter characteristic.

Questions 1-3
The figure below shows the path of a projectile fired by a toy cannon. In answering the related questions, assume frictional forces to be negligible.

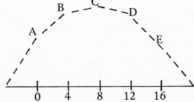

1.   The speed of the projectile as it leaves the miniature cannon is the same as its speed at
      (a)   none of the following
      (b)   B
      (c)   C
      (d)   D
      (e)   E

2. The horizontal component of the velocity of the projectile after it leaves the muzzle of the miniature cannon is
   (a) greatest at point A
   (b) greatest at point B
   (c) greatest at point C
   (d) greatest at point E
   (e) the same at all points

3. The vertical component of the velocity is zero at
   (a) A
   (b) B
   (c) C
   (d) D
   (e) E

All three of these items require learners to apply their knowledge of the resolution of velocity into its component vectors. Thus, each of these items requires youngsters to do more than recall, or recognize the answer, assuming this example was not discussed previously in class.

These examples reflect a number of characteristics that should be kept in mind when building multiple-choice items. These include:

1. The stem of each question should contain a central problem.
2. The stem should be long enough to express an idea without including extraneous information.
3. Double negatives should not be used in the stem or answer choices.
4. All distractors should be reasonable choices.
5. Whenever an item reflects a controversial option, an authority should be cited.
6. The distractors should be related, that is, on the basis of meaning, spelling, phonology.
7. Choices should be provided in an ordered sequence.
8. The correct response should not be consistently longer or briefer than the distractors.
9. Finally, make sure only one choice is correct.

Sample multiple-choice items, introduced previously, exemplify what good items should be. Below a number of additional multiple-choice questions illustrate instances of *inadequate* items.

1. To locate the section in the text that gives information on different models of instruction one should refer to the . . . .
   a. bibliography
   b. introduction
   c. table of content because major topics are identified there
   d. preface
2. Gubernatorial candidates for Missouri include . . . .
   a. Christopher Bond
   b. Warren Hearnes
   c. Joe Namath
   d. Little Abner
3. The chemical formula for muriatic acid which is a commercial grade of a common laboratory reagent is . . . .
   a. HCL
   b. HNO_3
   c. HCL
   d. H_2SO_4
4. All but one of the following balls are not examples of a pneumatic sphere; pick the example from the non-example.
   a. baseball
   b. golf ball
   c. basketball
   d. pool ball

The first example is a reasonable item with the exception of the correct answer, which is considerably longer than the other choices. This is a very common error, with the correct choice being either notably longer or shorter than the distractors.

The second example contains at least two serious flaws, one being the ambiguity of the stem; it is impossible to determine from the question stem which election year is being considered. Answer choices "a" and "b" are both correct the way the question is stated. But Christopher Bond and Warren Hearnes were not candidates during the same election. Another serious flaw with this example is revealed by an examination of the two other answer choices. Obviously, answers "c" and "d" are unlikely candidates. Thus, instead of four *plausible* answers, there are only two.

The third example contains a number of deficiencies. The question stem contains some unnecessary information. For example, the phrase, "which is a commercial grade of a common laboratory reagent," could be omitted without reducing the clarity of the stem. The question would then become "The chemical formula for muriatic acid is . . . ." The difficulty is not with the stem alone. Note that two of the answer choices are identical, and in this case both are correct. This mistake is an oversight that results from a failure to proofread the test before printing. Whether the error is an obvious duplication or an error due to a typographical mistake, the results negate the effort expended in developing that item.

The fourth example contains a double negative, which is confusing. Quite often items stated in the negative sense, for example, "all but one of the following do not represent an example. . .pick out the non-example," distort the question to the extent that a simple question becomes difficult and tricky. Such questions should be rephrased or excluded from the test. To illustrate this point, example four could be rephrased: "One of the following recreational balls is a pneumatic sphere; identify it from the following list."

A number of formats can be adopted for multiple-choice stems. Ordinarily, building an item is easier if the stem, initially, is written as a question. The use of a figure, illustration, or graph, cited earlier, provides an excellent background for a series of items. Another functional format is to use analogies such as the following:

Washington is to President as Marshall is to:
a.   Chief Justice
b.   U.S. Treasurer
c.   General of the Army
d.   Secretary of State

A problem statement is another format readily translated into multiple-choice stems. For example:

The prime factorizations for 50 are:
a.   5, 10
b. 5^2, 2
c.   25, 2
d.   50, 1

These examples provide a few ideas for formatting multiple-choice stems. Unfortunately, the development of the stem only partially completes the task of building a multiple-choice item. The number of answer alternatives is another issue to be resolved. It is better to develop four alternative answers for each question than three or five. Three options provide too few alternatives to assure variability of potential responses, while developing a fifth option takes time and adds little to strengthening the item. The following items are offered to illustrate possible answer choice formats.

> Pascal's principle is applied in hydraulic equipment such as:
> a.   pneumatic hammer
> b.   fork lift
> c.   both A and B
> d.   neither A nor B

This format reduces the number of alternatives that need to be developed and puts another dimension into the item. Rather than identifying one correct answer and stopping (since both may be correct), the learner must consider both options before making a decision. The following example represents an extension of the format used in the preceding item. In this instance three single options are possible, or a combination of two options, or a combination of three items.

> Which of the following statements represent the reason(s) for the present teacher surplus.
> a.   enrollment statistics indicate a decreasing rate of enrollment growth in public schools
> b.   government loans have encouraged students to enter teacher preparatory programs
> c.   ZPG (Zero Population Growth) is largely responsible for the smaller school enrollments
> d.   A, B
> e.   A, B, C

Hopefully, these examples and characteristics of multiple-choice items will be useful in the construction of test items.

Matching Items

Matching items are another type of test item that can be scored objectively. These items are well adapted for measuring lower levels of cognitive learning, namely, knowing and understanding. Generally, matching tests are easy to construct and use. These advantages suggest that matching items are viable for some objectives. On the other hand, when matching items are used too frequently, learners are encouraged to memorize facts and isolated details without integrating the information.

When constructing matching items, there is a need to recall that they may be constructed either with or without *distractors.* Distractors are terms or phrases that are added to make one list longer than the other. As with the various formats for answer choices of multiple-choice items, the addition of distractors adds a new dimension to the matching item. When distractors are present, the learner cannot rely on the process of elimination to make his final choices. For this reason, the use of distractors with matching items is recommended. Other suggestions for preparing matching tests include:

1. Use at least six but fewer than 12 responses in each test.
2. Use capital letters to identify the options.
3. Confine a matching question to a single space.
4. Use three or four additional options as distractors.
5. Use content related to a single objective in each test.
6. Place the list containing the longer statements on the left hand side of the page.
7. Define the basis for matching, i.e., synonyms, antonyms.

The following example and comments have been included to elaborate on these observations.

Directions: Match the names of these common compounds to the appropriate chemical formula. Place the letter indicating your choice in the appropriate blank.

.... 1.	Table salt	A.	$NaNo_3$
.... 2.	Ammonia	B.	$NaCl$
.... 3.	Muriatic acid	C.	HCl
.... 4.	Acetone	D.	HNO_3
.... 5.	Rubbing alcohol	E.	C_3H_7OH
.... 6.	Lead sulfate	F.	C_2H_5OH
.... 7.	Drinking alcohol	G.	$PbSO_4$
		H.	$PbSO_3$
		I.	NH_3
		J.	C_3H_6O

The number of responses called for on this item falls within the recommended limits. Although it is dangerous to generalize from one sample, brief mention of a specific case will illustrate a point. Recently a daughter of one of the authors brought home a test paper from school with a matching item containing 24 associations on one page and 30 completion items on the following page. Both sets of items were designed to seek identical information at the level of knowing and understanding. The young lady answered three times as many completion items correctly as matching items. Apparently, she became confused while taking the long matching test.

The reason for suggesting six to a dozen associations per test relates to the clarity of the item. With fewer than six associations, the time necessary to lay out the test and provide specific directions is great relative to the amount of information that can be gained. When more than a dozen associations are included in a test, learners are likely to become confused and receive low scores. Part of this confusion can be attributed to the number of bits of information a person can keep track of at any one time (seven bits is often cited). Consequently, with a long list of associations, the learner may simply miss some responses because he cannot keep track of all of the choices available. When this occurs, scores may go down.

A single matching test should be printed in its entirety on one page. It is very easy for youngsters to overlook parts of matching tests that continue on to a second page.

In constructing matching tests, it is desirable to list the longer terms on the left side. This is consistent with reading instruction that teaches learners to proceed from left to right on the page.

Finally, the directions should provide the learner with the basis of association as well as direct him how to respond to the associations. If directions are omitted, drawing lines from one list to another usually results. These lines often end up looking like a ball of tangled string. Omitting explicit directions for responding to any type of test items creates scoring problems, but this is especially pronounced with matching tests.

True-False Items

True-false items are used frequently in teacher-made instruments for a number of reasons. First of all, true-false tests are easy to prepare. Second, they can be scored quickly. Finally, they can be adapted to nearly any content.

Ironically, a disadvantage of true-false items is related to one of their positive traits. Since these items are so easy to construct, items often are developed that reflect little forethought concerning the uniformity of items and their relation to the unit's performance objectives. Another misuse of the true-false tests involves attempts to use them to assess learning at the higher levels of the cognitive dimension. Further, true-false items may be so ambiguous that a convincing argument can be made to support either answer. One other disadvantage is that guessing may play a role in test scores because of the dichotomous scoring structure of true-false items. An enterprising learner who knows a little about the content, who is wise to test-taking (if the item contains *never* or *always,* it is probably false), and is a little lucky, will probably reach criterion on most of the performance objectives which use true-false items. Suppose a performance objective has a stated degree (criterion level) which requires that eight of ten true-false items be answered correctly to satisfy the objective. Second, assume the learner knows the answers to six of the ten items and is able to make an educated guess about two more because of the way the items are stated. The learner may not need to answer either of the last two items correctly, but he has a fifty-fifty chance of getting each of them correct, since there are only two choices. Such a person, while not truly competent to the level necessary to achieve the performance objective, will attain a passing score because of the nature of the test items.

Careful test construction can do much to prevent high scores by students who really do not know the materials. Rules for constructing true-false items to enhance test validity include:

1. Make each item completely true or false.
2. Use nearly an equal number of true and false questions.
3. Never use statements that are stated exactly the same way in the text.
4. Avoid specific determiners. Words such as all, always, never, invariably, none, and no are usually associated with statements that are *false;* words such as "may," "probably," and "sometimes" are included in *true* statements.
5. Do not make a statement false by means of trivial detail.
6. Employ specific rather than general terms.
7. Resist using attitude and value questions among the list of items; terms such as "worst," "best," and "better than," indicate value questions are being used.
8. Provide succinct directions on how to mark an item and where to record the answer.

9. Use a single concept item; do not combine two ideas into one item.

Consider the following short true-false test items in terms of the guidelines above:

Directions: Mark T for true, O for false.
1. All birds that have colorful feathers destroy huge quantities of insects.
2. Pi (π) has a numerical value (rounded off) of 3.1416.
3. The volume of a mass of gas tends to decrease with an increase in temperature while the pressure increases.
4. The majority of microbes are not good for mankind.

The "directions" component of this test fails to provide learners with clear guidelines. Although true statements are to be designated with a "T," and false statements with an "O," learners are not told *where* answers should be recorded. In dealing with this issue, it makes sense to direct students to put responses on separate answer sheets. Such a practice can facilitate scoring and save paper. This practice, additionally, permits a single classroom set of questions to be used by a number of sections of a given course.

Item "1" in this set of questions is almost sure to be marked false by an alert learner who reacts to the words "all" and "every." Most course content presents few "absolute truths." Thus, when words implying absolutes, such as "all" or "every," appear in test items, many learners will surmise correctly that "false" has to be the proper answer. Item "1" is also deficient because of the use of indeterminant words such as "colorful" and "huge." Such references must be made specific to provide learners with a reasonable basis for judgment.

Item "2" is much better than item "1." Learners should not encounter difficulty in deciding what the item means. Item "3" illustrates an item that is confounding because more than one idea is referred to in a single statement. ("Volume of gas decreases with an increase in temperature" and "Volume of gas tends to decrease with an increase in pressure.") Given the information available in this example, the first idea is false and the latter is true. This error invalidates the item and demonstrates why it is necessary to refrain from combining ideas in true-false items.

Item "4" irresponsibly attempts to elicit a "true" or "false" response to a value-laden issue. Such improper use of true-false items frequently results when teachers err in selecting a true-false item rather than an essay to get a measure of learners' ability to analyze, synthesize, or evaluate.

These examples illustrate potential hazards to be avoided as true-false items are developed. As long as true-false items are used only for assessing knowing and understanding and are constructed according to the preceding rules of construction, true-false tests should be stable and valid indicators of learners' competence.

Completion Items

Completion items, like true-false items, are relatively easy to construct. Completion items share the characteristic of allowing for comprehensive coverage of content. The basic difference in the scope and purposes of the two forms is that true-false items require recognition of information and relations, while completion items demand *recall* of information and relations. Scoring completion items is more difficult than scoring true-false items, since a single completion item may contain more than one blank. Such tests are easier to correct when learners respond directly on the test instrument rather than on an answer sheet. Since answers are interspersed in the prose at different points (wherever a blank is provided), correction takes longer than in the case of true-false tests.

The following guidelines should be followed in preparing completion test items.

1. Do not copy sentences directly from the textbook.
2. Blanks should be placed at the end rather than at the beginning of a statement.
3. Do not use vaguely worded completion items.
4. Avoid using "a" and "an" immediately preceding the blank.
5. Words rather than phrases should be deleted from statements.
6. Correct answers should include synonyms of the "answer."

Consider the following items in the light of the guidelines for preparing completion tests.

Directions: Complete the following statements:
1. .... is credited with the invention of the electric light bulb.
2. Trees which shed their leaves annually are called .... trees.
3. The reaction of oxygen with iron to form iron rust is an
   ....
4. What is the length of a meter? ....

The "directions" component of this test lacks specificity. For example, it fails to indicate where the answers are to be placed. Directions should tell learners to write responses directly on the test in the blanks provided.

Item "1" violates the guideline that blanks be placed at the end rather than the beginning of a statement. The reason for this suggestion is simply that learners should have an idea about what they are being asked to respond to before encountering the blank. Although the same information is requested, learners would not be expected to restructure the sentence if item one were rephrased as follows:

1a. The invention of the electric light bulb is credited to ....

Item "2" appears to be a reasonable item, except it seems to have been removed verbatim from the course text, and the expected answer is *deciduous.* Unfortunately, when the statement is taken out of context, something is lost. Several answers that would not have been appropriate given the supporting information of the text are quite reasonable. For example, *elm, maple, oak,* or *hickory* fit logically and grammatically in the blank.

Item "3" gives perceptive learners who are wise to basic rules of grammar an edge in answering this question simply because they know the answer will begin with a vowel; the article *an* immediately precedes the blank. This clue might be offset simply by changing the *an* to *a(n)* thereby creating the possibility that either a vowel or consonant is appropriate.

Item "4" is a fair question providing the teacher is willing to accept answers varying in form. Correct answers to this question include: 1m, 100cm, 1000mm, .001km, 39.37in, 3.28ft, 1.093yd. These only begin to represent the possibilities. It is possible the question was intended to seek the number of centimeters in a meter; if so, the item could be rephrased:

4a. A measured length of one meter equals .... centimeters.

A vague completion item like item "4" creates a dilemma in

deciding which answers are acceptable. Each answer must be considered on its own merits, not merely compared with the answer key.

Two General Guidelines for Test Preparation

Preparing test directions is an essential function in developing tests of all kinds. Directions should be easily understood. They should be placed at the beginning of the test if the entire test consists of one item type, or at the beginning of each section where a change of item type occurs. Test directions should include all necessary information to prevent confusion and interruption. Information that should be made explicit in the directions include:

1. Indicate whether answers are to be put on the test or placed on the answer sheet.
2. Inform students whether to write on the test itself in making calculations or to make notes about the question on a separate calculation or note page.
3. Specify a time limit if necessary and indicate the number of test items per objective as well as the degree of attainment for each objective.
4. Explain how answers are to be recorded, that is, circle choice, draw a line through, mark T or O, mark A-D, etc.

Preparing an answer sheet for a test will pay dividends in terms of conserving time in scoring and recording learner performance. Also, answer sheets can quickly direct learners' attention to problem items when tests have been corrected. Answer sheets for multiple-choice and true-false items can be easily designed for use with an overlay key which can speed up the scoring process considerably. The answer sheet should be kept relatively simple and easy-to-use, so as not to become an additional distractor for the learner. In programs guided by performance objectives, it is a good idea to group items by objective and indicate the degree of attainment for the objective (i.e., eight of ten). This provides a ready reference to both learners and teachers in interpreting the results in terms of whether specific performance objectives have been achieved.

Evaluating the Worth of Tests

How much confidence should teachers place in tests they devise to measure attainment of performance objectives for each instructional unit? Do the test items really measure learners' functioning at the intended cognitive level? Are the tests stable? In other words, if the same test were administered to the same class twice, once today and again tomorrow, would the rank order of students in terms of performance on the test be unchanged? How can teachers check the quality of individual items?

Questions like these usually do not concern teachers too much while they are preparing a test, simply because of the effort and thought directed to the generation of sound test items. These questions, however, begin to surface during feedback sessions with the learners who, for example, may say, "These questions are unfair!" Additionally, colleagues may ask, "Just how sound *are* your tests?" In responding to this questions, some understanding is necessary of the measurement concepts of *validity, reliability,* and *item discrimination.*

For the sake of this discussion, *validity* is defined in terms of the relation between the test items and the behavior components of the performance objective. This type of validity is called "content validity." The relation of test items to objectives can be assured when a table of specifications described earlier (see Figure 7.3) is used as a basis for developing or compiling a test. Once the test items have been developed, it is helpful to have "judges" compare the items given in a table of specifications, with instructions to rule *yes* or *no* on the appropriateness of each item. Colleagues, especially those in one's department, are good candidates for judges, but they should be briefed on which items relate to specific cells in the table. To illustrate how the validity of an item is judged, consider the following behavioral component of an objective and the test items that are supposed to measure its attainment:

> Objective . . . distinguish the characteristics of four techniques which provide for individual differences in learners. This objective. . .
>
> *Related Items*
> 1. Individual differences of learners are taken into account in all of the following techniques *except*:
>   A. tutorial study

B. small group discussions
C. lecture
D. programmed instruction

2. A curricular movement that emphasized the need to study biology so the students learn to think like biologists would be classified as the ....
   A. individual needs
   B. human values
   C. content structure
   D. social realities

To begin the item evaluation process, note the cognitive level of the objective. The objective in this case is written at the knowing and understanding level. Directing attention to the items, it is clear that both test items are designed to measure recall, but different areas of content are being measured. Item "1" offers content consistent with the objective, while item "2" is concerned with different material. Given this information, the rulings rendered for these items would be "yes" for item "1" and "no" for item "2." If more than one judge critiques the items (four are recommended), it is to be expected that there will be some disagreement regarding the appropriateness of a given item. As a "rule of thumb," it makes sense to accept an item as sound when 75% or more of the judges concur. When disagreement is more pronounced, the item should be revised or discarded.

Reliability is another characteristic of a test that bears some relationship to *validity*. *Reliability* refers to the consistency of scores achieved by learners when reassessed with a test on different occasions or tested with different but equivalent instruments. It is possible to obtain consistent results on a test which bear little or no relation to the behavior stated in the performance objective. For example, suppose an objective required preservice teachers to be able to collect and interpret verbal interaction analysis data obtained from any secondary level classroom, but that test items developed to measure this objective were designed to determine the candidates' knowledge of the coding categories. If this test were then administered to teaching candidates on two occasions and the relative standing of student performance was found to be consistent, the test would be considered to have high reliability. However, the validity would be open to question because the test did not measure candidates' abilities to collect and interpret verbal interaction in classrooms.

Whereas it *is* possible to have high reliability and low validity, it *is not* possible to have high validity and low reliability. To establish validity of test responses, it is essential that repeated testing produce a similar pattern of scores. This consistency, of course, implies a high test reliability.

The notion of reliability can be shown by comparing test-retest results on some particular measure. Figure 7.4 illustrates the situation. The figure shows the scores obtained by ten learners on an arithmetic achievement test in which the second administration was given one week after the first.

Figure 7.4 illustrates that the rank of the students remained nearly the same between test administrations. This illustrates the consistency of results.

A concept strongly associated with reliability is *variance.* Variance comes from two sources: (1) *true variance,* the actual ability difference among learners; and (2) *error variance,* differences occurring among scores because of such factors as poor test

---

Figure 7.4

Score and Class Rank on an Achievement Test

Pupil	First Administration		Second Administration	
	Score	Rank	Score	Rank
Allan	24	10	27	10
Bob	65	1	68	2
George	30	8	37	8
Mary	38	7	40	7
Fred	29	9	29	9
Debbie	41	6	50	6
Nancy	50	5	55	4
Fred	52	4	54	5
Carol	64	2	69	1
Bill	57	3	56	3

Figure 7.5

Examples Illustrating Error Variance

	Example A		**Example B**		
				Measurements	
Trial	Jack's Height	Student	1st	2nd	Difference
1	71.5 inches	Jack	71.5 - 72.3		.8
2	72.0	Tom	68.9 - 69.3		.6
3	72.5	Fred	75.2 - 75.0		.2
4	72.3	John	72.3 - 72.8		.5
5	71.7	Sam	66.3 - 67.0		.7
6	72.6	Al	71.0 - 71.6		.6
7	72.0	Greg	69.3 - 69.1		.2

Average = 72.09 inches

ΣD = 3.6

Extreme - Average = Measurement
Measures   Error

Sum of ÷ No. of = Measure-
Difference Students ment Error

Measurement Error = + .55 inches

3.6 ÷ 7 = .51 inches

---

construction. To illustrate error variance, consider that in the measurement of height, one can take more than a single measurement. This is shown by the examples in Figure 7.5.

Example A in Figure 7.5 illustrates how error can result from multiple measurements of the same variable, while Example B shows an average error accumulated from a pair of measurements on a group of subjects. In either case, the point remains that error can result from measurement, and teachers must be aware of this phenomenon when constructing tests to measure cognitive achievement.

Suggestions cited earlier for improving the quality of individual test items influence the reliability of a test, i.e., clarifying vague items and directions. In addition, the reliability can be increased by simply adding good items to the test. This is illustrated in Example C in Figure 7.6. Suppose that three additional students, Denise, Jeff, and David, were measured and used to check the accuracy of measurement of a height determiner, used in Example B in Figure 7.5.

Figure 7.6

Adding Items to Increase Reliability

Example C

Student	Measurements 1st	2nd	Absolute Difference	
Jack	71.5	72.3	.8	
Tom	68.9	69.3	.6	
Fred	75.2	75.0	.2	
John	72.3	72.8	.5	
Debbie	66.3	67.0	.7	
Al	71.0	71.6	.6	
Greg	69.3	69.1	.2	Measurement error with 7 measures
Denise	67.3	67.0	.3	$3.6 \div 7 = .514$
Jeff	73.6	73.9	.3	
David	64.0	64.5	.5	
			4.7	Measurement error with 10 measures $4.7 \div 10 = .470$

Note that while the differences of measurements for these three additional students are similar to differences found in measurements of other learners, the total measurement error decreases. With other factors being equal, as the measurement error decreases the reliability of the instrument increases. This example illustrates that an increase in the number of scores enhances reliability.

Improving the *discrimination power* of criterion-referenced items is yet another way to increase reliability. The value of discrimination for each item is determined by comparing the performance of two groups of learners tested: (1) those who reached criterion on the related objective, and those who did not. More specifically, the value of discrimination of an item is calculated by determining the total number of learners who achieved the objective and scored the item correctly, while concurrently determining the total number of learners who did not achieve the objective but scored the item correctly. After these subtotals have been compiled, subtract the non-mastery total from the mastery total and divide the difference by the number of learners taking the test. If the numerator is positive, the mastery group collectively has performed better on the item than the non-mastery group. In such cases the item is said to discriminate "positively." This reflects quantitatively that mastery students will do better on this item than non-mastery students.

Assigning Grades

Teachers are responsible for making evaluative judgments about learner achievement and development. Reporting systems provide the means of communicating these judgments to students, parents, other teachers and schools, and potential employers. Although the periodic evaluation of learners has been a constant concern of teachers and administrators, the rising expenditures for education have resulted in increased public interest in educational accountability. Certainly, one aspect of accountability is the quantity and quality of learning that occurs during a certain instructional period. Grading practices that report A, B, C, etc., in English or reading fail to indicate just *what has been accomplished* by the individual learner. Consequently, reporting systems that convey what has been learned and to what degree the information or skill has been learned are being recommended to replace conventional grading practices.

What a Grade Means

Decisions about a grade's meaning ought to precede determination of a grade for an individual. A single grade under different circumstances can be so specific as to indicate precise standards of achievement, as, for example, in typewriting based on accuracy and speed. On the other hand, a given grade can be so global as to include an appraisal of the learner's attitude, industry, conduct, punctuality, attendance, and growth in skill. The grade may also represent an estimate of how well the pupil *is* doing compared to how well the teacher thinks he *should be* doing. With the variety of criteria on which grades are based, it is little wonder that teachers and learners alike feel something drastic should be done to rationalize the process.

By design, grading is a subjective process. The end product, the grade, usually represents a composite evaluation of pupil achievement of specific course or unit objectives. Much data presumably have been accumulated to support the awarding of a particular grade, but the final judgmental process integrates these data according to whatever educational philosophy operates at a particular school and with a certain teacher. Whatever guides grade determination, once decisions have been made, grades must be reported. For reporting to be effective, the meanings must be known to both the evaluator and the recipient, or they will be of little value.

Grading and reporting are made less subjective by precise definitions of the meaning of each grading symbol. It is common to find authorities who feel that subject matter achievement should be separated from attitude, effort, and behavior.

Grading systems are often classified in terms of their point of reference. *Absolute grading systems* try to express how nearly a learner's performance approaches an ideal performance, while *relative grading systems* attempt to express how well a learner's performance compares with the performance of peers. Relative grading systems are currently more popular than absolute systems. Common letter grades assigned to student performance include:

    A—outstanding performance
    B—above average performance
    C—average performance
    D—below average performance
    F—failure

One major difficulty with this relative grading system is the lack of a standardized achievement level which is typical of the peer group. This results in the possibility of rating an individual high when his performance is not outstanding or above average. For example, in a class with very poor scholars, a "top" score might be only 15 out of a possible 100. Under a relative system, students with scores of 15 would be "A" students.

The statistical rationale for this system is based on the premise that achievement is a normally distributed trait among the total student population. Further, this assumption of normality is generalized so that achievement in each particular class is also normally distributed. Given these assumptions, the percentage of class members receiving the various letter grades ranges from 3.6 to 45.2. A complete listing of the percentages and the respective grades are provided in Figure 7.7.

As in shown in Figure 7.7, the various percentage values represent the percent of total area under the curve within each

Figure 7.7

Statistical Basis for Relative Grading Systems

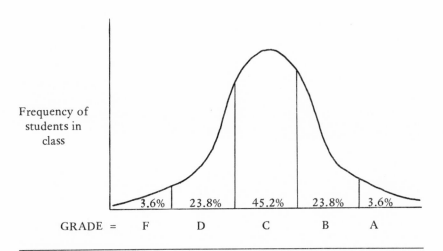

Frequency of
students in
class

| | 3.6% | 23.8% | 45.2% | 23.8% | 3.6% | |
GRADE = F   D   C   B   A

grade distribution. This procedure is clearly logical and based on accepted statistical procedures. The difficulty with this grading approach is that the basic assumptions frequently are not valid. For example, if a class is highly selective, such as a senior level physics class, the class distribution will likely approximate a skewed distribution, not a normal distribution. The normality assumptions are violated on purpose in school systems that practice homogeneous grouping to "provide for individual differences."

Yet relative grading systems are so entrenched in educational thinking that rather than adopt an absolute system, numerous adjustments have been tried with the relative system. One approach utilizes letter grades, but directs teachers to assign only A and B grades in the upper achievement groups and to transfer a learner who does not deserve a high grade to a lower group. In this approach teachers are prevented from awarding an A grade to learners in the lower or middle groups except in unusual cases. Pupils in the lowest groups are categorized, in advance, for D or F grades. Another approach utilizes the A to F scale for all classes regardless of the group classification. The learners are judged on the basis of their achievement in relation to other students in the class. However, a stigma is attached to learners by the addition of a subscript to the letter grade to indicate the group in which the learner earned the grade (A-slow group, B-accelerated group, etc.).

These "adjusted relative grading systems" are embarrassments to education. It is appalling that such insensitive policies could occur in schools. The authors are convinced that absolute grading systems provide a more humane, fair, and logical approach for determining grades, regardless of the composition of individual classes.

Absolute grades are usually expressed in percentage values. A grade of 100 percent indicates that a pupil has achieved all that is possible to learn in a particular course. A grade of 0 (zero) indicates that a student has failed to learn anything. Under this system, 70 percent is often established as a minimum passing score. Usually, the percentage grades are translated into letters, i.e., A = 90-100, B = 80-89, etc.

One difficulty with an absolute grading system is that it is difficult to determine a total amount of learning that represents a perfect performance in a course. Moreover, the idea of establishing percentage ranges for grades is arbitrary, and measuring human behaviors to two-place accuracy with the tests now in use is difficult. On the other hand, an advantage of absolute grading is that such systems diminish the possibility of an incompetent performance receiving a high grade simply because it is the "best" performance. In addition, an absolute system provides an opportunity for all learners in the course to earn the highest grade possible.

In the following paragraphs two absolute grading approaches, objective attainment and performance contracts, will be described. Either one of these approaches can be used to complement the instructional model promoted and discussed throughout this book.

Grade determination via objectives achieved is a straightforward approach to grading that promotes the use of performance objectives to structure instruction. To illustrate this grading policy, consider the following example.

> Your grades will be determined on the basis of the number of objectives mastered. If you do not succeed at mastering the objective on the first attempt, recycling should occur until you

achieve the objective. Since this system assures success, everyone should earn an "A." This is hopefully what will happen. However, there are some administrative problems that may interfere with this "ideal system." As you well know, this course is scheduled into a definite number of class periods. Suppose it is necessary for a learner to recycle through five additional activities during the semester to accomplish all of the objectives. Instead of taking 16 weeks, it may require 20 weeks to master all of the objectives for the course. This is where the mastery learning concept comes into direct conflict with the traditional semester schedule. In order to work around this problem, two alternatives are possible; get a time extension or devise some means of assessing a "grade" on what's been accomplished up to that time.

According to the rules and regulations concerning student grades, a short extension is possible, and this option may be used. Very brief extensions will be considered if this unusual situation arises, but this alternative is administratively undesirable under the present program. This leaves the determination of the grade on what's been accomplished at the end of the semester as the more appropriate option. Since there are 38 objectives in this course, letter grades will be assigned based upon the present scale recognized by the district for designating grades.

Grade	Objectives Mastered
A*	38-33
B	32-29
C	28-25
D	24-22

*In order to quality for an "A" grade you must submit work and participate in activities for *all modules* of the course; merely satisfying the minimum for an "A" grade, i.e., 33 objectives achieved, will not suffice.

A final examination will be administered at the conclusion of the course to determine the strengths and weaknesses of the instructional program. Your performance on this test will not affect your course grade.

This example signals a potential difficulty with this approach when mastery is required; that is, expiration of an administratively established time period. Either an extension must be negotiated with the administration, or an arbitrary but acceptable plan for assigning grades on the basis of what has been accomplished at the end of the grading period must be established. The latter approach works fairly well, without seriously compromising the tenets of the program.

Since the course grade depends on objective achievement, the criterion level of the performance objective must specify the standard to be attained to signal accomplishment. The evaluation must provide appropriate test items consistent with the objective to enable the learner to demonstrate mastery. Further, the recording system must indicate performance objectives achieved rather that simply scores or grades from tests and homework assignments. An ordinary grade book can be organized to record performance objective achievement simply by labeling the columns for objectives rather than for daily grades or test scores.

Advantages accrued through the use of the performance objectives-based grading approach include:

1. The system is logical and easy to monitor. Once an objective is achieved it is simply recorded.

2. Reporting grades can be accompanied by the list of skills and knowledges which have been demonstrated while earning the grade.

3. This approach can be readily integrated into a grading policy based on percentages. Rather than calculating the percentage on the total score accumulated, the number of objectives achieved is used.

4. This system encourages learners to use performance objectives as study guides, since accomplishment of the objectives is the basis for their grades.

Grade determination via performance contracts is an approach that has gained popularity in programs stressing individualized instruction. The name for this approach is derived from the contractual agreement that is made between individual learners and the teacher. Customarily, learners are given a list of tasks and are informed that their unit grades depend on the number of tasks performed satisfactorily. These tasks may include reading assignments, written exercises, problems, laboratory work, quizzes, etc. Each task is rated on a pass-fail basis, with unsatisfactory performances repeated. Essential parts of the unit are required in order to receive a passing grade. Often the essential tasks to be completed are listed for either a D or C grade. Successful completion of these tasks and a minimum performance on a progress test are usually necessary requisites for a B grade. The grade of A often requires, in addition to successful completion of all basic tasks, a higher level of performance on the progress test, and an in-depth project related to the unit.

Formal contracts require the learner to sign a written statement affirming his intent to achieve a particular grade, such as the following:

> I, ..., hereby declare my intention of achieving a grade of .... in this unit. I understand that in order to attain this grade, the following requirements must be completed within a time period of .... class days: (List of requirements.)

Informal contracts, on the other hand, require only that a verbal commitment be made to the teacher. Requiring learners to contract for a grade by either approach has the advantage of compelling them to evaluate their own capabilities.

Advantages of using a grading contract center on the idea that an entire class can work on the same general objectives, while at the same time provision can be made for individual differences. For this reason, the approach is popular in individualized instructional programs. Moreover, work and effort can be rewarded by providing some credit for optional activities. This is especially good for classes containing learners who do not do well on written tests, but who try hard. For example, a learner could earn a B or a C by doing a good deal of extra project-type work even if he had only moderately high test scores.

Grading contracts differ from the objective attainment approach in a number of ways. Certainly, the effort of detailing each task in advance is one difference. An implied difference is the *focus* of the grading system, that is, what counts for the grade. Attainment of the performance objective is central to grade attainment in one approach, while task completion and documentation is pivotal in performance contracts—with secondary emphasis placed on objective attainment. Unfortunately, documentation of task completion often results in an inordinate number of worksheets to be completed and submitted to the teacher, either as separate sheets or in a notebook at the end of the unit. If a decision is made to use a grading contract, there is a need to resist using worksheets simply to document that an activity has been completed. It is questionable whether proof of an activity being *completed* means that *competency* has been attained. For this reason, documentation of *activities* completed is a demanding task that provides little important information. Documentation of test performance requires fewer records and provides teachers with insights that are much more useful.

Evaluating the Quality of Instruction

Instructional quality discussions often highlight conferences, workshops, and even departmental faculty meetings. Usually, responses to the issue tend toward the philosophical rather than the practical. Only rarely do such discussions result in identification of practical procedures that can be used to assess the instructional program. Moreover, there is little time available for reflection on program quality. Except for inservice training days and, possibly, time at the conclusion of the school year, little systematic attention is devoted to the issue.

The authors believe that instructional programs can be assessed by referring to test data collected through the year to measure learners' growth. Not only can the results of pretests, progress tests, and final posttests indicate whether learners have the requisite knowledge and skills called for by the performance objectives, but also these data, taken collectively, provide valuable information for program evaluation. Achievement data from these sources may provide information concerning the number of objectives achieved on the pretests, the number of objectives achieved on the first administration of a progress test, and the number of objectives that require remediation and retesting. Such information says much about individual components of the instructional program.

For instance, if 40 percent of the class were able to "test-out" of an objective in unit three on the pretest, the teacher should question whether that objective and the related activities were appropriate for the unit or for the course. In such circumstances, it would be logical to assume that the content associated with the objective had been learned at an earlier time. Conversely, if another objective in unit three were recycled by 30 percent of the learners in class, apparently a difficulty existed, either with the objective, the learning experiences, the test items, or combinations of these possibilities. To pinpoint the specific difficulty, it would be necessary to scrutinize each of these program elements to identify the source of the problem. If test items and the performance objective are found to be adequate, the difficulty probably would lie with the instructional activities. In such an instance, the teacher should examine the activity with respect of the tenets presented in Chapter 5 ("Selecting Instructional Strategies") to determine if the activity is related logically to the guiding performance objective.

In addition to using pretest, progress test, and posttest data to assess the quality of instructional units, an attitude scale, labeled an *affective antenna,* is also useful. Use of the affective antenna provides data to complement information obtained from the progress tests and final posttests. This instrument requests learners to provide perceptions relating to the quality of the activities, the degree of organization in the unit, and the amount of content overlap with other units and courses. Information gleaned from this source provides attitudinal information with regard to the instructional unit. An example of an affective antenna, at the college level, is provided below in Figure 7.8.

These suggestions on how to use learner achievement data coupled with learner perceptions about the quality of the instructional program offer a means of evaluating the instructional program with little additional instrumentation and effort. In addition, using learner achievement data for dual functions (learner evaluation *and* program evaluation) should encourage teachers to develop instruments that are as sound as possible, since the data obtained must serve a number of important instructional functions.

Summary
Material in this chapter has been addressed to the issue of evaluation. A case has been made for using criterion-referenced instruments to assess the impact on learners of instructional programs. Since performance objectives play a central role in the diagnosis of entry levels of learners as well as the selection of instructional activities, it is natural that remarks on learner assessment center on evaluation tools which measure attainment of those objectives.

Types of criterion-referenced tests (pretests, progress tests, and final posttests) have one function in common. All are designed to measure the learners' facility with behaviors set forth in perform-

Figure 7.8

Example of an Affective Antenna

The following questions are being asked during the current school year of all students taking courses. We want you to carefully think about the unit (or topic or module) you have just finished in the course listed below and give your instructor your evaluation of the material covered. Rate the content of the unit, *not* the instructor.

Course Number ....   Section Number .....   Unit Name .....

Rate the unit on each of the following dimensions by putting an X for each dimension.

1. ineffective	.....	.....	.....	.....	.....	effective
2. active	.....	.....	.....	.....	.....	passive
3. boring	.....	.....	.....	.....	.....	interesting
4. valuable	.....	.....	.....	.....	.....	worthless
5. organized	.....	.....	.....	.....	.....	unorganized

Now rate the unit on several other aspects by putting an X for each question.

6. To what degree were the objectves clearly stated?
Very clear   ....   Very unclear

7. Compared to other courses you are taking this semester, how would you rate the clarity of objectives in this unit?
Very high   ....   Very low

8. To what degree were the unit written materials well organized?
Very poor   ....   Very well

9. To what degree were the unit activities reasonable (in time and effort)?
Very reasonable   ....   Very Unreasonable

10. To what degree has the content of this unit been covered in a previous course?
Totally   ....   Not at all

Name the course(s) with this content ....

11. Does this unit need to be modified before it is used again?
                    Yes .....   No .....

Additional Comments:

ance objectives. But each type of test has its own specific function. For example, a pretest usually contains a diagnostic component which is designed to determine the individual learner's entry level into an instructional program. Progress tests monitor growth toward objective attainment and provide values for grading purposes. Final posttests, though they may be used for grade determination, more properly function as a program assessment tool to determine the relatively long-term effects of instruction.

Regardless of the type of criterion test developed, guidelines for the development of sound items needs to be observed.

The *validity* of a test is important because test results are used for both learner assessment and program evaluation. Learner assessment ordinarily leads to a grade determined either by a performance contract or an objective attainment system. The latter approach is less demanding in terms of scheduling and more stringent in terms of demonstrated competence. Both systems provide specific criteria for attaining a letter grade. Thus documentation is readily available of what the grade represents in terms of demonstrable behavior.

Learner assessment for the purpose of assigning grades requires that teachers consider *individual* achievement data. Conversely, program evaluation examines the same data *collectively* to determine whether the instructional elements are effective in promoting the acquisiton of the designated behaviors. Achievement data combined with learner perceptions regarding the quality of the instructional unit provide information about how well the instructional system is functioning. These two sources of data, however, do not automatically suggest specific program alterations. Specific changes are accomplished only after individual "soft spots" have been identified and possible causes diagnosed. Once this information is in hand, the teacher can return to the "instructional drawing board" in the hope of devising new procedures that will strengthen the unit the next time it is taught. There is "artistry" in this effort, but, because specific problem areas have been identified, it is "focused artistry." The authors believe that, out of such efforts, outstanding instructional programs can evolve.

References

GLASER, R. *The Designed Programming of Instruction* (Reprint 43). Pittsburgh: University of Pittsburgh, Learning Research and Development Center, 1968.

SCRIVEN, Michael. *The Methodology of Evaluation*. AERA Monograph Series on Curriculum Evaluation. Chicago: Rand McNally, 1967.

Additional Professional Study

Books

BEGGS, Donald L. and Ernest L. LEWIS. *Measurement and Evaluation in the Schools*. Boston, Mass.: Houghton Mifflin Co., 1975.

BLOOM, Benjamin S., J. Thomas HASTINGS, and G.F. MADAUS. *Handbook on Formative and Summative Evaluation of Student Learning*. New York: McGraw Hill Book Co., 1971.

BRACHT, Glenn H., Kenneth D. HOPKINS, and Julian C. STANLEY. *Perspectives in Educational and Psychological Measurement*. Englewood Cliffs, N.J.: Prentice-Hall, Inc., 1972.

BROWN, Frederick G. *Principles of Educational and Psychological Testing* (2nd edition). New York: Holt, Rinehart, and Winston, 1976.

CHASE, Clinton I. *Measurement for Educational Evaluation*. Reading Mass.: Addison-Wesley Publishing Co., Inc., 1974.

COLLINS, Harold W., John H. JOHANSEN, and James A. JOHNSON. *Educational Measurement and Evaluation: A Worktext* (2nd edition). Palo Alto, Calif.: Scott, Foresman and Co., 1976.

EBEL, Robert L. *Essentials of Educational Measurement*. Englewood Cliffs, N.J.: Prentice-Hall, Inc., 1972.

GLASER, R. *The Designed Programming of Instruction* (Reprint 43). Pittsburgh: University of Pittsburgh, Learning Research and Development Center, 1968.

GREEN, John A. *Teacher-made Tests*. New York: Harper and Row, 1975.

GRONLUND, Norman E. *Preparing Criterion-Referenced Tests for Classroom Instruction*. New York: Macmillan, 1973.

MARSHALL, Jon Clark, and Loyde Wesley HALES. *Essentials of Testing*. Reading Mass.: Addison-Wesley Publishing Co., 1972.

PAYNE, David A. *The Specification and Measurement of Learning Outcomes*. Waltham, Mass.: Blaisdell Publishing Co., 1968.

POPHAM, W. James. *Educational Evaluation*. Englewood Cliffs, N.J.: Prentice-Hall, Inc., 1975.

SAX, Gilbert. *Principles of Educational Measurement and Evaluation.* Belmont, Calif.: Wadsworth Publishing Co., Inc., 1974.

SCANNELL, Dale P. and D.B. TRACY. *Testing and Measurement in the Classroom.* Boston, Mass.: Houghton Mifflin Co., 1975.

SCRIVEN, Michael. *The Methodology of Evaluation.* AERA Monograph Series on Curriculum Evaluation. Chicago: Rand McNally, 1967.

STOREY, Arthur G. *The Measurement of Classroom Learning.* Chicago: Science Research Associates, 1970.

Periodicals

BOEHM, Ann E. "Criterion-Referenced Assessment for the Teacher." *Teachers College Record* (September 1973), 117-126.

DENTON, Jon J. "Pretests: How Do You Construct Them?" *The Science Teacher* (April 1974), 42-43.

DENTON, Jon J., Walter F. STENNING, and Phillip C. LIMBACHER. "A Field Tested Assessment Model to Evaluate the Effectiveness of a CBTE Program." Paper presented to Association of Teacher Education Conference, New Orleans, February, 1975.

LACROIX, William J. "Evaluating Learner Growth." *Man/Society/Technology* (February 1974) 133-136.

MILLER, Anthony G. and Ron G. WILLIAMS. "Constructing Higher Level Multiple Choice Questions Covering Factual Content." *Educational Technology* (May 1972), 39-42.

SWADENER, Marc and D. Franklin Wright. "Testing in the Mathematics Classroom." *The Mathematics Teacher* (January 1975), 11-17.

Chapter 8

Selecting Content and Planning Units

OBJECTIVES

This chapter provides information to help the reader to·

1. point out defining attributes of "concepts."

2. point out defining attributes of "generalizations."

3. develop a planning grid for organizing subject matter based on the use of concepts and generalizations.

4. identify components of a framework for systematic unit planning.

5. prepare units with elements interrelated according to a systems approach.

_____

Each of the five preceding chapters has focused intensively on a major instructional skill. Once basic elements of these skills have been mastered, it is time to put them together into systematic units of instruction for classroom use. Before these skills can be deployed to prepare a unit, decisions must be made regarding organization of the subject matter that will be the unit focus. The next section introduces a procedure that can be used to impose some logical order on the content selection process.

Using Generalizations and Concepts
to Organize Topics Within Subjects

"There is so much to teach and so little time to do it!" This faculty lounge lament points up one of the professional educator's most persistent frustrations. Difficulties associated with responsibly selecting content material around which to organize experiences for learners are most pronounced when curriculum guides are not available. Few teachers feel complete confidence in their abilities to make sound decisions lacking guidelines of some kind. But even when curriculum guides are available, teachers must make decisions due to the usual practice of including a number of alternative instructional suggestions. Whether guides are available or not, there is a need for a methodology that makes possible responsible selection of options so that content can be organized intelligently and systematically.

One commendably workable procedure for structuring subject matter content is based on the use of generalizations and concepts. If generalizations and concepts are viewed as "building blocks" of the subject curriculum, then they can be arranged in a framework that can guide selection and development of specific performance objectives, instructional strategies, and evaluation procedures. Assume, for example, that the following generalization had been selected to guide part of an instructional unit focusing on 19th century European history:

> Wars in the 19th century resulted in a diffusion of political decision-making into the hands of economic classes who had had no such authority in the 18th century.

Having selected this generalization, instruction could be organized through the use of learning experiences logically related to the generalization. In some cases, this might mean selection of certain passages from a textbook. But other materials might serve equally well, if not better. Use of generalizations as organizers results in instruction centering on these key propositions rather than following a page-by-page sequence laid out by the author of a given textbook. To develop an appreciation for how generalizations can function as instructional guides, it will be necessary to take a close look at their defining characteristics.

Generalizations

Simply stated, *generalizations* are propositions whose validity are tested by reference to evidence. Generalizations that have been tested and verified repeatedly in a variety of settings and that seem to have a universality of application are sometimes termed *principles.*

There are no "true" or "false" generalizations. By definition, generalizations represent tentative statements of relationship. A generalization's worth is measured by its ability to stand up under the scrutiny of skeptics armed with evidence. Most frequently, "facts" are used to test the veracity of a generalization.

Which facts should be taught? For teachers using generalizations to guide their instructional programs, the answer to that question is clear. Facts that have the capability of testing the veracity of and illuminating guiding generalizations ought to be included. Facts that bear no such connection to these generalizations fulfill no substantive function, and requiring learners to master them serves no useful purpose.

Generalizations tend to follow a predictable semantic form. Though not all contain the words "if" and "then," most generalizations can be re-written in an "if X, then Y" format. Further, the statement of relationship implied by the "if X, then Y" situation typically is qualified by a condition. In a generalization, the statements of relationship are between and among *concepts.* Consider the following generalization:

> An increase in the money supply taken together with a decrease in the number of goods available for purchase results in an inflation of prices.

Concepts involved in this generalization include "increase," "money supply," "decrease," "goods," "purchase," "inflation," and "prices." Clearly, several of these concepts are more complex than others and, thus, more likely to cause difficulty for learners. The concepts "money supply" and "inflation" would seem the most likely sources of learner problems in this list.

This generalization does include a *condition* that must obtain for the relationship among the concepts to hold. The generalization states that inflation results under the presence of a condition of an increase in the money supply and a decrease in the number of goods available for purchase. Of course, learners could not be expected to learn the generalization without understanding the meaning of the concepts involved. The next section will examine the nature of concepts.

Concepts

Whereas generalizations are *propositional* in nature, concepts are *definitional.* Concepts are stipulative. They mean what they say because of their defined characteristics. Concepts are akin to axioms in plane geometry. They are not testable propositions, but "givens." For example, if *lawn grass* were defined as "a (1) green plant with (2) jointed stems and (3) slender leaves," and someone were to find something growing in his yard that was (1) a *brown* plant with (2) jointed stems and (3) slender leaves, then that individual does *not* have *lawn grass* in his yard. By definition, *lawn grass* is *green.*

Individual concepts are defined by reference to specified qualities that *all* examples of a given concept must have. These qualities are referred to as the *attributes* of a concept. For example, Martorella (1972) has noted that the concept "parallelogram" has four attributes: (1) closed, (2) two-dimensional, (3) four-sided figure including (4) two pairs of parallel sides. To be properly labeled an example of the concept "parallelogram," any figure must possess each of these four attributes.

Unfortunately for teachers, few concepts that learners need in order to understand generalizations are so simple as "parallelogram." Teachers must deal with such complex concepts as "culture," "capital," "exchange," "diffusion," and other abstractions that have large numbers of defining attributes. Problems in dealing with these complex concepts frequently are exacerbated when the defining attributes, themselves, contain abstractions which students do not grasp.

A further difficulty teachers face has to do with the tendency of some older students to use concept *labels* in proper contexts even when there is no genuine understanding of the defining attributes of those concepts. Imagine a situation in which a high school teacher asked a student this question: "What do you like best about our country?" A clever student might reply, "our democratic way of life," knowing that (1) the label "democratic way of life" has some logical connection to the question, and (2) this answer might please the teacher. Of course, such an answer cannot be taken as evidence that the student has a solid understanding of the many attributes of the complex concept, "democratic way of life." Alert teachers recognize that fine-sounding verbalisms do not necessarily imply genuine understanding.

Perhaps more widespread than problems associated with learner verbalisms are difficulties associated with concept complexity. Suppose, for instance, that the concept *equator* has been identified as one learners need to know. The *equator* might be defined as "the imaginary line around the earth that is everywhere equidistant from the two poles." *Poles, equidistance,* and even *earth* may be concepts that are unknown to some learners. It is evident that if concepts contained in statements of definition have not been mastered, learners will experience great difficulty in acquiring the concept being defined. The implication for teachers is that when concepts that students must understand in order to grasp guiding generalizations are identified, there is a need to identify, at the same time, potentially confusing subordinate concepts contained in the description of the key concepts' attributes.

Steps in Subject
Matter Organization

In some school districts, curriculum guides identify a number of potentially useful generalizations and supporting concepts. When such guides are available, selection of specific generalizations can be accomplished quickly, and teachers can move on to the task of preparing specific performance objectives derived from the guiding generalizations.

When good curriculum guides are not available, teachers must develop their own schemes for organizing subject matter in a rational way. A five-step process such as the following will result in the development of a suitable organizational framework:

1. Identify, by name, unit topics to be covered.
2. For each unit topic, identify generalizations to be used to guide instruction.
3. Identify concepts embedded in generalizations and important sub-concepts contained in their defining attributes.
4. Arrange generalizations and embedded concepts in a logical sequence.
5. Develop a framework for instructional planning for each generalization and its set of embedded concepts.

Once generalizations and concepts have been identified, specific planning can begin for each instructional skill area. A useful device

Figure 8.1

Planning Grid Checklist

Major Concepts	FOLKLORE		CULTURE			VALUES		GENERATION		
Sub-Concepts	Customs	Tales	Food	Shelter	Environment	Feelings	Attitudes	Life Span	Offspring	Line of Descent
Performance Objectives	✓	✓	✓	✓	✓	✓	✓	✓	✓	✓
Diagnostic Procedures	✓	✓	✓	✓	✓	✓	✓	✓	✓	✓
Instructional Strategeis	✓	✓	✓	✓	✓	✓	✓	✓	✓	✓
Interacting with Learners	✓	✓	✓	✓	✓	✓	✓	✓	✓	✓
Evaluation: In-progress	✓	✓	✓	✓	✓	✓	✓	✓	✓	✓
Final Posttest	✓	✓	✓	✓	✓	✓	✓	✓	✓	✓

for ensuring that planning considers all identified concepts and all instructional skill areas is the "Planning Grid Checklist." An example is provided in Figure 8.1.

A procedure of "checking off" each cell in this grid as unit planning goes forward will assure that no important area is overlooked. Since other instructional considerations derive directly from performance objectives, they should be developed first, once guiding generalizations and concepts have been identified. Once these are completed and there are "checks" all the way across the "performance objective" row of the planning grid, then consideration can be given to the development and selection of diagnostic procedures, instructional strategies, modes of interacting with learners, and evaluation techniques. After these decisions have been made, it is useful to lay out the instructional plan according to a format that makes clear the interrelationships existing among program components. Figure 8.2 represents a workable response to this need.

When this unit planning framework is used, it is possible, subsequent to instruction, to review program elements with sufficient specificity to pinpoint those features that worked well along with those that caused difficulties. Armed with information of this nature, the revision process can go forward with a confident focus on those sub-components of the program that require work. In the absence of a planning structure that permits individual program elements to be examined in isolation, there may be a tendency to believe that an entire program may not be worth salvaging, when in reality some imaginative tinkering with one or two program elements might be all that is required to produce an outstanding revision.

In addition to using a framework for unit planning, some teachers find it useful to develop lesson plan outlines in advance of program implementation. Many excellent formats are available for this purpose. One such format is displayed in Figure 8.3.

Most categories indicated on the sample lesson plan form in Figure 8.3 are self-explanatory. Note that the "expected outcomes" section and the "evaluation procedures" section are derived directly from performance objectives. This procedure assumes that, in most cases, daily lessons will be guided over a number of consecutive days by the same performance objective.

Figure 8.2

A Framework for Unit Planning

A Guided Unit

Title of Unit

_____

Name of Unit Developer

_____

Figure 8.2
(Continued)

Title of Unit

....

General Goal of the Unit (In one or two sentences explain what learners
should get out of the unit. Two examples: "This unit is designed to
help learners understand how secret international agreements contributed to the outbreak of World War I." "This unit is designed to help
learners identify members of of the halogen family using appropriate
procedures.")

....

....

....

....

....

....

....

....

Focusing Generalizations for the Unit (no more than four or five)

....

....

....

....

....

....

....

....

....

....

....

....

....

....

....

....

....

....

....

....

Figure 8.2
(Continued)

Concepts Learners Must Know to Understand These Generalizations

....	....	....
....	....	....
....	....	....
....	....	....
....	....	....
....	....	....
....	....	....
....	....	....
....	....	....
....	....	....
....	....	....
....	....	....
....	....	....
....	....	....

Performance Objectives

Obj. No.	Type	Level	
....	....	....	....
....	....	....	....
....	....	....	....
....	....	....	....
....	....	....	....
....	....	....	....
....	....	....	....
....	....	....	....
....	....	....	....
....	....	....	....
....	....	....	....
....	....	....	....
....	....	....	....
....	....	....	....
....	....	....	....
....	....	....	....
....	....	....	....
....	....	....	....
....	....	....	....
....	....	....	....

Figure 8.2
(Continued)

Diagnostic and Remediation Procedures (Derive prerequisite knowledges, prerequisite skills, and hoped-for attitudes from performance objectives. Identify diagnostic techniques to be used to gather data regarding each area. Prepare prescription options for learners found to have deficiencies.)

Prerequisite Knowledges	*Prerequisite Skills*	*Hoped-for Attitudes*
....	....	....
....	....	....
....	....	....
....	....	....
....	....	....
....	....	....
....	....	....
....	....	....

Diagnostic Procedures to Gather Information Regarding:

Prerequisite Knowledges	*Prerequisite Skills*	*Hoped-for Attitudes*
....	....	....
....	....	....
....	....	....
....	....	....
....	....	....
....	....	....
....	....	....
....	....	....

Prescription Options

....
....
....
....
....
....
....
....
....
....
....
....

Figure 8.2
(Continued)

Instructional Strategies:
   *Techniques to Be Used with Learners During This Unit Will In-
   clude:*

....
....
....
....
....
....
....
....
....
....
....
....

Evaluating Instruction
   In-progress evaluation will be provided as follows for:

Objective 1   ....
Objective 2   ....
Objective 3   ....
Objective 4   ....
Objective 5   ....
Objective 6   ....
Objective 7   ....
Objective 8   ....
Objective 9   ....
Objective 10   ....

   The following objectives will be posttested as indicated:

Objective 1   ....
Objective 2   ....
Objective 3   ....
Objective 4   ....
Objective 5   ....
Objective 6   ....
Objective 7   ....
Objective 8   ....
Objective 9   ....
Objective 10   ....

Figure 8.2
(Continued)

Post Teaching Assessment of Unit
  Features of the unit that worked out well:

....
....
....
....
....
....
....
....

Features of the unit that did not work out well:

....
....
....
....
....
....
....

Specific changes that would be desirable before re-teaching unit:

....
....
....
....
....
....
....

Other general comments about the unit:

....
....
....
....
....
....
....

Figure 8.3

Lesson Plan Format

Subject: ....

General Purpose: ....
....

Expected Outcomes (Audience and Behavior components of relevant performance objectives)		
Sequence of Teacher Activities	Sequence of Learner Activities	Specific Materials Needed
Evaluation Procedures (Condition and Degree components of relevant performance objectives)		

There will be few occasions when a given performance objective can be mastered by learners after exposure to a single day's lesson. Indeed, in such cases, it might be well to examine the performance objective itself with a view to determining whether it might be too narrowly conceived. When lesson plans are viewed as vehicles for guiding instruction over several consecutive days, fragmentation of instruction resulting from using a single-day's teaching as the organizational unit can be avoided.

Formats for units and for lesson plans such as those introduced in Figures 8.2 and 8.3 can be understood better when actual units developed according to these guidelines are available for inspection. To illustrate how actual classroom units and lesson plans look that have been organized according to these formats, Appendices A, B, and C are provided following this chapter.

Each of these units has its strengths and weaknesses. However, each is organized so that the teacher can review systematically program strengths and weaknesses at the conclusion of the unit. In instances where these programs work well, teachers involved can identify components that contributed to the unit's success. When results are disappointing, "soft spots" in the program can be identified. This capacity for refining program analyses to avoid massive program revision makes good sense, given teachers' heavy time commitments.

Summary

In this chapter, use of generalizations and concepts was recommended as a means of identifying areas to be emphasized within a given subject field. Characteristics of both generalizations and concepts were described. A framework was introduced according to which generalizations and concepts can be used to guide instructional planning.

Guidelines were introduced for organizing instructional planning decisions into unit plans. Possibilities of utilizing systematically organized units for tightly-focused program revision were discussed. Finally, three examples of actual instructional units are provided (see Appendices A, B, and C) that were developed according to the framework presented in this chapter.

A Final Thought

Teachers labor in a political and social world that is more

inclined to place new demands on their services than to provide new resources to help them meet those demands. Given this reality, there is a need to deploy resources that *are* available. By careful planning, it is possible to identify those learner behaviors that are the proper professional concern of teachers and to distinguish them from other behaviors. Hopefully, procedures outlined here may help educators everywhere to function as clear-headed professionals, sure of their direction, and confident of their ability to manage credibly those areas in which schools have a legitimate and a compelling interest.

Additional Professional Study

References

MARTORELLA, Peter J. *Concept Learning: Designs for Instruction.* Scranton, PA: Intext Educational Publishers, 1972.

Books

BANATHY, Bela. *Instructional Systems.* Palo Alto, Calif.: Fearon Publishers, 1968.

BRIGGS, Leslie J. *et al. Instructional Design: Principles and Applications.* Englewood Cliffs, N.J.: Educational Technology Publications, 1977.

JOYCE, Bruce R. and Berj HAROOTUNIAN. *The Structure of Teaching.* Chicago: Science Research Associates, Inc., 1967.

MERRILL, M. David and Robert L. TENNYSON. *Teaching Concepts: An Instructional Design Guide.* Englewood Cliffs, N.J.: Educational Technology Publications, 1977.

POPHAM, W. James and Eva L. BAKER. *Systematic Instruction.* Englewood Cliffs, N.J.: Prentice-Hall, 1970.

Periodicals

ASCHERMANN, Jerry R. "Catalogue Unit." *Media and Methods* (February 1974), 67.

BLANC, Sam S. "Planning a Teaching Unit for the Primary Grades." *Science and Children* (April 1972), 21-24.

EDIGER, Marlow, "Development of Teaching Units." *School and Community* (January 1974), 23.

EIGL, Pierre von. "Concise Building Scheme for Instructional Modules." *Educational Technology* (February 1976), 33-35.

FERGUSON, Thomas A. and Susan O. REPASS. "Developing a Measurement Unit for Primary Children." *Science and Children* (March 1975), 31-33.

PAUTLER, Albert J. "Computer-Based Curriculum Planning." *Man/Society/Technology* (February 1972), 150-151.

SWYERS, Betty J. "That Little Old Module-Maker, You!" *Grade Teacher* (May 1972), 4-5.

Appendix A

A Guided Unit

Title of Unit

Temperature and Heat

Name of Unit Developer

Brenda Doe

Title of Unit
  Temperature and Heat

General Goal of the Unit
  This unit seeks to help learners understand how temperature and heat can be measured and how they affect the environment.

Focusing Generalizations for the Unit
  1. Temperature can be measured by a variety of procedures that have been validated by scientists.
  2. When temperatures go down, objects contract; and when temperatures go up, objects expand.

Concepts Learners Must Know to Understand
These Generalizations

fixed points	evaporation
calorie	condensation
heat capacity	boiling
heat of fusion	boiling point
molecules	vaporization
atoms	contraction
element	expansion
compound	water cycle
internal energy	melting
temperature	freezing

Performance Objectives
  1. (Cognitive: Knowing and Understanding) Each student in the ninth grade physical science class will define ten thermal energy terms on a true-false/multiple-choice test by responding correctly to at least eight of the ten items.
  2. (Cognitive: Applying) Each student in the ninth grade physical science class will find the heat capacity of substances by solving correctly at least seven of ten problems provided on a worksheet.
  3. (Cognitive: Applying) Each student in the ninth grade physical science class will compute the heat of fusion of substances by solving correctly at least four of every five problems on worksheets provided.
  4. (Cognitive: Applying) Each student in the ninth grade physical science class will find the melting point, heat of fusion, heat capacity of solids, heat capacity of liquids, and boiling point of several substances. Each student will achieve this objective by responding correctly to at least eight of ten questions on a graph quiz.
  5. (Attitudinal) Each student in the ninth grade physical science class will show an increased interest in the topics of temperature and heat as a consequence of this unit. This increase will be reflected in higher

indicated preferences for the topics of heat and temperature on an interest inventory given at the conclusion of the unit than on an interest inventory given before the unit begins.

Diagnostic Tests and Proposed Remediation Procedures

Prerequisite Knowledges   Prerequisite Skills   Hoped-for Attitudes

Knowledge of this
term:

heat   ----   --

Diagnostic Test
Instructions: This is a true-false test. Write a *T* in the blank to the left of each true statement. Write an *F* in the blank to the left of each false statement.

..... 1. Heat is a form of energy.
..... 2. Heat is something a person can feel.
..... 3. Heat is a fluid.
..... 4. Heat can be given off by live objects.
..... 5. Heat can be given off by objects that are not alive.
..... 6. We have ways of measuring heat directly.
..... 7. There are no ways to conserve heat in containers.
..... 8. When an object is heated, the molecules move very slowly.
..... 9. Heat is not involved in the change of state of an object from a solid to a liquid.
..... 10. When water is heated, the temperature rises and the rate of evaporation increases.

(Students who miss more than one-half of these items will be provided with the supplementary reading material.)

Supplement for Learners with Low
Diagnostic Test Scores
What *is* heat? For centuries, one phenomenon involving heat has been known. That is, when hot water is added to cold water, the hot water becomes cooler and the cold water becomes warmer. This appeared to indicate that there was a flow of something from the hot to the cold or from the cold to the hot. Interested 18th century scientists were curious to know whether this flow might alter the mass of the water. Results of their experiments indicated that no change of mass occurred as the hot water cooled off when cold water was added. These 18th century scientists reached the following conclusions about heat:

1. Since heat flows it must be a fluid which
2. does not have mass.

These conclusions became a part of the *caloric theory of heat.* This theory stated that caloric fluid is present in all matter and moves from the hot substance to the cold substance. This theory explained heat transfer from hot to cold objects fairly well, especially heat transfer in water. However, the theory did not explain how heat results when two solid objects are rubbed together. That is, why does friction cause heat?

Although the caloric theory was generally accepted as the correct explanation of heat transfer, some people supported the view that heat was a form of energy. James Prescott Joule (1818-1889) was one of the scientists favoring this position. He believed that heat was a form of energy, and he conducted a series of investigations to test this view.

Joule used a variety of devices in his experiments. His most famous study was performed with an apparatus in which descending weights caused a paddle wheel to turn in a can of water. Friction between the wheel and water generated heat, which heated the water. After many repetitions, Joule concluded that the quantity of heat produced by friction was proportional to the kinetic energy released by the falling weights. In other words, energy had changed from energy of motion (kinetic) to heat. The view that heat is energy, proved experimentally by Joule, continues today to be the accepted explanation for the phenomenon.

Instructional Strategies

(In support of performance objective #1) Short lecutre to introduce topic. Following filmstrips: "Thermometers"; "Contraction and Expansion." Debriefing utilizing questioning strategies.

(In support of performance objective #2) Team learning focusing on materials on heat capacity worksheets. Questioning strategies.

(In support of performance objective #3) Concept attainment strategy focusing on "heat of fusion." Team learning on worksheets focusing on same concept. Short lecture to conclude material on this topic.

(In support of performance objective #4) Short lecture to introduce heat change during phase change. Student laboratory exercises. Questioning strategies. Data retrieval charting as a summary activity.

(In support of performance objective #5) Provision of opportunities to express relative interest in topics contained in unit.

An Example of a Daily Lesson Plan to Be Used During the Unit
Day 7
General Purpose of the Lesson: Acquaint students with heat capacity and the measurements needed to compute it.

Expected Outcomes: Each student will be able to compute the heat capacity of iron.

Sequence of Teacher Activities:
1. Discuss how to find the heat capacity of a metal.
2. Go over laboratory procedures (4-6).
3. Have students work in pairs to complete lab.
4. Have students compare results and analyze reasons for errors.
5. Assessing Perspective 4-4 and question 16.

Sequence of Learner Activities:
1. Read "Unit of Heat" and "Heat Capacity."
2. Read Experiment 4-6 ("The Heat Capacity of Iron.")
3. Work through lab procedures in pairs and collect appropriate data.
4. At the conclusion of the experiment, make computations.
5. Participate in post-lab discussion.
6. Study Perspective 4-4 and answer question 16.

Materials Needed:
1. two styrofoam cups
2. blackboard and chalk
3. balance
4. six iron washers
5. thermometer

Evaluation Procedures: These objectives will be achieved by each student when he solves accurately at least 70 percent of the problems provided on a worksheet.

Evaluating Instruction

(Evaluation for performance objective #1) Ten true-false/multiple-choice items on the unit progress test.

(Evaluation for performance objective #2) Ten problems on a worksheet.

(Evaluation for performance objective #3) Five problems on each of several worksheets.

(Evaluation for performance objective #4) Ten questions on a graph quiz.

(Evaluation for performance objective #5) An interest inventory to be administered at the beginning and again at the conclusion of the unit.

These progress tests will be administered at various times throughout the duration of the unit, as appropriate. A final posttest will be constructed, consisting of a sampling of items from the several progress tests.

Unit Progress Tests

Performance Objective #1

True-False: Place a *T* to the left of each true statement and an *F* to the left of each false statement.

..... 1. Evaporation is a change of state from solid to gas.
..... 2. Condensation is a change of state from gas to liquid.
..... 3. Temperature is related to the enery of molecules.
..... 4. The boiling point of a substance is the temperature at which the substance changes from a solid to a liquid.
..... 5. The process in which a substance changes from a liquid to a vapor is called vaporization.
..... 6. Fixed points on a thermometer refer to the temperature at which water freezes and boils.

Multiple-Choice: Circle the letter preceding the *best* response.

7. If a large amount of water and a small amount of water are both at $0°$ C, the one which contains more internal energy is
   a. the large amount of water, because the mass is greater.
   b. the small amount of water, because the large amount would have to be heated longer to make it boil.
   c. neither, because they are at the same temperature.
   d. neither, because neither contains any internal energy.

8. Evaporation differs from boiling because
   a. a liquid changes to a vapor.
   b. boiling occurs only at the surface of the liquid.
   c. evaporation occurs at a particular temperature.
   d. evaporation occurs at all temperatures.

9. A calorie is defined as . . .
   a. the unit of measure of heat.
   b. the amount of heat required to raise the temperature of one gram of water through one Celcius degree.
   c. both a and b
   d. neither a nor b.

10. Melting and freezing
   a. are the same temperatures between the solid and liquid states.

b. are the same temperatures between the liquid and gas states.

c. both a and b.

d. niether a nor b.

Performance Objective #2

Worksheet: Write answers beneath each problem, showing all work.

1. Compute the amount of heat needed to raise the temperature of 100 g of alcohol from 20° C to 45° C.

2. Compute the amount of heat needed to raise the temperature of 765 g of silver from 5° C to 30° C.

3. The heat lost when the temperature of 100 g of aluminum was lowered from 62° C to 32° C was _____?

4. What is the mass of a block of copper if 2,500 calories raises its temperature from 15° C to 45° C?

5. A sample of warm water at 50° C is added to 80 g of aluminum at 15° C. The temperature of the mixture is 25° C. Calculate the mass of the warm water.

6. A 450 g piece of glass at 20° C absorbs 1500 calories of heat. What is the new temperature of the glass?

7. Compute the amount of heat needed to raise the temperature of 75 g of mercury from 10° C to 40° C.

Refer to the following graph in answering questions 8 and 9.

Temperature
in degrees C.

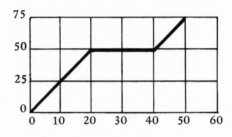

(This graph is for
one gram of some
substance.)

Heat added in Calories

8. Compute the heat capacity as a solid.

9. Compute the heat capacity as a liquid.

10. What is the heat gained when the temperature of 100 g of
    mercury is raised from 225° C to 70° C?

Performance Objective #3

Worksheet: Write answers beneath each problem, showing all work.

1. What mass of ice at 0° C must be added to 150 g of hot coffee at
    85° C to give cold coffee at 10° C? (Heat capacity of coffee =
    heat capacity of water) (Heat of fusion of ice = 80 cal/g)

2. If 45 g of ice at 0° are added to 175 g of water at 40° C, what is
    the temperature of this mixture? (Heat of fusion of ice = 80
    cal/g)

3. If the temperature of a mixture is 65° C and to get this you added 150 g of water at 50° C to _____ g of ice at 0° C, how many grams of ice did you add to the H_2O?

4. What mass of ice at 0° C must be added to 100 g of tea at 60° C to give cold water at 15° C? (Heat capacity of tea = heat capacity of water) (Heat of fusion of ice = 80 cal/g)

5. If 70 g of ice at 0° C are added to 165 g of water at 45° C, what is the temperature of the mixture? (Heat of fusion of ice = 80 cal/g)

Performance Objective #4

Worksheet: Write answers beneath each problem, showing all work.

Questions 1 through 5 refer to the graph below:

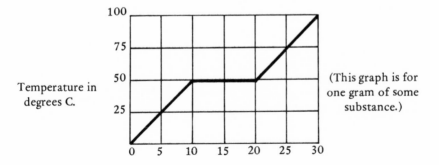

Temperature in degrees C.

(This graph is for one gram of some substance.)

Heat added in Calories

1. Compute the heat capacity as a solid.

2.   Compute the heat capacity as a liquid.

3.   Compute the heat of fusion.

4.   What is the melting point of the substance?

5.   What is the freezing point of the substance?

For questions 6 through 10, refer to the following graph:

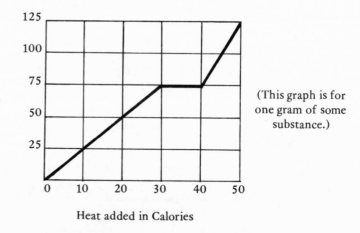

Temperature in degrees C.

(This graph is for one gram of some substance.)

Heat added in Calories

6.   Compute the heat capacity as a solid.

7.   Compute the heat capacity as a liquid.

8. Compute the heat of fusion.

9. What is the melting point of this substance?

10. What is the freezing point of this substance?

Performance Ojbective #5

Interest Inventory: Below you see listed the topics we have prepared for this physical science course. Please place a "1" before the topic that interests you most, a "2" before the next most interesting, and continue on in the same fashion until you conclude with an "8" in the blank before the topic you consider least interesting.

..... 1. motion

..... 2. temperature and heat

..... 3. force

..... 4. astronomy

..... 5. electricity

..... 6. sound

..... 7. machines

..... 8. gravitational force

Appendix B

A Guided Unit

Title of Unit

Pollution and Health

Name of Unit Developer

Jean F. Johnson

Title of Unit
Pollution and Health

General Goal of the Unit
This unit seeks to help learners understand what pollution is. More specifically, the unit will help learners to appreciate how air pollution, water pollution, noise pollution, and landscape pollution can be detrimental to the physical health of human beings.

Focusing Generalizations for the Unit
1. Survival in the earth's environment depends upon the ability people have to sense various phenomena through the senses.
2. Any substance that adversely affects the ability of the senses to perceive various phenomena through the senses with reliability may be regarded as a "pollutant."
3. Different pollutants affect health in different ways depending on the senses involved and the levels of concentration of the pollutant present at a given time.

Concepts Learners Must Know to Understand
These Generalizations

earth's environment	concentration
element	survival
five senses	stimulant
pollutant	

Performance Objectives
1. (Cognitive: Knowing and Understanding) Each student in the seventh grade science class will identify the concept "earth's environment" by answering correctly at least seven out of ten matching items on a unit progress test.
2. (Cognitive: Knowing and Understanding) Each student in the seventh grade science class will identify the concept "pollution" by responding correctly to at least seven out of ten true-false items on a unit progress test.
3. (Cognitive: Applying) Each student in the seventh grade science class will categorize selected pollutants as being either air, water, noise, or landscape pollutants by responding correctly to at least seven out of ten multiple-choice items on a unit progress test.
4. (Cognitive: Applying) Each student in the seventh grade science class will determine which categories of pollution are associated with various business and social practices by responding correctly to at least seven out of ten multiple-choice items on a unit progress test.
5. (Cognitive: Applying) Each student in the seventh grade science class will point out several ways pollution can influence health adversely by responding correctly to at least seven out of ten true-false items on a unit progress test.

6. (Cognitive: Analyzing) Each student in the seventh grade science class will take a position regarding the desirability of committing a large scale effort directed toward elimination of pollution of all kinds in the United States. To accomplish this objective, each student will prepare an essay, at least two pages in length, to be submitted at the conclusion of the unit. Each essay must include specific references to (1) air pollution, (2) water pollution, (3) noise pollution, and (4) landscape pollution.

7. (Cognitive: Knowing and Understanding) Each student in the seventh grade science class will identify important persons and events associated with the history of the struggle against pollution by responding correctly to at least seven out of ten matching items on a unit progress test.

8. (Attitudinal) Each student in the seventh grade science class will write an essay, no more than three pages in length, in which he expresses his feelings about the relative seriousness of pollution in his own community to be submitted at the end of the unit

Diagnostic Tests and Proposed Remediation Procedures

Prerequisite Knowledges	*Prerequisite Skills*	*Hoped-for Attitudes*
Knowledge of these terms	----	-------
earth's environment	------	------
pollution	-----	-----
respiratory ailment	-----	----

Diagnostic Test

Instructions: Circle the letter preceding the "most correct" answer for each of the following multiple-choice items.

1. The following are all states of matter that are included in the earth's environment *except for*
   a. solids.   c. quasars.
   b. gases.   d. liquids.

2. The following is an example of an organic constituent of the earth's environment:
   a. an air conditioner   c. a cement brick
   b. a blade of grass   d. a plastic and metal chair

3. Naturally occurring inorganic elements of earth's environment most often are found
   a. at or beneath the ground level.
   b. 1 to 5 feet above ground level.
   c. 50 to 600 feet above ground level.
   d. 5,000 to 50,000 feet above ground level.

4. The following is an example of air pollution:
   a. carbon monoxide
   b. dry ice
   c. any gas present in excessive amounts in the atmosphere
   d. water vapor

5. The following is an example of water pollution:
   a. factory wastes dumped into a public stream
   b. melting snow
   c. natural plant life in a fishing pond
   d. animal wastes deposited into a river in less than excessive amounts

6. Noise pollution is measured using the following units:
   a. millimeters
   b. gallons
   c. hectares
   d. decibels

7. The following is an example of landscape pollution:
   a. an oak tree
   b. cattle grazing in a pasture
   c. roadside billboards
   d. flocks of wild birds

8. Constant exposure to severe air pollution can result in serious lung and respiratory ailments such as
   a. measles.
   b. asthma.
   c. mumps.
   d. chicken pox.

9. A well-known conservation organization which is fighting to reduce pollution in the United States is
   a. OPEC
   b. National Audubon Society
   c. The World Bank
   d. The British Garment Workers Union

(Students missing more than one-half of these items will be provided with the supplmentary reading material.)

Supplement for Learners with Low
Diagnostic Test Scores

We live in earth's environment. This environment is composed of three different states of matter. They are (1) gases, such as those that make up the air; (2) liquids, such as water; and (3) solids, such as rocks and trees. Some of these elements are *organic.* These are things that are living themselves or come from living things. Examples of organic elements are rabbits, worms, wood, flowers, fish, and wool. Anything that is not living and is not derived from a living thing is called *inorganic.* Inorganic elements include glass, plastic, most rocks, and metal.

We are part of our environment. Many parts of the environment make up *ecosystems.* All the parts of an ecosystem (trees, animals, water, soil, etc.) are dependent on one another. We call these interdependent elements the *components* of the ecosystem.

When all is normal, these components exist in harmony. If a disruptive element, such as smog, oil slicks, or a deforested hillside is introduced, the harmony is broken. Such a disruptive force is called a *pollutant.*

Pollution has, in many cases, far reaching influences on an ecosystem. Very often, pollution causes disease in plants and in animals. It would be well for all of us to learn how to recognize pollution. Then we can work together to eliminate it. When we have conquered pollution, we all will be able to lead safer and healthier lives.

Instructional Strategies

(In support of performance objective #1) Lecture will be used to introduce the concept of "earth's environment."

(In support of performance objective #2) Taba's concept attainment strategy will be used to introduce the concept of "pollution."

(In support of performance objective #3) Taba's concept attainment strategy will be used to help students learn how to categorize air, water, noise, and landscape pollution.

(In support of performance objective #4) A data retrieval chart will be used to help students associate certain kinds of pollution with selected industrial and social situations.

(In support of performance objective #5) Brainstorming will be used to assist students in identifying possible health consequences of pollution.

(In support of performance objective #6) Team learning will be used as students analyze effects of pollution on various aspects of life in the United States.

(In support of performance objective #7) A lecture, supplemented by hand-outs, will introduce students to the history of pollution. A game will be used to reinforce these understandings.

(In support of performance objective #8) Students will have an opportunity to review a case study of pollution in a local community.

An Example of a Daily Lesson Plan to Be Used During the Unit

Day 1

General Purpose of the Lesson: Introduce unit on pollution by defining the parameters of the concept "earth's environment" and introducing some fundamental ecological principles.

Expected Outcomes: Each student will point out characteristics of the concepts "earth's environment" and "pollution."

Sequence of Teacher Activities:
1. Lecture, hand-outs, and readings will be used, in that order, to introduce the topic: "earth's environment."
2. Taba's concept attainment strategy will be used to introduce the concept "pollution."

Sequence of Learner Activities
1. Students will listen, take notes, read, and ask questions regarding the topic "earth's environment."
2. Students will participate in the concept attainment exercise by identifying examples and non-examples of "pollution." They will conclude this exercise by constructing a definition of "pollution."

Materials Needed:
1. Podium for lecture; chalk; chalkboard.
2. Poster-sized illustrations of examples and non-examples of "pollution."

Evaluation Procedures: These objectives will be achieved when students respond correctly to seven out of ten matching items and seven out of ten true-false items on the unit test.

Evaluating Instruction

(Evaluation for performance objective #1) Ten matching items on the unit progress test.

(Evaluation for performance objective #2) Ten true-false items on the unit progress test.

(Evaluation for performance objective #3) Ten multiple-choice items on the unit progress test.

(Evaluation for performance objective #4) Ten multiple-choice items on the unit progress test.

(Evaluation for performance objective #5) Ten true-false items on the unit progress test.

(Evaluation for performance objective #6) An essay to be submitted at the conclusion of the unit.

(Evaluation for performance objective #7) Ten matching items on the unit progress test.

(Evaluation for performance objective #8) An essay to be submitted at the conclusion of the unit.

Elements of the unit progress test described here will be administered, as appropriate, at various times during the actual teaching of this unit. As a means of testing for retention of materials presented throughout the entire unit, a final posttest will be constructed. This final posttest will be comprised of a sampling of test items included in progress tests for each performance objective. The final posttest will not assess behavior relevant to performance objectives assessed by submissions of essay responses at the conclusion of the unit (performance objectives 6 and 8).

Unit Progress Tests
Performance Objective #1

Matching: In the columns of information below, phrases in the left-hand column describe terms in the right-hand column. For each phrase in the left-hand column, find the term being described in the right-hand column. Place the letter of the term in the right-hand column in the blank before the correct phrase in the left-hand column.

..... related to living things	a. inorganic
..... a mixture of gases	b. solids
..... an environment in which plants and animals depend on one another and are in balance	c. biosphere
	d. green plants
..... the most abundant natural liquid	e. organic
..... thin layer of soil, water, and air covering the earth's surface	f. air
	g. ecology
..... transform sunlight into food	

..... not derived from living things

h. water

..... feed on materials built by producers

i. ecosystem

..... study of the relation of living things to their environment and to each other

j. consumers

k. herpetology

..... substances with high molecular density

l. quasar

m. cytokinesis

n. penguins

o. evolution

Performance Objective #2

True-False: Indicate whether each of the following statements is true or false by placing a *T* for true and an *F* for false in the space provided.

..... 1. Smog is a form of pollution.
..... 2. Any addition of man-made products to the environment that endangers the health of survival of people, plants, or animals is called *pollution*.
..... 3. Water pollution often is caused by fish that inhabit this environment.
..... 4. Pollutants are agents that man uses to fight pollution in his environment.
..... 5. Pollution in the United States has never been serious enough to cause real concern.
..... 6. Industry has been blamed, in the past, for much of the pollution found in the United States.
..... 7. Pollution can be categorized either according to the type of disturbance it causes or according to the specific nature of the polluting agent.
..... 8. Oxidation is a form of pollution.
..... 9. Pollution did not exist on earth until man began living in cities.
..... 10. The automobile is a major source of air pollution in the United States.

Performance Objective #3

Multiple-Choice: Select the most appropriate answer from among the four possibilities. Indicate your choice by circling the letter of that response.

1. Gasoline fumes are an example of
   a. air pollution.　　　　　c. noise pollution.
   b. water pollution.　　　　d. landscape pollution.

2. Roadside billboards contribute to
   a. air pollution.　　　　　c. noise pollution.
   b. water pollution.　　　　d. landscape pollution.

3. Mufflers are placed on cars to help control
   a. air pollution.　　　　　c. noise pollution.
   b. water pollution.　　　　d. landscape pollution.

4. In an urban setting, smoke from burning leaves is an example of
   a. water pollution.　　　　c. landscape pollution.
   b. air pollution.　　　　　d. none of these

5. Run-off pesticides into streams, rivers, and oceans typifies
   a. air pollution.　　　　　c. noise pollution.
   b. water pollution.　　　　d. landscape pollution.

6. Decibels are used to measure levels of
   a. air pollution.　　　　　c. noise pollution.
   b. water pollution.　　　　d. landscape pollution.

7. Telephone poles and power lines are examples of
   a. air pollution.　　　　　c. noise pollution.
   b. water pollution.　　　　d. landscape pollution.

8. When cruise ships dump their garbage into the sea, they contribute to
   a. air pollution.　　　　　c. noise pollution.
   b. water pollution.　　　　d. landscape pollution.

9. Large cities are often the places where one finds
   a. air pollution.　　　　　c. noise pollution.
   b. water pollution.　　　　d. all of these.

10. Cigarette smoke is a form of
    a. air pollution.　　　　　c. noise pollution.
    b. water pollution.　　　　d. landscape pollution.

Performance Objective #4

Multiple-Choice: Select the most appropriate answer from among the four possibilities. Indicate your choice by circling the letter of that response.

1. Industry has contributed to
    a. air pollution.   c. noise pollution.
    b. water pollution.   d. all of these.

2. The era of rock music has led to some problems in the area of
    a. air pollution.   c. noise pollution.
    b. water pollution.   d. fire pollution.

3. A chemical factory dumping wastes into a public stream is guilty of
    a. air pollution.   c. noise pollution.
    b. water pollution.   d. landscape pollution.

4. A boisterous crowd at a football game might be guilty of
    a. air pollution.   c. noise pollution.
    b. water pollution.   d. all of these.

5. A boy rowing a boat across a lake is guilty of
    a. air pollution.   c. noise pollution.
    b. water pollution.   d. none of these.

6. A television antenna on every house may be viewed as an example of
    a. air pollution.   c. noise pollution.
    b. water pollution.   d. landscape pollution.

7. A loud party in an apartment complex late at night might be thought by some people to produce
    a. air pollution.   c. noise pollution.
    b. water pollution.   d. landscape pollution.

8. Bicycles contribute, when properly used, to
    a. air pollution.   c. noise pollution.
    b. water pollution.   d. none of these.

9. A farmer who lived down wind from a chicken ranch might have reason to complain about
    a. air pollution.   c. noise pollution.
    b. water pollution.   d. landscape pollution.

10. Heavy growths of aquatic algae usually indicate
   a. air pollution.
   b. water pollution.
   c. noise pollution.
   d. landscape pollution.

Performance Objective #5

True-False: Indicate whether each of the following statements is true or false by placing a *T* for true and an *F* for false in the space provided.

..... 1. Water pollution can lead to contaminated tuna being sold in grocery stores.
..... 2. Air pollution can cause such respiratory ailments as asthma and emphysema.
..... 3. Landscape pollution frequently causes permanent blindness.
..... 4. Noise pollution, if very severe, can rupture the ear drum.
..... 5. Water pollution is responsible for epidemics of common mumps.
..... 6. Smoking is the leading cause of diseases caused by air pollution.
..... 7. Water pollution most often has adverse effects on plants and animals as opposed to human beings.
..... 8. Mental disorders have resulted from severe cases of landscape pollution.
..... 9. Water pollution is a leading cause of tooth decay.
..... 10. Water pollution has caused a great reduction in plant and animal life in the Houston ship channel.

Performance Objective #6

Essay: Write an essay, at least two pages in length, on the topic "What Should the United States Do About Pollution?" In your essay make specific references to problems associated with (1) air pollution, (2) water pollution, (3) noise pollution, and (4) landscape pollution. Describe specific steps that might be taken to deal with each problem you identify. Include some information regarding financial costs and other consequences of a large-scale effort to remedy these problems. The essay will be due at the conclusion of of the unit.

Performance Objective #7

Matching: Phrases in the left-hand column describe terms listed in the right-hand column. For each phrase in the left-hand column, find the appropriate term in the right-hand column. Place the letter of the term in the right-hand column in the blank before the correct phrase in the left-hand column.

..... First noticeable air pollution	a. Great Britain
..... First book written about air pollution	b. Smoke from wood fires
	c. 1948
..... Clean Air Act of 1956	
	d. United States
..... Disaster in Donora	
	e. Landscape pollution
..... Discovery of photochemical smogs	
	f. Sanitary landfill
..... Environmental Protection Agency	g. Noise pollution
..... Water Pollution Control Act	h. Helps modern communities build sewage-treatment plants
..... Regulated by state laws	
	i. Los Angeles
..... Voluntary control by individuals	j. 1661
..... Method used as an alternative to burning garbage in city dumps	k. 903 B.C.

Performance Objective #8

Essay: Write an essay, no more than three pages in length, in which you identify pollution in your own community. What are your feelings about these problems? What would your attitude be about various methods of dealing with pollution problems here? Or, is pollution not really a serious problem here? Be honest. Give your own opinion. There are no "right" responses to these questions.

Appendix C

A Guided Unit

Title of Unit

The "Inner Struggle" Theme

in American Literature

Name of Unit Developer

Robert Smith

Title of Unit

The "Inner Struggle" Theme in American Literature

General Goal of the Unit

This unit is designed to help learners become familiar with a section of American literature dealing with the "inner struggle," develop understandings of the terms "conflict," "climax," "setting," "characterization," and "plot," and add to their vocabulary during the reading of the literature.

Focusing Generalization for the Unit

Much of American literature can be viewed through the theme of the "inner struggle" and can be understood better through an analytical application of the concepts of "conflict," "climax," "setting," "characterization," and "plot."

Concepts Learners Must Know to Understand
These Generalizations

theme	setting
conflict	characterization
climax	plot

Performance Objectives

1. (Cognitive: Knowing and Understanding) Each student in the eleventh grade English class will match 75 vocabulary words with their definitions. The vocabulary words will be organized into three separate matching tests to be administered at different times during the course of the unit. Each student must match the words and definitions with 80 percent accuracy on each of the three tests.

2. (Cognitive: Knowing and Understanding) Each student in the eleventh grade English class will identify conflicts in short stories and poems on three tests to be given at different times during the unit by responding correctly to at least four of six true-false items on each of the three tests.

3. (Cognitive: Applying) Each student in the eleventh grade English class will reveal his interest in the unit on the "inner struggle" by identifying correctly the central climax of a short story he has not seen before. Responses will take the form of an essay that must include at least two specific reasons that a specific episode was identified as the "climax."

4. (Attitudinal) Each student in the eleventh grade English class will reveal his interest in the unit on the "inner struggle" by submitting a two-page paper at the conclusion of the unit in which he describes his feelings regarding the unit topic.

5. (Cognitive: Applying) Each student in the eleventh grade English class will describe, in a short essay, how each author of short stories studied during the unit dealt with the "inner struggle" theme. For

each author, one example must be provided illustrating how he worked with the "inner struggle" theme in his short story.

6. (Cognitive: Knowing and Understanding) Each student in the eleventh grade English class will identify elements of "plot," "setting," and "characterization" on three tests to be given at different times throughout the unit. Each student must respond correctly to at least eight of ten multiple-choice items on each test.

Diagnostic Tests and Proposed Remediation Procedures

Prerequisite Knowledges	*Prerequisite Skills*	*Hoped-for Attitudes*
Knowledge of terms used in literary analysis, including:		
plot	-----	------
conflict	------	------
setting	----	------
climax	-----	------
setting	------	-----
theme	----	-----

Diagnostic Test

Instructions: Circle the letter preceding the "most correct" response for each of the following multiple-choice items.

1. The struggle which grows out of the interaction between the two opposing forces in a story is called
   a. plot   c. conflict
   b. climax   d. setting

2. The point of highest interest in a story or the point at which the reader makes his greatest emotional response to a story is the _____ of a story.
   a. climax   c. conflict
   b. characterization   d. moment of illumination

3. The central or dominating idea in a literary work is the
   a. plot.   c. setting.
   b. theme.   d. conflict.

4. The flow of the action in a story is termed the
   a. climax   c. moment of illumination
   b. theme   d. plot

5. The physical, sometimes spiritual, background against which the
   action of a story takes place is the _____ of a story.
   a. setting   c. conflict
   b. plot   d. climax

6. The presentation of characters through their personalities and
   actions in a story is the _____ of a story.
   a. setting   c. moment of illumination
   b. characterization   d. conflict

(Students missing more than one-half of these items will be supplied
with a short hand-out focusing on concepts included in the diagnostic
test.)

Supplement for Learners with Low
Diagnostic Test Scores

Conflict is the struggle which grows out of the interaction between two
opposing forces in a story or in a plot. At least one of the opposing forces is
usually a person. This person may be involved in conflicts of four different
kinds: (1) he may struggle against the forces of nature; (2) he may struggle
against another person; (3) he may struggle against society as a force; (4) two
elements within him may struggle for mastery.

The *climax* is the point of highest interest in a short story or novel. It is
the point at which the reader makes his greatest personal response to the
story or is most interested and involved in the story.

The *theme* is the central or dominating idea in a literary work. In
non-fiction prose, the theme may be thought of as the general topic of
discussion. In poetry, fiction, and drama, it is the abstract concept which is
made concrete through its representation in person, action, and image in the
work.

The *plot* is the ordering of events in a story. The plot covers the main
events that happen in a story. It includes the sequence of the action.

Setting includes the physical, and sometimes spiritual, background against
which the action of a short story or novel takes place. The elements which go
together to make up a setting are: (1) the actual geographic location, its
topography, scenery, and such physical arrangements as locations of windows
and doors in a room; (2) the occupations and daily manner of living of the
characters; (3) the time or period in which the action takes place; and (4) the
general religious, mental, moral, social, and emotional environment in which
the characters and the narrative move.

Characterization involves the development of the characters by means of
description of their personalities and actions in a short story or novel.

Instructional Strategies

(In support of performance objective #1) A team learning procedure will be used as learners use dictionaries to look up words and develop sentences illustrating their correct use. Further, each student will keep a personal notebook of new words encountered in each short story and poem.

(In support of performance objective #2) A short lecture will introduce students to the concept "conflict." Subsequently, questioning strategies will be employed to probe for student understanding of this concept following the completion of each short story and poem.

(In support of performance objective #3) A short lecture will introduce students to the concept of "climax." A data-retrieval chart technique will be used after several poems and short stories have been completed to enable students to compare and contrast nature of the climaxes in each of these works.

(In support of performance objective #4) Questioning strategies will be used as students attempt to gain insights into the dimensions of the "inner struggle" theme and how this theme may be operating in their own lives.

(In support of performance objective #5) A short lecture will introduce the concept of "theme." Using a team learning approach, students will work in groups as they attempt to identify the themes of a number of short selections.

(In support of performance objective #6) A brief introductory lecture on how to identify the "plot," "setting," and "characterization" of a work will be given. After the lecture, students will be divided into several groups and encouraged to create plot, setting, and characterization schemes of their own. A class discussion will follow that will center on some of the more creative schemes developed. Questioning strategies will be employed at this time.

An Example of a Daily Lesson Plan to Be Used During the Unit
Day 8
General Purpose of the Lesson setting, and characterization in literary works.

Expected Outcomes: Each student will be able to identify correctly elements of plot, characterization, and setting in selections introduced during the unit.

Sequence of Teacher Activities:
1. Short lecture on how to identify the plot, setting, and characterization of a work.
2. Divide students into groups and encourage them to create their own plot, setting, and characterization schemes.
3. Lead a class discussion centering on plot, setting, and characterization proposals developed by each group.

Sequence of Learner Activities:
1. Take notes on short lecture focusing on plot, setting, and characterization schemes.
2. Work in teams and develop plot, setting, and characterization schemes.
3. Participate in discussion centering on plot, setting, and characterization proposals developed by each of the groups.

Materials Needed:
1. chalk
2. chalkboard

Evaluation Procedures: Achievement of the objective related to this lesson will require each student to respond correctly to at least eight of ten multiple-choice questions on each of three unit progress tests.

Evaluating Instruction

(Evaluation for performance objective #1) Three separate matching tests to be administered at different times throughout the unit.

(Evaluation for performance objective #2) Three separate true-false tests to be administered at different times throughout the unit.

(Evaluation for performance objective #3) An essay question to be administered after students have been introduced the concept of "climax."

(Evaluation for performance objective #4) A two-page paper to be submitted at the conclusion of the unit.

(Evaluation for performance objective #5) An essay to be administered as a progress test after students have read works by each author to be studied during the unit.

(Evaluation for performance objective #6) Three separate multiple-choice tests to be administered at different times throughout the unit.

Elements of the unit progress tests, described above, will be administered at various times throughout the course of the unit, as appropriate. To test for retention of all unit-related material, a final posttest will be constructed and administered. This final posttest will include a sample of items from progress tests designed to assess student performance on objectives 1, 2, and 6.

Unit Progress Tests

Performance Objective #1, Test One, Part A

Matching: Match the definitions on the left with the correct vocabulary words on the right. Place the letter of the word in the blank in front of its definition.

..... 1. to examine closely		a. lithograph
..... 2. epidemic; plague		b. concoct
..... 3. summon up; call		c. cosmopolitan
..... 4. quiet; peaceful		d. idolatrous
..... 5. distress; displeasure		e. insinuate
..... 6. proverb		f. maxim
..... 7. wordly		g. chagrin
..... 8. to hint		h. conjure
..... 9. blindly devoted; worship		i. tranquil
..... 10. to make up; invent		j. subtly
..... 11. fat		k. pestilence
..... 12. done without notice		l. corpulent
		m. scrutinize
		n. pedagogue

Performance Objective #1, Test One, Part B.

Matching: Match the definitions on the left with the correct vocabulary words on the right. Place the letter of the word in the blank in front of its definition.

..... 1. whims   a. cutlass

..... 2. tendencies; bent   b. confounding

..... 3. illnesses   c. sartorial

..... 4. long knife; sword   d. intricate

..... 5. doorway   e. omnipotence

..... 6. coiling; twisting together   f. catechism

..... 7. unwanted visitation   g. vestibule

..... 8. basic principles of a religion   h. convolution

..... 9. very detailed   i. intrusion

..... 10. offensiveness   j. repugnance

..... 11. drawing stressing facial features   k. caricature

..... 12. all powerful   l. infirmities

                                               m. propensities

                                               n. confiscating

Performance Objective #1 Test Two, Part A.

Matching: Match the definitions on the left with the correct vocabu-
           lary words on the right. Place the letter of the word in the
           blank in front of its definition.

..... 1. slope or inclination of the earth   a. configuration

..... 2. amazing   b. acclivity

..... 3. outward shape or figure; outline   c. pommel

..... 4. open air encampment   d. equestrian

..... 5. of or like a lion   e. mettle

..... 6. lofty; grand; exhalted   f. impetuous

..... 7.	the front part of a saddle	g. ventricle
..... 8.	lassitude; weariness	h. incredible
..... 9.	pertaining to or consisting of air	i. leonine
..... 10.	projecting part of a fortification	j. aerial
..... 11.	pertaining to horses or horsemanship	k. salient
..... 12.	courage; daring; bravery	l. sublime
		m. bivouac
		n. serendipity

Performance Objective #1 Test Two, Part B

Matching: Match the definitions on the left with the correct vocabulary words on the right. Place the letter of the word in the blank in front of its definition.

..... 1.	current	a. reconcile
..... 2.	make up	b. omen
..... 3.	vomiting	c. militia
..... 4.	you	d. wholly
..... 5.	questioning	e. willy-nilly
..... 6.	whether desired or not	f. retching
..... 7.	sign of something to come	g. eddy
..... 8.	mixture	h. canard
..... 9.	band to hold a saddle in place	i. quizzically
..... 10.	totally; sum total	j. medley
..... 11.	local military unit	k. vulnerable

..... 12. easily destroyed or hurt

                                          l. girth

                                         m. thee

                                         n. baffle

Performance Objective #1, Test Three, Part A

Matching: Match the definitions on the left with the correct vocabulary words on the right. Place the letter of the word in the blank in front of its definition.

..... 1. sly, furtive look	a. sultry
..... 2. hot, close, and oppressive	b. extreme
..... 3. pale, sickly	c. wan
..... 4. suffering without complaint	d. belligerent
..... 5. perturbation; stirred up	e. spurious
..... 6. combination of two or more forces	f. agitation
..... 7. hidden; dim	g. reconciliation
..... 8. strategic movement	h. stoical
..... 9. doubtful	i. maneuvers
..... 10. renewal of friendship	j. leering
..... 11. quarrelsome; warlike	k. dubious
..... 12. at the utmost point or degree	l. obscure
	m. bloc
	n. tangential

Performance Objective #1, Test Three, Part B

Matching: Match the definitions on the left with the correct vocabulary words on the right. Place the letter of the word in the blank in front of its definition.

..... 1.   critical   a. foe

..... 2.   enemy   b. frenzied

..... 3.   impudent   c. surreptitious

..... 4.   guided by will only; high-handed   d. harangues

..... 5.   furtive   e. cower

..... 6.   cluster   f. conglomeration

..... 7.   crouch because of fear   g. thwart

..... 8.   loud, passionate speech   h. arbitrary

..... 9.   hinder or frustrate   i. affirmative

..... 10. mad; agitated   j. brazen

..... 11. positive   k. fanatical

..... 12. over-enthusiastic   l. crucial

                                               m. progeny

                                               n. postulate

Performance Objective #2, Test One

True-False: This section deals with "conflict." Write a *T* in the blank to the left of the number if the statement is true. Write an *F* in the blank to the left of the number if the statement is false.

..... 1.   The main conflict in the story "William Wilson" is the one between William Wilson and his "double."
..... 2.   There is a conflict between Dr. Bransby and William Wilson.
..... 3.   There is a minor conflict between William Wilson and Glendenning, the Oxford student.
..... 4.   There is a conflict between John March and Kualai in "You Can't Do That."

..... 5. In "You Can't Do That" there is a conflict between Moses March and Captain Griggs.
..... 6. There is a conflict between Captain Griggs and John March because of Captain Griggs' manner of trading.

Performance Objective #2, Test Two

True-False: This section deals with "conflict." Write a *T* in the blank to the left of the number if the statement is true. Write an *F* in the blank to the left of the number if the statement is false.

..... 1. There is a conflict between Josh and his parents over the issue of whether he should go into battle and kill.
..... 2. Josh has an inner conflict in which he needs to prove his manhood by fighting and killing.
..... 3. The issue of whether or not Morgan's raiders will succeed in taking Vernon is not a conflict.
..... 4. There is a conflict between two lovers' tastes in "Ballad."
..... 5. George Soyonovich's inner conflict involves an important moral issue.
..... 6. George faces a conflict in that he cannot decide whether to develop himself as fully as he can or not.

Performance Objective #3

Essay: Read the short story beginning on page 113 in the text. Write a short essay, no more than a page in length, in which you identify the central climax of the story. Provide at least two reasons that led you to select that particular episode as the climax.

Performance Objective #4

Short Paper: Prepare a short paper, approximately two pages in length, on the subject "What the 'Inner Struggle' Means to Me." Feel free to express your own opinion. Papers will be due at the end of this unit of study.

Performance Objective #5

Essay: Using no more than four or five sentences for each selection, explain how the authors of each of the following dealt with the "inner struggle" theme: (1) "William Wilson;" (2) "You Can't Do That;" (3) "The Battle of Finney's Ford;" (4) "A Horseman in the Sky;" (5) "I looked Down Into My Open Grave;" (6) "A Summer's Reading."

Performance Objective #6, Test One

Multiple-Choice: Circle the letter of the most appropriate response.

1. The setting of "William Wilson" is
   a. a boy's school in England.
   b. Oxford.
   c. Europe.
   d. a, b, and c above.

2. The main characters of "William Wilson" are
   a. William Wilson.
   b. William Wilson's "double."
   c. Dr. Bransby.
   d. both a and b.
   e. both a and c.

3. A minor character in "William Wilson" is
   a. Dr. Bransby.
   b. William Wilson's "double."
   c. John March.
   d. Mr. Preston.

4. William Wilson kills
   a. Dr. Bransby.
   b. Edgar Allan Poe.
   c. Captain Griggs.
   d. none of these.

5. William Wilson's "double" really is his
   a. cousin.
   b. twin.
   c. conscience.
   d. imagination.

6. The main characters in "You Can't Do That" include
   a. John March.
   b. Captain Griggs.
   c. Kualai.
   d. a, b, and c.

7. The time period in which the story "You Can't Do That" takes place is
   a. the early 1800's.
   b. the 1700's.
   c. the early 1900's.
   d. the late 1800's.

8. The main setting of "You Can't Do That" is
    a. a voyage to Europe.
    b. a voyage to the Sandwich Islands.
    c. a voyage to California.
    d. a voyage to Russia.

9. What was given to John March to symbolize his honesty?
    a. a boat.
    b. a musket.
    c. a feather cloak.
    d. some wood.

10. John March was sent on the trading mission to
    a. learn the business.
    b. take a vacation.
    c. make money.
    d. see the world.

Performance Objective #6, Test Two

Multiple-Choice: Circle the letter of the most appropriate response.

1. What period of time did Birdwell live in?
    a. during the Revolutionary War.
    b. during the War of 1812.
    c. during the Civil War.
    d. during the French and Indian War.

2. How was Josh wounded in "The Battle of Finney's Ford?"
    a. He fell into a creek.
    b. He was shot by rebels.
    c. He was shot by a farmer.
    d. He was kicked by his horse.

3. Josh and his friends were trying to defeat
    a. Robert E. Lee.
    b. John Hunt Morgan.
    c. Jeb Stuart.
    d. Home Guardsmen.

4. All of these characters play roles in "The Battle of Finney's Ford" *except*
    a. Josh Birdwell.
    b. Labe Birdwell.
    c. Carter Druse.
    d. Ben Whitey.

5. Josh Birdwell and his family are
   a. Quakers.
   b. Amish.
   c. Mormons.
   d. Protestants.

6. Who was the horseman in the sky?
   a. Carter Druse.
   b. Druse's father.
   c. Druse's brother.
   d. Druse's best friend.

7. Private Carter Druse was assigned to what job?
   a. to tend the horses.
   b. to a guard post.
   c. to set up camp.
   d. none of the above.

8. The setting of "A Horseman in the Sky" is
   a. Georgia.
   b. Kentucky.
   c. Virginia.
   d. Mississippi.

9. Carter Druse is a
   a. rebel.
   b. deserter.
   c. Yankee.
   d. none of the above.

10. Carter Druse's father told him
    a. not to join the Union army.
    b. to join the Union army.
    c. not to leave him.
    d. to always do his duty.

Performance Objective #6, Test Three

Multiple-Choice: Circle the letter of the most appropriate response.

1. Edmond G. Ross looked down into his open grave when he
   a. had to start over.
   b. was voted not guilty.
   c. a and b.
   d. neither a nor b.

2. Why did George finally decide to start reading those 100 books?
   a. Sophie made him do so.
   b. He had nothing else to do.
   c. He was ashamed of himself.
   d. None of the above.

3. The story "I Looked Down into My Open Grave" took place in the
   a. 1790's.
   b. 1810's.
   c. 1860's.
   d. 1910's.

4. The President they were trying to impeach in the story "I Looked Down into My Open Grave" was
   a. Abraham Lincoln.
   b. Andrew Jackson.
   c. John F. Kennedy.
   d. Andrew Johnson.

5. In the poem "Ballad," the soldiers are after
   a. the woman.
   b. her lover.
   c. the farmer.
   d. the parson.

6. Which of these characters does not play a part in "A Summer's Reading?"
   a. George.
   b. Sophie.
   c. Mr. Cattanzara.
   d. the librarian.

7. The result of Senator Ross' vote was
   a. to impeach the President.
   b. to save the President from impeachment.
   c. to save the nation.
   d. both a and c.
   e. both b and c.

8. Senator Ross was a Senator from
   a. Kansas.
   b. Nebraska.
   c. Iowa.
   d. Pennsylvania.

9. Two lovers do not have the same tastes in life in
   a. "Parting Without a Sequel."
   b. "Wild Peaches."
   c. "Ballad."
   d. none of the above.

10. After breaking with her sweetheart, what emotion does the lady in "Parting, With a Sequel" show?
    a. relief.
    b. hatred.
    c. indecision.
    d. none of the above.

Glossary

Aim
This term expresses a relation between subject-area generalizations and the educational goals of the school. Aims identify the intellectual skills to be acquired by the learner, without indicating levels of performance.

Analyzing
The category of cognitive functioning which requires the learner to break down known information and observations into less complex parts. This level of mental operation assumes the learner has not performed this type of mental task previously.

Anecdotal Record
Brief written summaries that describe specific classroom incidents involving a particular learner. This information is usually retained in the personal file of the learner.

Applying
The category of cognitive functioning which requires the learner to apply previously learned information to new situations.

Attitudinal Dimension
The classification of performance objectives concerned with learner attitudes and feelings about school experience.

Audience
This is one of the four components of a performance objective. The "audience" component indicates which learner or learners must demonstrate a behavior.

Behavior
This term represents a description of the skill or content the

learner must acquire. The "behavior" component of a performance objective states what a learner should be able to do as a consequence of instruction.

Behavior Modification

A strategy to influence human behavior based on the assumption that human behaviors result as a consequence of their being reinforced by certain features of the external environment.

Brainstorming

A process-centered activity channeled through learners which attempts to unleash learners' untapped reservoirs of thinking talent by encouraging them to pour forth as many ideas as possible that relate to a narrowly defined topic situation.

Case Study

The case study is an instructional strategy that seeks to promote close learner involvement with a specific situation by presenting that situation in such a way that learners identify closely with it. Case studies focus on a single incident, and they typically describe interaction patterns of people.

Centering Question

Teacher questions which help learners to establish a tighter focus on the topic under consideration.

Checklist

A diagnostic technique which can be used by the teacher to obtain information on the learner's attitude toward a topic or instructional activity.

Cloze Procedure

A diagnostic procedure which enables the teacher to determine the learner's ability to function with specific printed material.

Cognitive Dimension

The intellectual or academic aspect of the thinking process. Cognitive dimension performance objectives focus on academic aspects of schooling.

Completion Test Items

An objective type test item consisting of a statement with one word or phrase deleted. This type of test item measures *recall* of particular phenomena rather than *recognition* of those phenomena.

Concept

A term that applies a common label to a class of phenomena sharing certain characteristics. Concepts are mental constructs used to organize and categorize phenomena encountered in the "real world."

Concept Attainment Strategy (Taba Strategy)

A systematic approach based on a set of structured teacher questions designed to (1) familiarize the learner with the name of the concept, (2) enable the learner to recognize the defining characteristics of the concept, and (3) distinguish between examples and non-examples of the concept.

Conditions

A statement of the circumstances and limitations that will be present during the test performance of the behavior.

Conference

A diagnostic technique which can be used by the teacher to obtain information about the learner's needs and concerns. This technique is a planned conversation between the learner and the teacher.

"Content-Centered" Performance Objective

An objective in which the teacher has total interest in promoting learner mastery of a specific body of subject matter and no interest in promoting learner internalization of a content processing technique.

Criterion-Referenced Test

An instrument designed to measure learners' performance by reference to a predetermined standard.

Data-Retrieval Chart

A process-centered activity channeled through the teacher which enhances the development of analytical skills of learners. Data retrieval charts are two dimensional matrices which enable learners to organize large quantities of information in a systematic manner.

Deductive Learning Experiences

Learning activities which present an instructional sequence based on deductive logic. In this approach, learners are provided with theories and generalizations as "givens." Learning proceeds through an examination of specifics in terms of their relationship to these theories or generalizations.

Degree

The degree component of a performance objective indicates the extent to which the learner is to demonstrate on identified behavior.

Diagnosis

This is a process of instruction whereby efforts are made to determine (1) learner readiness to begin a sequence of instruction, (2) learner attitudes, and (3) learner needs and interests.

Discrimination Power

The utility of a test to identify the high-ability individuals with respect to a cognitive skill addressed by the test. A test with high discrimination power effectively identifies the very capable learners with respect to a specific cognitive skill.

Error Variance

The variability of learner performance due to spurious measurements obtained by inaccurate and imprecise instrumentation.

Essay Test Item

An item designed to measure a learner's ability to *analyze, synthesize,* and/or *evaluate* concepts and relations between concepts.

Evaluating

The category of cognitive functioning which requires the learner to state criteria for making a judgment followed by a decision based on the stated criteria.

Expansion Question

Teacher questions that require learners to move beyond a simple knowledge and understanding to apply previously learned information and to make inferences about new situations.

Experimentation Question

Learner questions used in a Suchman inquiry exercise to determine the consequence of some change by the learner on a given phenomenon.

Feedback

Information provided to the learner on the appropriateness of his answers on a test or assessment instrument.

Flow of Activity

A characteristic of an instructional strategy which is based on the actors in a communication interchange. In general, two "flow of activity" types exist, namely, teacher-centered, and learner-centered strategies. Talk and activities channeled through the teacher are teacher-centered strategies, while activities where primary patterns of communication flow between learners and need not be channeled through the teacher are labeled learner-centered strategies.

Fry Readability Graph

A diagnostic procedure which enables the teacher to determine the reading level of printed material.

Generalization

Propositions whose validity are tested by reference to evidence.

Goal

Educational goals are statements which indicate the general direction and focus of school curriculums.

Hoped-For Attitude

Learner attitudes toward a topic or course of study which the teacher intends to engender through teaching a unit.

Hypothesis Checking Question

Learner questions used in a Suchman inquiry exercise to obtain a verification of a hypothesis suggested by the learner.

Inductive Learning Experiences

Learning activities which present an instructional sequence based on inductive logic. In this approach specific information is presented, with the outcome depending on assimilating the information into a *generalization.*

Instructional Skill

A process conducted by a teacher engaged in teaching. More specifically, this term is used to denote the five categories of the teaching model espoused in this book, i.e., specifying performance objectives, diagnosing learners, selecting instructional strategies, interacting with learners, and evaluating instruction.

Instructional Strategy

A plan which incorporates a series of instructional activities to enable the learner to gain an intellectual skill delineated by a performance objective.

Interaction

Communication between two or more individuals. Customarily the communication is verbal, but signals, gestures, and written messages are included among human behaviors from which communication may occur.

Interest Inventory

A diagnostic technique which is useful when the teacher wishes to gather information regarding learners' relative ranking of a subject or topic before a new unit of instruction begins.

Knowing and Understanding

This is the category of cognitive functioning which includes the recognition and recalling of information.

Large Group Instruction

Instructional activities designed for more than eight learners. Activities such as lectures and discussions between teacher and entire class are common large group activities.

Lecture

A content centered activity channeled through the teacher. A good lecture is characterized by (1) responsiveness to audience, (2) good organization, (3) variety of stimuli, and (4) brevity.

Mastery Learning

An instructional expectation that most students can master what is expected of them, and it is the task of instruction to make this learning possible.

Matching Test Items

An objective type test item consisting of two lists of terms which contain interrelated pairs. This type of test item measures *recognition* of relations between terms in each of the two lists.

Model of Teaching

A conceptual framework to guide the instructional practices of teachers.

Multiple-Choice Items

An objective type test item consisting of a stem which presents a speculation, then presents three or four foils as well as the correct answer to the question. This type of test item measures *discrimination* of the most appropriate alternative from among four or five choices.

Necessity Question

Learner questions used in a Suchman inquiry exercise to determine what conditions may or may not be present for a given phenomenon to exist.

Negative Reinforcement

An environmental event that, when removed, prompts an increase in frequency of the behavior preceding that removal.

Norm-Referenced Evaluation

An evaluation interpreted in terms of group performance. An individual's performance is expressed in terms of his relative performance compared to the other members of the group.

Normal Curve

Term which refers to the distribution of a human trait in the population. This expression often occurs when an individual's performance is compared to the performance of the group on a particular skill.

Objective Attainment Grading

Evaluation policy whereby a learner earns grade credit on the basis of the number of performance objectives achieved.

Performance Contract

Evaluation policy whereby a learner completes a specified number of learning activities for a minimum grade. Higher grades are often contingent on the learner's performance on a test over the material related to the instructional activities in the contract.

Performance Objective

A statement or combination of statements which delineate the intellectual skills to be learned by the student. In addition, the performance objective specifies the attainment level and the testing conditions under which the objective will be achieved.

Positive Reinforcement

An environmental event whose occurrence results in an increase in frequency of the behavior it follows. Often this event is in the form of praise or rewards given after a successful performance.

Posttest

An assessment administered to learners at the conclusion of a grading period, such as semester tests.

Predetermined Role Group

A small-group activity whereby each learner in the group is charged with reacting to a particular situation as a given character might be expected to react.

Premack Principle

This states that behaviors which occur frequently can be used to reinforce behaviors occurring less frequently. Example: "If you behave, you can play bingo."

Prerequisite Skill

Behaviors the learner must have before instruction can begin.

Prescription

An instructional program based on the available activities which are designed to rectify learning deficiencies identified by the instructional diagnosis process.

Pretest

An assessment administered to learners at the outset of an instructional unit.

"Process-Centered" Performance Objective

An objective in which the teacher has total interest in promoting learner mastery of a content processing technique and no interest in promoting learner mastery of a specific body of content.

Progress Test

An assessment administered to learners at the conclusion of a one to two week instructional unit.

Psychomotor Dimension

The classification of performance objectives dealing with fine muscle control.

Punishment

A behavior technique which consists of either the imposition of an external event the learner does not like or the removal of an environmental event the learner does like.

Questioning Strategy

A content-centered activity channeled through the teacher, whereby the teacher requests information from the learners.

Reality Therapy

Technique to help learners identify and resolve their own behavioral problems.

Reinforcer

An environmental event that increases the probability of recurrence of the behavior it follows.

Relative Grading System

Evaluation policy whereby grades are based on a learner's performance compared to other learners in the class (group).

Reliability

A concept which refers to the relative degree of consistency and precision with which the test measures what it purports to measure.

Remediation

Instructional activities designed for learners not achieving the performance objectives for a particular unit on the initial progress test. Remediation activities occur after feedback on the progress test has been received by the learner.

Research Group

A small group activity which depends on individuals fulfilling different roles and cooperatively working together to solve a problem.

Role Playing

A content centered activity not channeled through the teacher. Role playing promotes tolerance and acceptance of diverse viewpoints by requiring learners to assume roles and portray those roles in a social situation.

Simulation

A content centered activity not channeled through the teacher. Simulations present participants with opportunities to focus on selected features of a "real world" situation.

Small Group Instruction

Instructional activities designed for four to seven learners.

Social Praise

A reinforcer commonly used in classrooms. Social praise often is used by a teacher following a student contribution during a discussion, or for a successful performance by the learner.

Suchman's Inquiry Strategy

A process centered activity channeled through the teacher which promotes active student involvement in the process of generating and testing hypotheses. The Suchman Strategy is unique among inquiry approaches in that the teacher functions as an information source that learners must interrogate as they attempt to formulate and test hypotheses.

Synthesizing

The category of cognitive functioning which requires the learner to develop responses that go beyond a simple recitation of the available facts; information bits must be put together to form new information.

Table of Specifications

A two dimensional matrix which presents the content elements being addressed in a performance objective along one dimension and the cognitive level of the objective along the other dimension. The table displays the content elements in an instructional unit with the corresponding relations among the elements inherent in the instructional plan.

Task-Choice Group

A small group activity whereby learners work at a given learning center. Group membership changes in this type of group.

Teacher-Administered Test

An assessment instrument developed and implemented by the instructor.

Team Learning

A content-centered activity not channeled through the teacher. A small group activity through which subject matter is processed by learners from work sheets and brief synopses of papers and textual material.

"Test-Out" Criterion

The level of performance that a learner must attain on a pretest in order to forgo the instructional activities related to the pretest.

"Test-Out" Option

A component of pretests which enable the learner to demonstrate competence of a performance objective before the instructional unit begins.

True-False Test Item

An objective type test item consisting of a statement whose veracity must be determined by the learner. This type of test item primarily measures *recognition* of phenomena.

True Variance

The variability of learner performances due to real differences of ability among learners of a given population.

Tutorial Group

A small group activity whereby the teacher presents information to a select number of learners.

Validity

A concept which refers to the degree of accuracy with which a test measures what it purports to measure.

Variance

The range of learner performance scores within a group of learners or between groups of learners.

Verification Question

Learner questions used in a Suchman inquiry exercise to determine the existence or non-existence of a certain piece of information.

Work Sample

Examples of previous work submitted by learners, such as examinations, projects, papers, and laboratory write-ups, that are retained by the instructor for diagnostic purposes.

Index